PYTHON PROGRAMMING

Python Machine Learning

Python data analytics

The ultimate guide for beginners

Tony f. Charles

Chapter 4: Building Machine Learning Models

Chapter 5: Machine Learning Algorithms ... **269**

Python machine learning

Introduction

The world continues to advance every day. Every now and then, we find humanity discovering newer realms and expanding the horizon far beyond what we once thought possible. That is the magic of science. However, this entire feat was probably not possible without the invention of computer programming languages. Every major success we have had in terms of technology comes from some form of computer programming.

Today, the world is awash with programming languages such as the R, C# (called C Sharp), JavaScript, the list is just endless. While we continue to search for new languages to further explore new possibilities, one language stands out for its sheer effectiveness, simplicity and exceptional use in the world of today. Created by Guido Van Rossum, Python has become a new benchmark for beginners and experts alike.

Leading platforms around the world are using Python as their core programming language. Whether we speak about social media giants such as Instagram, or the latest radar-guided and satellite-guided self-driven cars, Python is found to be in the heart of the entire success. It is because of Python that the world has now taken an interest in Data Science and Machine learning, the two leading frontiers of technology.

Naturally, it makes great sense for any programmer to seek guidance to learn and master the technicalities involved behind these two, which is where this book will step in.

Unlike many other books, we will jump straight to the good bits and keep it true to the "clean code writing" practice as possible. You will get ample explanation only where they may be required; the rest are self-explanatory by nature.

What exactly is machine learning? While the book talks about the more advanced aspects of machine learning, here's a little explanation for anyone who is thinking about taking up Machine Learning as their choice of field.

Generally speaking, we human beings learn from our past experiences and correct our headings to ensure the results we desire are obtained. Machines, on the other hand, are programmed by us, without the option of allowing them to learn from their past experiences. With Machine Learning, we now have the option to allow the machines to learn from their past experiences. Sure enough, the machine cannot do anything unless we allow it to carry out a specific task. In this case, we will become the trainer and the machines will become the students. We will use this book to have a look into what are some advanced ways to ensure that we train our machine, test out their capabilities, check their accuracy and quite a lot more.

The idea to write a book with practical codes is one that has been taken up by quite a lot of esteemed authors and publishers, however, this book was created to ensure a good chunk of such codes and variations were used. We will encounter quite a few terminologies that may seem daunting at first, but the explanations provided should be easy to understand.

Python Machine Learning is a book that ensures all technicalities are catered and applied to examples to showcase their unique features and differences. Through carefully created codes and snippets, it would be easy to draw a conclusion and learn a thing or two about the various methods used within this book.

While there are quite a few graphs that were omitted, owing to the fact that these were almost identical in nature, readers are encouraged to try to manipulate the data to see the minor yet existing differences.

To get the most out of this book, there is only one thing you can do: Practice. The more you practice your coding skills, the better you learn and understand matters. In the interest of advanced learning, we will not be visiting any basics but instead will be focusing on advanced terminologies, methods, and their usages only.

If you have just started using Python, it is best that you create a good understanding of how to code with Python before embarking on a journey to the world of Machine learning.

Who should read this book?

This book ideally aims to provide a learning experience to professionals who are practicing machine learning tools to investigate real-world issues. This book is an advanced level of learning and requires some basic knowledge of machine learning and artificial intelligence (AI). There is quite a lot of software that can be used for applying machine learning algorithms, but we will focus on using Python along with a few selected software's and libraries. It is understood that by reading this book, you have a basic understanding of what libraries are and how they are used in python for algorithm development. You must be familiar with the basics of NumPy, Matplotlib and Scikit-learn as these will be our primary sources to work with.

If you have yet to come across these libraries and software's, it is probably best to acquire the required knowledge first prior to reading the content within this book. While there is no harm in doing so, there is a good possibility that you might be overwhelmed with commands, functions, libraries, and other methods used within the book if you have never used them before.

There will be times where you might feel overwhelmed by the sheer number of codes used within this book. If you are not sure about some of these, you can always browse the internet to gain a better perspective. These codes were designed with specific datasets and hence some functions, methods and parameters were used that were related to these codes. For a list of complete methods and functions, be sure to visit websites pertaining to said libraries to find a list of these. We will not be going through all of them within this book.

Before you do go ahead and start your journey, it is essential to know that you will need to use the latest version of Python on your system. It does not matter whether you are using Windows, Macintosh OS or any distribution of Linux, the coding will remain universal. However, having Python-2 will surely have a few troubles. Therefore, it is essential that you use Python-3.x.x (whichever is applicable) to follow the book without encountering any errors.

Purpose of this book

There are many books written on python and machine learning. It is only natural that you might be asking how is this book any different. Most of these books either dive deep into theories behind python and machine learning unnecessarily or gave simple generic examples consisting of general problems. This book deals with only real-world problems and applies almost all methods of machine learning to make you gain a better understanding of algorithms and provide you with a practical way to resolve and investigate real-world issues.

At the end of reading this book, you will be able to compare all methods of machine learning and ready to apply these algorithms both efficiently and effectively. This book is to be taken as a reference book and does not necessarily guarantee that the content shown here would work on future versions of the language or software's used. All commands, libraries, coding methods used here were valid at the time of writing this book. If you run into such issues where certain methods, functions or commands no longer work, use the Python community to seek answers.

Python is one of the most well-documented languages in existence that allows you to learn almost everything about the language by scrolling through the community forums. You are encouraged to take advantage of it when and where possible to help you further accelerate your learning.

It is imperative that you understand that we will be using Anaconda as our prime environment for development purposes as it contains all the necessary packages and libraries that we need in order to try out, test, and learn machine learning. The datasets used within the book are predefined and available within Scikit-Learn. Should you find yourself in a spot of trouble, you can always search for those online to find out how to access them.

The Python version in use throughout the book will be 3.x.x as Python 2 is slightly different and will run out of services soon. If you do not have Python 3 installed, head over to www.python.org to download the latest version of Python 3.

Although the book provides various examples and data visualizations, it is not to be taken as the only guide to learn from. This book covers all the bases of Machine Learning and puts various methods to use with numerous scenarios. You can visit online repositories to gain access to all of these datasets and libraries. Use this book as your reference, and aim to learn and develop a sound understanding of matters involved in machine learning. By the end of this book, we aim to allow a student or an aspirant to have enough confidence to carry out various experiments using their own imaginations, scenarios and codes.

If you encounter errors during the process of executing codes or during the installation of any of the libraries, software or plugins, ensure to visit the concerned websites or ask the ever-active community of Python programmers and Machine learners on various platforms.

All the codes written were tried and tested during the writing of this book. All of these were found to be working and result-oriented. However, it is not to be taken for granted that these codes will work perfectly in future releases of any of the components involved.

Lastly, the book was written after thorough research and wishes to provide more practical coding than theory. Should you feel overwhelmed at any point, stop and take a bit of a break. Do not try and pace through the lines. Sometimes, a glass of water and some fresh air might be just what you need to get you back into the productive zone.

Take this book as your ultimate reference book and extract as much knowledge from this book as possible. Always remember that you can and will encounter errors. There is nothing to be alarmed about any of those as these errors will not affect or jeopardize your system as a whole. Upon encountering an error, debug the code and correct the values, parameters or arguments to ensure the code is able to work perfectly.

Chapter 1: Getting Started With Machine Learning

Machine learning is a method that is used to get information from the given data sets. These data sets are then used to train systems using the provided information so that they can be used to provide output of corresponding input when any input is given. It has numerous applications. Although it can be used for both small and sizeable data, usually it is mainly used to process a high quantity of data in quick time and then return the output in relation to the input provided.

Machine learning is what allows AI to gain the ability to self-learn and improve itself through various occurrences and experiences. There is a reason that this field has quickly garnered quite a lot of attention from the rest of the world. More and more people are now willing to learn Python to understand Machine Learning and be able to write and execute programs that can further enable their AIs to become intelligent systems.

We already have an example of how this sublime technology is being used in weather systems. Through carefully designed architectures and programs, the system now has the ability to comprehend, understand and then predict what the weather conditions will be like in the coming days. This is made possible through effective use of AI. Take the machine learning away, and we might be back to computing individual variables and data for hours before realizing that the results are in a little too late.

What is Machine Learning?

By now, you may have already acquired an idea as to what machine learning is. It is an efficient way to process large quantities of data in the smallest amount of time and allow systems to gain the ability to learn from the given data. It is used to provide prediction of future values by training itself with current and old values. It is used in many cases these days such as the automatic recommendation regarding best movies, ordering the best food, and buying the best products.

Similarly, it is used to recognize your friends in photos stored on Facebook and other social platforms through facial recognition. It is also used in platforms such as Amazon and Netflix. Hence, machine learning can be used in many ways, and that is precisely why it is necessary to gain an understanding at an advanced level so that it can be used to solve multiple problems and deliver various services to ease the users further.

In the old days, "if and else" statements were used for processing of data or adjusting user input in order to make intelligent applications. There was a spam filter that was used to transfer specific emails to spam folder. How do you think this was done with emails to categorize them as spam?

Spam filter used a list of blacklisted words that helped the filter to identify spam. This filter can be used as one of the examples of intelligent applications. This problem can be solved by a human as well, but in that case, a person requires enough understanding of processes to come up with such a model. Manual or hand-coded rules can be useful but not in every case, as mentioned above. It can have some disadvantages as follows:

· The code or system will work for a specific problem; any change in the problem can lead to failure of that code or system.

· A human being may not be able to develop such a thorough understanding quickly and might consume quite a lot of time to carry out such work.

Similarly, there is one more example in which the hand-coded method fails, and that is the detection of a face in an image. Although every smartphone these days can detect and identify faces in the pictures, these were not identified successfully in the past. The reason behind failure in detection and identification of faces in an image in the recent past is the difference in perception of pixels between a human and a computer.

Computer perceives images differently as compared to humans. The improvement from failure to success in detection of a face in an image is due to the utilization of machine learning algorithms. The machine learning-based program contains large samples of pictures, which is enough to detect and identify various faces within an image.

Types of learning and their examples

Just a few minutes ago, we discussed the use of spam filters within our emails and how it transfers individual emails to our junk mail folder while retaining the others in the inbox. The machine learning algorithm can perform this work efficiently. All it requires is a sample of spam words or emails for the training of the model, and then that model will categorize spam emails. In reality, that model will predict emails as spam or otherwise.

The model that requires training needs machine learning. Furthermore, the selection of methods depends on the situation of the problem at hand.

If the problem provides the information of categorization as an input, it is known as supervised learning. On the other hand, if the problem does not provide the information of categorization as an input, it is known as unsupervised learning. Clustering is a perfect example of unsupervised learning, while classification and regression are examples of supervised learning.

The term 'Supervised' learning is recognized from the term supervision, just as a teacher supervises his/her students on a specific task and guides them regarding inputs and outputs. In doing this, they learn the sequence of that particular problem.

Likewise, supervised learning takes inputs and learns its outputs as well, and when other data is given to it, it can predict its output using the trained model.

Supervised learning can further be explained, and to do that, let us assume another example situation. Suppose that you are presented with three similar pills of the same dimensions and all are of the same color.

- Pill A - five grams
- Pill B - six grams
- Pill C - 7 grams

We have the weights. Here, the weight will turn into a component called 'feature,' which we will be using shortly to classify these. Let us assume that we have another data that is already defined in the machine. The machine will cross-check with the data and immediately recognize these pills based on their 'features' and provide them with their names. Names are defined as labels. Your end result may look like this:

- (name of drug) - 5 grams
- (name of drug) - 6 grams
- (name of drug) - 7 grams

Here, the name of the drug can be anything that is predefined. The same can be used to identify coins, metals, ornaments, and objects.

In the above example, we have features and the machine uses labeled data to identify these and provide outputs accordingly.

On the other hand, unsupervised learning has no awareness of outputs to specific inputs, and when a different data set is given, it can just categorize outputs on the basis of some parameters such as Euclidean distance, etc. To put it in plain terms, unsupervised data works on unlabeled data and provides outputs in cluster forms.

We will see some more examples of both supervised learning and unsupervised learning to develop a better understanding of these schemes. One of the most common examples of supervised learning is the identification of zip codes from handwritten digits on an envelope.

In this example, you have scans of handwriting as input, and zip code is the desired output. You need to collect multiple envelopes to create datasets for the training model. Hence, when any handwritten digits are provided to the system as an input, the algorithm will provide the zip codes as output.

Another example of supervised learning is determining whether the tumor is benign in a medical image. Here, you have the medical images as input, and the desired output will inform whether the tumor is benign or not. You would need to collect multiple medical images to make datasets for the training model. Hence, when any medical image is fed to the system as an input, the algorithm will come into play and inform regarding the intensity of the said tumor. Machine learning is used quite often in the field of medical imaging.

To quote yet another example of supervised learning, it is the detection of fraudulent activity in the transactions of credit cards. Following the same pattern as above, you have credit card transactions as input, and the output will determine whether the said transaction is legitimate or fraudulent in nature. Once again, you will need to collect credit card transactions to make datasets for the training model. Hence, when any credit card transactions are fed to the system as inputs, the algorithm will produce the results accordingly.

With a bit of an understanding of how supervised learning works, let us now look at some examples of unsupervised learning. One of the examples of unsupervised learning is the identification of topics in blog posts.

The large number of textual data that you have represents these blog posts as input, and you want to summarize the themes of these posts. Since you don't know about these topics, the outputs are unknown. Hence, without any known corresponding outputs of these inputs, you need to summarize the themes of these posts. This can pose a bit of a challenge as you will need to rely on other methods to gather the related information and categorize them accordingly. See how supervised learning is much more efficient?

Another example of unsupervised learning is the segmentation of customers into groups with similarities. In this example, you have a massive number of customer records as input, and you want to identify which customers have similarities.

Customers can be parents, book buyers or gamers. You don't know about these groups, and naturally the output is unknown. Hence, without any known corresponding outputs of these inputs, you need to identify similarities among customers and then segment them on the basis of those similarities on your own.

Finally, we have an example of unsupervised learning for the detection of abnormal access patterns to websites. Here, you have a large number of website access records as input and you want to identify which access is classified as abnormal. The abnormal accesses will be different from each other. Since you have no idea about these accesses and how they are organized, the outputs are unknown. Therefore, without any known corresponding outputs of these inputs, you now need to identify which access is abnormal on your own.

By no means are we stating that of these two methods only one is usable. There are cases where both can be used, depending on the input and output of the scenario. However, as the book progresses, you will soon learn why the former is favored over the latter.

Now that we have seen a few examples where Machine Learning is applied, let us now shift our attention to the more technical aspects, one where we start setting up our environment, gathering the right tools and starting our own venture.

Installing Machine Libraries in Your System

Before we commence, the readers are reminded that this book is meant for intermediate to advanced users, which is why we will not be explaining the basic terminologies involved in Python and programming in general, such as libraries, classes, arrays, lists, tuples and so on.

There are multiple libraries that are required to be installed in Python in order to apply Machine learning. Some of them are basic libraries, while some are more advanced in nature. Each library has its own usage. These are usually used for performing specific operations.

First, we have Scikit-learn. Scikit-learn is a free-to-use package, hence it is also known as an open-source package. It is being developed much throughout the world, and it is being used by many programmers. It is quite a great package, and almost every advanced program should be able to recognize it.

It contains many Machine learning-based algorithms. This package relies on other two packages of Python; SciPy and NumPy. Furthermore, you will need to install additional packages of Python, such as matplotlib for plotting, and Jupyter Notebook for development.

There are some distributions of Python that automatically install some packages when installed. Anaconda is one of them. It is used for large-scale processing of data, scientific computing, and analyzing of prediction. It automatically installs Scipy, NumPy, pandas, matplotlib, Jupyter Notebook, IPython, and Scikit-learn.

Enthought Canopy is another distribution of Python, which is usually used for scientific computing. It automatically installs Scipy, NumPy, pandas, matplotlib, IPython, and Jupyter Notebook. However, it does not automatically install the Scikit-learn package, especially with the free version.

Python (x,y) is another distribution of Python, which is also used for scientific computing. It is a free version. It automatically installs Scipy, NumPy, pandas, matplotlib, IPython, and Scikit-learn. If you have installed Python, you need to use pip command to install all of the above mentioned package.

```
$ pip install scipy numpy matplotlib pandas ipython scikit-learn
```

Once done, we are ready to proceed to the next step.

How to import libraries

To import libraries and verify their versions, run the following line of codes:

Input:

```
import sys

print("Version of Python: {}".format(sys.version))
```

Output:

```
Version of Python: 3.6.5 |Anaconda, Inc.| (default, Mar 29 2018, 13:32:41) [MSC v.1900 64 bit (AMD64)]
```

In order to import pandas:

Input:

```
import pandas as pd
```

```
print("Version of pandas: {}".format(pd.__version__))
```

Output:

```
Version of pandas: 0.23.0
```

In order to import matplotlib:

Input:

```
import matplotlib
print("Version of matplotlib: {}".format(matplotlib.__version__))
```

Output:

```
Version of matplotlib: 2.2.2
```

In order to import SciPy:

Input:

```
import scipy as sp
print("Version of scipy: {}".format(sp.__version__))
```

Output:

```
Version of scipy: 1.1.0
```

And then for the rest:

Input:

```
import IPython
print("Version of IPython: {}".format(IPython.__version__))
```

Output:

Version of IPython: 6.4.0

Input:

import sklearn

print("Version of sklearn: {}".format(sklearn.__version__))

Output:

Version of sklearn: 0.19.1

You may have noticed that we are always demanding the console to print out the version information. This part is to ensure that we know which versions we are using as some of these commands may stop working in future releases.

We are all set to move toward our next chapter. This is where we will learn in detail about supervised learning and how we can apply it in various circumstances.

Chapter 2: Supervised Machine Learning for Discrete Class Label

Supervised learning holds quite a significance in the field of Machine Learning. We can already sense a feeling that the word 'supervised' has something to do with supervision. It is just as a teacher would teach and guide students about which inputs can provide outputs of desired types. But, when we mention supervised learning, you will come across another term that tags along with supervised learning: Classification.

Understanding the Concept of Classification

Supervised machine learning is divided into two types, classification, and regression. Classification is used to predict discrete labels. It is further divided into two categories, binary classification and multi-classification. Binary classification is used to divide two classes while multi-classification is used to separate multiple classes. We can safely say that binary classification yields us either a yes or a no. We discussed the example of classification of emails as either spam or not in the previous chapter as an example. That example relates to the binary classification.

On the other hand, regression is used to predict continuous numbers or floating-point numbers. Its examples are: prediction of an individual's annual income from his/her education, age, and residence. While predicting annual income, the predicted output will be an amount that will be of any value. Similarly, predicting the yield of a cornfield by providing number of features such as previous yields, weather, and the number of employees allocated on that farm is an example of regression. The predicted output can be any number.

It is very important to distinguish between classification and regression. You can distinguish between these two terms by figuring out whether predicted output contains any continuity or not; if yes, then it is an example of regression. In the example of the annual income of individuals, you can see how it is an example of regression.

Suppose you need to translate the language of any website, you can translate that language completely with a single click. This is an example of classification.

Overfitting and underfitting

While training datasets, you need to take care of some of the factors. Assuming that you are training datasets to make a model. You are sure that your dataset or model will work on your test data, but will that model work on a new test data? Are you quite sure about it? Will you need to completely change the model to work for other test data?

To explain further, let us take this statement as an example:

"People older than 40 want to buy a boat."

This statement can explain the behavior of all the customers; you know you just need to create a threshold of 40. Any other person that has an age of less than 40 will be considered as not willing to buy a boat. But on the other hand, you cannot simply tell any simple rule for this problem at first look. If you make a very complex model that will work for that specific problem, and it fills too closely to that specific problem, it is called overfitting. On the flip side, if you make a very simple model that is not taking care of all aspects of data, your model will neither work for the test data nor will it work effectively for the training set as well. This problem is called underfitting.

The reason behind these errors is that with making complex models, you allow your model to perform well on training data. But when you create too complex of a model, you force yourself to think more and more and in return you come up with taking care of each and every data point, and that might be counterproductive. Although that model will work on your training data but it will not work with new data. Similarly, a model that is too simple leads us to failure in prediction. You need to trade-off between overfitting and underfitting to get the right balance and get the optimum output.

Along with these factors, you need to keep in mind the time required in simulation of any algorithm. The more complex you create your algorithms, the more time it will consume for simulation. Sometimes, we are bound by time limits and require quicker results, and in such cases, we need to keep our algorithms simple. We will encounter all these factors while performing classification methods. It is recommended that you try out executing the programs and methods with numerous values. It is a good practice to develop an understanding.

Machine Learning Methods

K-Nearest Neighbors

Suppose you have an individual profile and you have successfully gathered some data pertaining to the liking and disliking of a person for movies. Based on the data we have gathered, let us assume the following situations:

- Mr. A loves to watch horror movies
- Mr. A prefers watching movies based on Science Fiction
- Mr. A dislikes watching romance films
- Mr. A prefers watching movies based on true stories
- Mr. A watches movies that are 90 minutes long

Now we have some general data, and if we map these values on a graph, where the x-axis represents genres and the y-axis represents the runtime of the film, we can easily visualize the data. So far, so good.

Let us bring a little technicality in this mix. Suppose there is a new movie out that is around 100 minutes long, and it is an action movie. This will now pose a problem for us.

In the initial data that has been gathered, there is no mention of the word 'action' and we already have a 90 minutes runtime mark established. Will Mr. A like this movie? This is where the K-Nearest Neighbors method comes into play.

It is the simplest machine learning algorithm to be used for the classification process. It has become a very popular machine learning algorithm for both classification and regression processes. It takes K nearest neighbors (KNN) to calculate a new data point for a given data. If the value of k is one, then it will be in its simplest form, which will take only one nearest neighbor to calculate a new data point from a given data. It will operate the same way for calculating new data points for all the given data.

To put things in the simplest words, the KNN method will take into consideration the nearest data points and gauge the majority. If the model sees that similar items are more in number compared to the ones that Mr. A dislikes, it will end up recommending this movie to Mr. A. Quite similar to how we see recommendations on YouTube, Netflix, and other streaming platforms.

Now, let us dive in a little deeper into the technicalities and see how KNN works with datasets. We will apply KNN on both Iris and Breast cancer datasets to perform classification process and we will then check its performance.

Applying KNN on Breast cancer dataset

Let us see how KNN works with a relatable example, as shown under:

Input:

```
# Importing required libraries

from sklearn.datasets import load_breast_cancer as cancer

from sklearn.neighbors import KNeighborsClassifier as KNN

import matplotlib.pyplot as plt


# Loading input data

value = cancer()

Data = value.data

Target = value.target


# Splitting input data into training and testing data

ts = len(Data)

trs = round(0.7*ts) #You can change this partition and the
```

```
remainder will be for testing

Data_trn = Data[0: trs]

Target_trn = Target[0: trs]


Data_tst = Data[trs:]

Target_tst = Target[trs:]



# Printing size of training and testing data

print(Data_trn.shape)

print(Data_tst.shape)

Output:

(398, 30)

(171, 30)


Input:

accuracy_trn = []

accuracy_tst = []


limit = range(1, 11)

for i in limit:

# Training the model
```

```python
knn = KNN(n_neighbors = 2)

knn.fit(Data_trn, Target_trn)

# Calculating accuracy of Training Data

accuracy_trn.append(knn.score(Data_trn, Target_trn))

# Calculating accuracy of Testing Data

accuracy_tst.append(knn.score(Data_tst, Target_tst))


# Plotting accuracy of training and testing data

plt.plot(limit, accuracy_trn, label = "Accuracy of Training Data")

plt.plot(limit, accuracy_tst, label = "Accuracy of Testing Data")

plt.xlabel("Value")

plt.ylabel("Accuracy")

plt.legend()
```

Output:

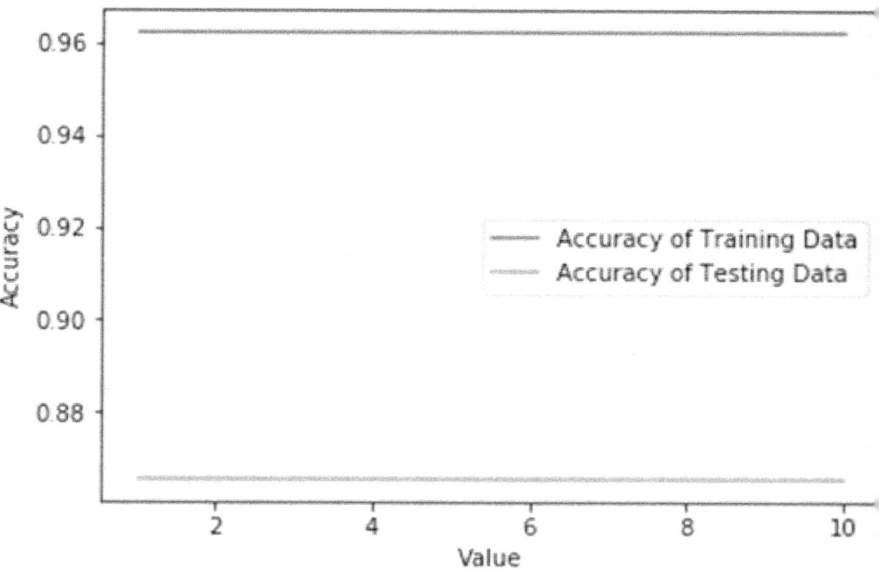

Accuracies of training and testing on Breast cancer dataset using
KNN with 2 neighbors without split command

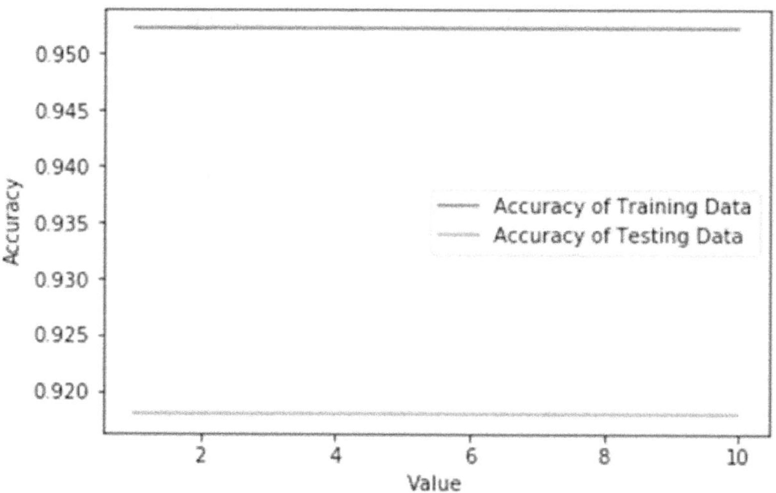

Accuracies of training and testing on Breast cancer dataset using

KNN with 3 neighbors without split command

By change in value of n_neighbors (representing the number of neighbors) from 2 to 3 in the below-mentioned command, you can observe the increase in accuracy of the KNN algorithm. As with the increase in the value of the nearest neighbors, the accuracy of the KNN algorithm increases. But by increasing too many nearest neighbors, the complexity, and simulation time will be increased as well.

```
knn = KNN(n_neighbors = 2)
```

You need to change parameters of algorithms to check their performances. You can change number of neighbors. Can you change it to 10? Why not try it out yourself? What do you suppose the output will be? Will it change the accuracy?

Currently, this example is using 70% of data for training and 30% data for testing. Try and change the partition to 50% each and see what the results are. You can do that by altering the value in "trs = round(0.7 * ts)". Remember, the percentage you use here will automatically assign the remainder to the testing data. Check the results by changing these values for the testing data. You will notice how the changes take effect.

It is to be kept in mind that 70-30 partition is only applicable in this specific dataset. It is a good likelihood that this might not work in other cases. Therefore, we will now look at how to deal with such cases the split command.

Applying KNN on Breast cancer dataset with the split command

Input:

```
# Importing required libraries
```

```python
from sklearn.datasets import load_breast_cancer as cancer

from sklearn.neighbors import KNeighborsClassifier as KNN

from sklearn.model_selection import train_test_split as tss

import matplotlib.pyplot as plt


# Loading input data

value = cancer()


# Splitting input data into training and testing data

Data_trn, Data_tst, Target_trn, Target_tst = tss(value.data,
                         value.target, random_state=10)


# Printing size of training and testing data

print(Data_trn.shape)

print(Data_tst.shape)
```

Output:

(426, 30)

(143, 30)

Input:

```python
accuracy_trn = []
```

```python
accuracy_tst = []

limit = range(1, 11)
for i in limit:
    # Training the model
    knn = KNN(n_neighbors = 2)
    knn.fit(Data_trn, Target_trn)
    # Calculating accuracy of Training Data
    accuracy_trn.append(knn.score(Data_trn, Target_trn))
    # Calculating accuracy of Testing Data
    accuracy_tst.append(knn.score(Data_tst, Target_tst))

# Plotting accuracy of training and testing data
plt.plot(limit, accuracy_trn, label = "Accuracy of Training Data")
plt.plot(limit, accuracy_tst, label = "Accuracy of Testing Data")
plt.xlabel("Value")
plt.ylabel("Accuracy")
plt.legend()
```

Output:

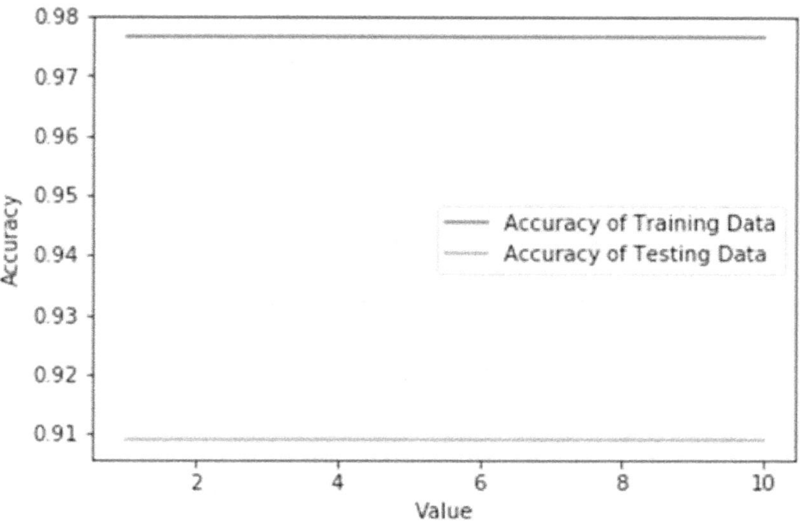

Accuracies of training and testing on Breast cancer dataset using
KNN with 2 neighbors with split command

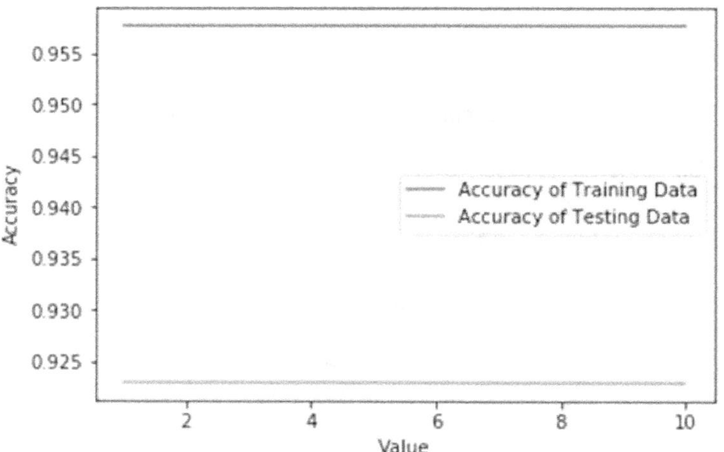

Accuracies of training and testing on Breast cancer dataset using
KNN with 3 neighbors with split command

Again, you can observe that by changing the value of n_neighbors from 2 to 3 in the below-mentioned command, accuracy of KNN algorithm will increase.

knn = KNN(n_neighbors = 2)

Play with this code again. Try to change the parameters of algorithms to check their performances. Can you change number of neighbors to 5? What output will you get now? Will it change the accuracy? Remember, through trial and error, we get to learn a lot. Do not be overwhelmed by any error you might encounter as this is a part of the learning.

Decision Tree

The decision tree method is another example of machine learning, which is used for both classification and regression processes. They work on making trees based on decisions to classify the datasets. This method contains if and else statements. The tree starts with data points having maximum probability among others. It makes multiple trees that are connected with each other. We will apply Decision tree on both Iris and Breast cancer datasets to perform classification process and then we will check its performance in terms of accuracy.

Applying Decision Tree on Breast cancer dataset

Input:

Importing required libraries

from sklearn.datasets import load_breast_cancer as cancer

```python
from sklearn.tree import DecisionTreeClassifier as DTC

from sklearn.model_selection import train_test_split as tss

import matplotlib.pyplot as plt


# Loading input data

value = cancer()


# Splitting input data into training and testing data

Data_trn, Data_tst, Target_trn, Target_tst = tss(value.data,
            value.target, random_state=10)


accuracy_trn = []

accuracy_tst = []


limit = range(1, 11)

for i in limit:


    # Training the model

    dtc = DTC(criterion = 'entropy', min_samples_split = 50,
            max_features = 3, max_depth = 2)

    dtc.fit(Data_trn, Target_trn)

    # Calculating accuracy of Training Data

    accuracy_trn.append(dtc.sccre(Data_trn, Target_trn))
```

Calculating accuracy of Testing Data

accuracy_tst.append(dtc.score(Data_tst, Target_tst))

Plotting accuracy of training and testing data

plt.plot(limit, accuracy_trn, label = "Accuracy of Training Data")

plt.plot(limit, accuracy_tst, label = "Accuracy of Testing Data")

plt.xlabel("Value")

plt.ylabel("Accuracy")

plt.legend()

Output:

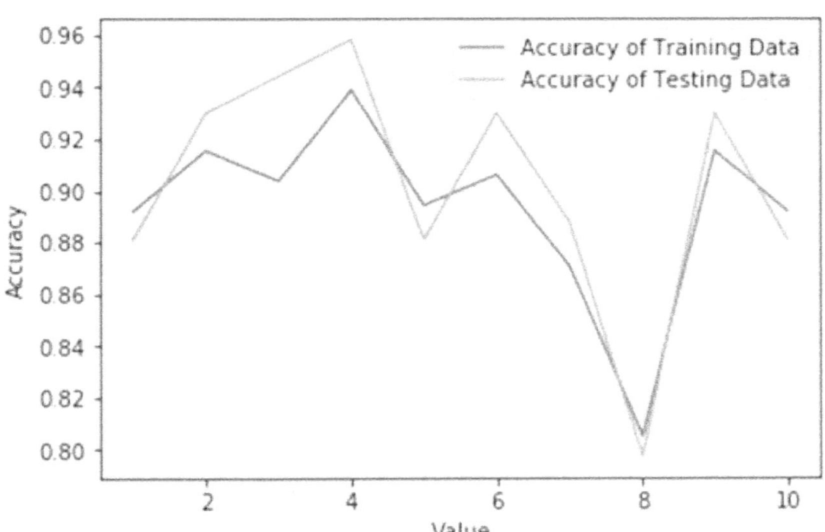

Accuracies accuracy of training and testing of Breast cancer dataset using DTC with 3 features

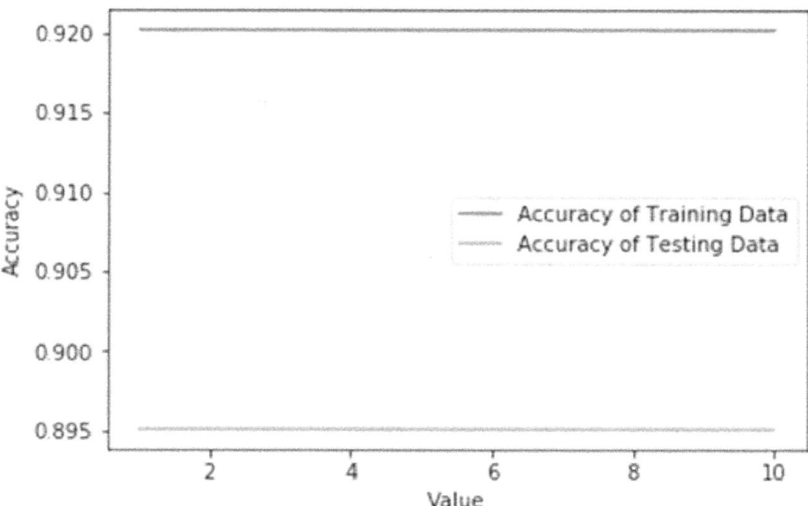

Accuracies of training and testing of Breast cancer dataset using DTC with 30 features

If you change the value of max_features (representing maximum features) from 3 to 30, the accuracy of DT algorithm will increase. Accuracy is increased with increase in number of features because the dataset contains 30 features. When the algorithm uses all features, the algorithm classifies effectively and hence accuracy is increased. While the accuracy of the DT algorithm increases with the increase in numbers and features, complexity and simulation time will increase as well.

```
dtc = DTC(criterion = 'entropy', min_samples_split = 50,
          max_features = 3, max_depth = 2)
```

Change parameters of DTC to check the results. You can see the effects of changing maximum features. If you try to change the value of features to more than 30, what will be the result?

You will be encountered with an error. Do not be alarmed as it can easily be explained. We have just surpassed the maximum value of features, which is why the program is unable to compute and hence returns an error.

Applying Decision Tree on Iris dataset

Input:

```python
# Importing required libraries

from sklearn.datasets import load_iris as iris

from sklearn.tree import DecisionTreeClassifier as DTC

from sklearn.model_selection import train_test_split as tss

import matplotlib.pyplot as plt


# Loading input data

value = iris()

Data = value.data

Target = value.target


# Splitting input data into training and testing data

Data_trn, Data_tst, Target_trn, Target_tst = tss(value.data,
value.target, random_state=10)
```

```python
# Printing size of training and testing data

print(Data_trn.shape)

print(Data_tst.shape)


accuracy_trn = []

accuracy_tst = []


limit = range(1, 11)

for i in limit:

# Training the model

dtc = DTC(criterion = 'entropy', min_samples_split = 50,
          max_features = 3, max_depth = 2)

dtc.fit(Data_trn, Target_trn)

# Calculating accuracy of Training Data

accuracy_trn.append(dtc.score(Data_trn, Target_trn))

# Calculating accuracy of Testing Data

accuracy_tst.append(dtc.score(Data_tst, Target_tst))


# Plotting accuracy of training and testing data

plt.plot(limit, accuracy_trn, label = "Accuracy of Training Data")

plt.hold
```

```python
plt.plot(limit, accuracy_tst, label = "Accuracy of Testing Data")

plt.xlabel("Value")

plt.ylabel("Accuracy")

plt.legend()


# Plotting prediction

plt.figure(2)

plt.plot(Data_trn[Target_trn == 0,0], Data_trn[Target_trn == 0,1],
            'rs', label = value.target_names[0])

plt.hold

plt.plot(Data_trn[Target_trn == 1,0], Data_trn[Target_trn == 1,1],
            'g.', label = value.target_names[1])

plt.legend()

plt.xlabel(value.feature_names[0])

plt.ylabel(value.feature_names[1])
```

Output:

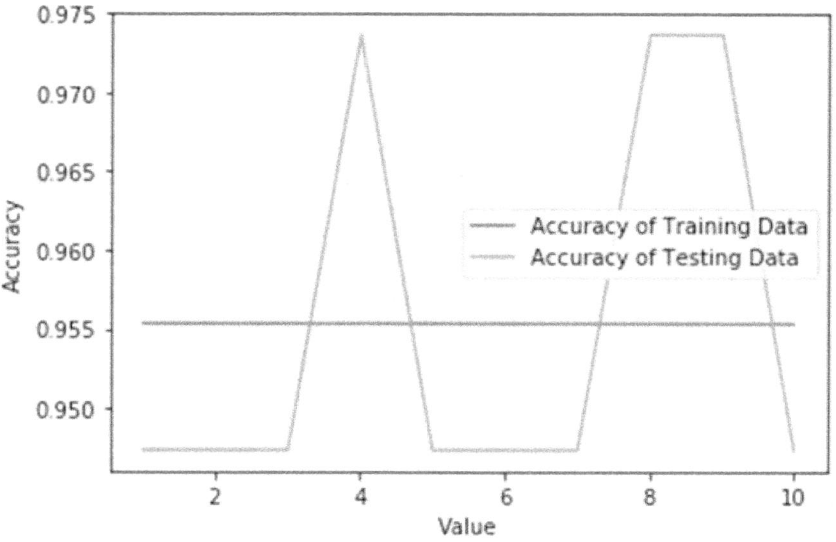

Accuracies of training and testing of iris dataset using DT with 3
features

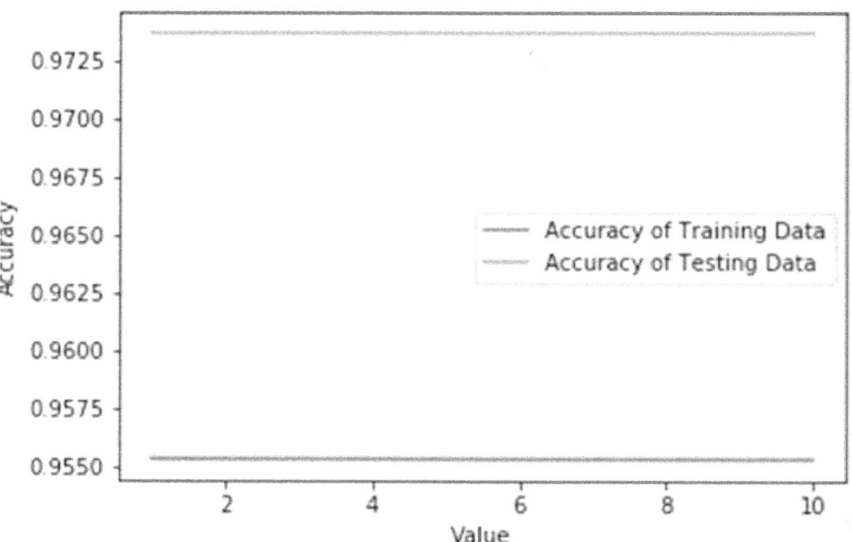

Accuracies of training and testing of iris dataset using DT with 4

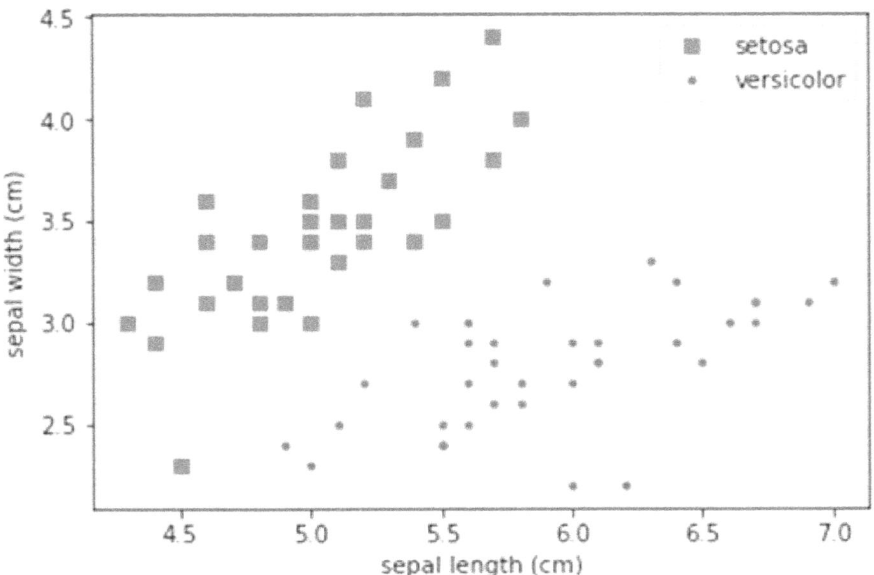

Predictions of iris dataset using DT with 3 features

By changing the value of max_features representing maximum features from three to four, you can observe that the accuracy of DT algorithm increases. As dataset contains four features and when algorithm uses all features, the algorithm classifies effectively and hence accuracy is increased and simulation time as well. Prediction achieved using four features instead of three is visually same, hence its plot is not shown.

```
dtc = DTC(criterion = 'entropy', min_samples_split = 50,
          max_features = 3, max_depth = 2)
```

Try changing the value to more than four. What results do you believe you will obtain? Again, do not worry should you encounter an error. This is to familiarize yourself with such situations and understanding the maximum values of such components. It is not necessary that these maximum values are predefined as we will look further in detail in future chapters.

Support Vector Machine

Support vector machines (SVM) are another example of machine learning, which is also used for both classification and regression processes. As it is used for supervised machine learning, labeled training data is given to a model. That model then assigns new values to these datasets. It works by creating categories separated by clear gap. The data belongs to a class, which is near to the line representing specific classes. This process proceeds until each dataset gets assigned.

Applying support vector classification on Breast cancer dataset

Input:

```python
# Importing required libraries

from sklearn.svm import SVC

from sklearn.datasets import load_breast_cancer as cancer

from sklearn.model_selection import train_test_split as tss

import matplotlib.pyplot as plt


# Loading input data

value = cancer()
```

```python
# Splitting input data into training and testing data

Data_trn, Data_tst, Target_trn, Target_tst = tss(value.data,
          value.target, random_state=10)


accuracy_trn = []

accuracy_tst = []


limit = range(1, 11)

for i in limit:

    # Training the model

svc = SVC(C = 1.0, gamma = 'auto', kernel = 'rbf')

svc.fit(Data_trn,Target_trn)

    # Calculating accuracy of Training Data

accuracy_trn.append(svc.score(Data_trn, Target_trn))

    # Calculating accuracy of Testing Data

accuracy_tst.append(svc.score(Data_tst, Target_tst))


# Plotting accuracy of training and testing data

plt.plot(limit, accuracy_trn, label="Accuracy of Training Data")

plt.plot(limit, accuracy_tst, label="Accuracy of Testing Data")

plt.xlabel("Neighbors")

plt.ylabel("Accuracy")
```

```
plt.legend()
```

Output:

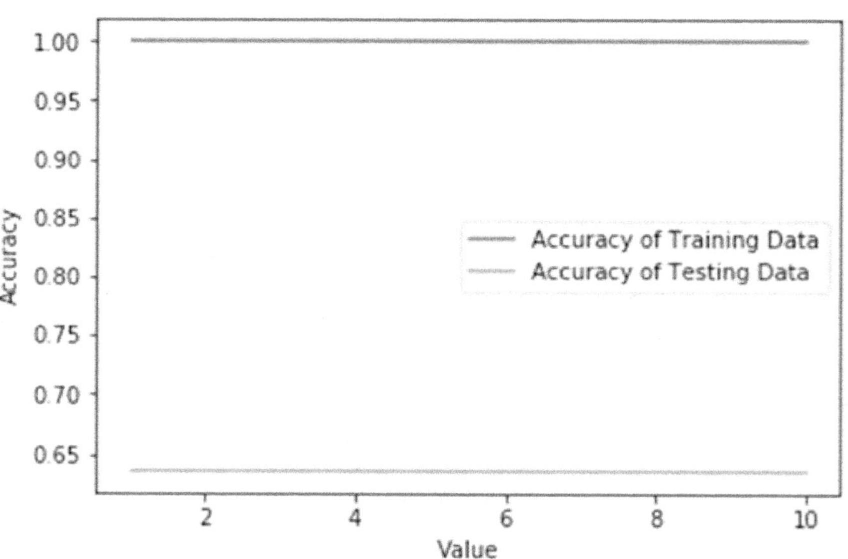

Accuracies of training and testing of Breast cancer dataset using
SVC with rbf kernel

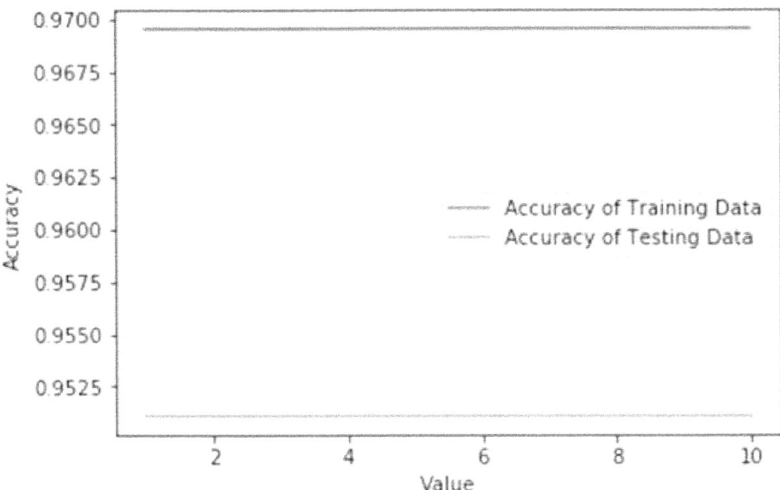

Accuracies of training and testing of Breast cancer dataset using SVC with linear kernel

By changing the kernel from 'rbf' to linear, it leads to better accuracy. The accuracy is increased because the problem is linear. The rbf can also work fine but in cases where problem is nonlinear.

svc = SVC(C = 1.0, gamma = 'auto', kernel = 'rbf')

Applying support vector classification on Iris dataset

Input:

Importing required libraries

from sklearn.svm import SVC

from sklearn.datasets import load_iris as iris

from sklearn.model_selection import train_test_split as tss

import matplotlib.pyplot as plt

Loading input data

```python
value = iris()


# Splitting input data into training and testing data

Data_trn, Data_tst, Target_trn, Target_tst = tss(value.data,
                         value.target, random_state=10)

accuracy_trn = []

accuracy_tst = []


limit = range(1, 11)

for i in limit:

    # Training the model

    svc = SVC(C = 1.0, gamma = 'auto', kernel = 'rbf')

    svc.fit(Data_trn, Target_trn)

    # Calculating accuracy of Training Data

    accuracy_trn.append(svc.score(Data_trn, Target_trn))

    # Calculating accuracy of Testing Data

    accuracy_tst.append(svc.score(Data_tst, Target_tst))


# Plotting accuracy of training and testing data

plt.plot(limit, accuracy_trn, label = "Accuracy of Training Data")

plt.plot(limit, accuracy_tst, label = "Accuracy of Testing Data")

plt.xlabel("Value")
```

```python
plt.ylabel("Accuracy")

plt.legend()



# Plotting prediction

plt.figure(2)

plt.plot(Data_trn[Target_trn == 0,0], Data_trn[Target_trn == 0,1],
         'rs', label = value.target_names[0])

plt.hold

plt.plot(Data_trn[Target_trn == 1,0], Data_trn[Target_trn == 1,1],
         'g.', label = value.target_names[1])

plt.legend()

plt.xlabel(value.feature_names[0])

plt.ylabel(value.feature_names[1])
```

Output:

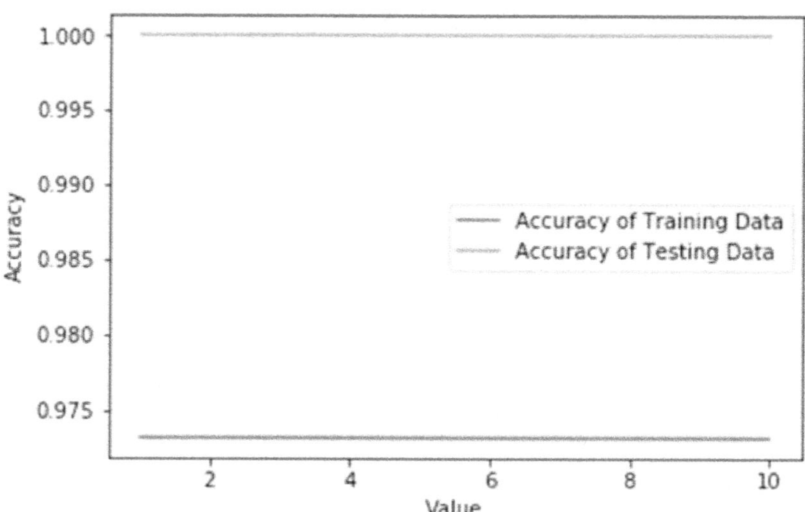

Accuracies of training and testing of iris dataset using SVC with rbf kernel

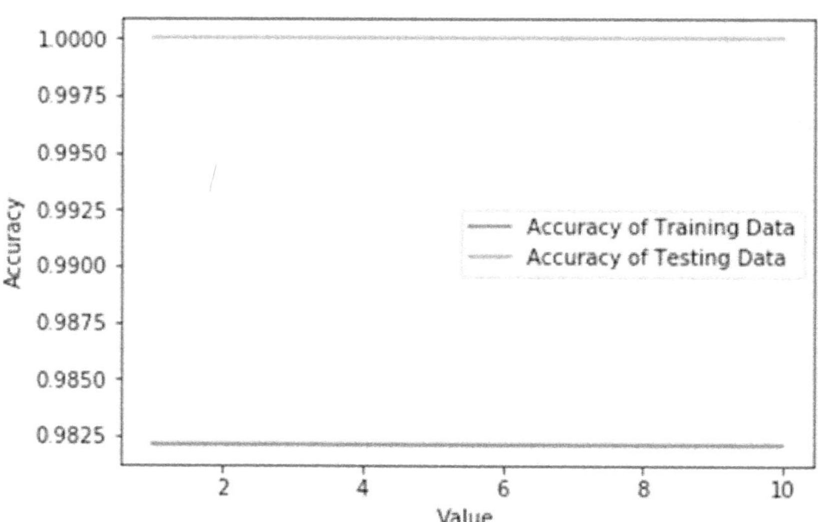

Accuracies of training and testing of iris dataset using SVC with linear kernel

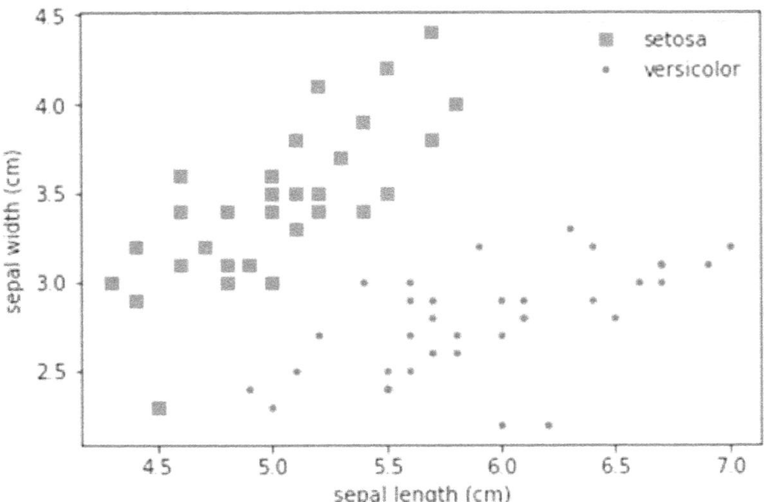

Predictions of iris dataset using SVC with rbf kernel

Again you can observe that by the change in the value of kernel from RBF to linear, the accuracy of the SVC algorithm increases. Accuracy is increased because problem is linear. The RBF can also work fine, but generally it is used in other cases where the problem is nonlinear. Predictions achieved using linear kernel instead of rbf kernel are visually the same and hold very minor details, not enough to be mapped or displayed, hence its plot is not shown.

svc = SVC(C = 1.0, gamma = 'auto', kernel = 'rbf')

Naive Bayes Classification

Naive Bayes classification method is another example of machine learning, which is used for classification process. This works by calculating probabilities of each dataset and assigns them new values depending on the value of their probabilities. This process continues until each dataset is assigned. Like previous methods, Naive Bayes will also be applied on both Iris and Breast cancer datasets for classification and then performances will be evaluated.

Remember, you can use your preferred datasets instead of the ones shown in the book. The aim here is to provide you with a visual data representation of how accuracy varies and how we can use various methods on the same datasets to bring out unique results, based on the situation.

Applying naive Bayes classification on Breast cancer dataset

Input:

```
# Importing required libraries

from sklearn.naive_bayes import GaussianNB as NB

from sklearn.datasets import load_breast_cancer as cancer

from sklearn.model_selection import train_test_split as tss

import matplotlib.pyplot as plt


# Loading input data

value = cancer()


# Splitting input data into training and testing data

Data_trn, Data_tst, Target_trn, Target_tst = tss(value.data,
value.target, random_state=10)


accuracy_trn = []

accuracy_tst = []


limit = range(1, 11)
```

```python
for i in limit:

    # Training the model

    nb = NB()

    nb.fit(Data_trn, Target_trn)

    # Calculating accuracy of Training Data

    accuracy_trn.append(nb.score(Data_trn, Target_trn))

    # Calculating accuracy of Testing Data

    accuracy_tst.append(nb.score(Data_tst, Target_tst))


# Plotting accuracy of training and testing data

plt.plot(limit, accuracy_trn, label = "Accuracy of Training Data")

plt.plot(limit, accuracy_tst, label = "Accuracy of Testing Data")

plt.xlabel("Value")

plt.ylabel("Accuracy")

plt.legend()
```

Output:

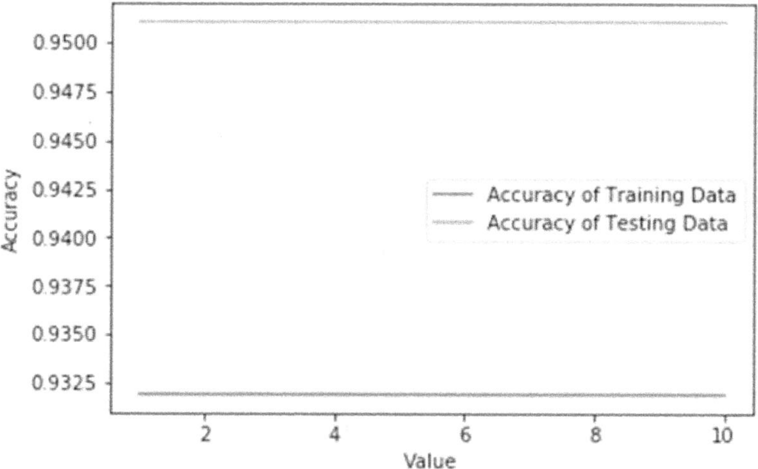

Accuracies of training and testing of Breast cancer dataset using NB

Naive Bayes method is applied with default settings of parameters. You can play with command below by passing various arguments:

nb = NB()

Applying naive Bayes classification on Iris dataset

Input:

Importing required libraries

from sklearn.naive_bayes import GaussianNB as NB

from sklearn.datasets import load_iris as iris

from sklearn.model_selection import train_test_split as tss

import matplotlib.pyplot as plt

```python
# Loading input data

value = iris()


# Splitting input data into training and testing data

Data_trn, Data_tst, Target_trn, Target_tst = tss(value.data,
             value.target, random_state=10)


accuracy_trn = []

accuracy_tst = []


limit = range(1, 11)

for i in limit:

    # Training the model

    nb = NB()

    nb.fit(Data_trn, Target_trn)

    # Calculating accuracy of Training Data

    accuracy_trn.append(nb.score(Data_trn, Target_trn))

    # Calculating accuracy of Testing Data

    accuracy_tst.append(nb.score(Data_tst, Target_tst))


# Plotting accuracy of training and testing data

plt.plot(limit, accuracy_trn, label = "Accuracy of Training Data")
```

```python
plt.plot(limit, accuracy_tst, label = "Accuracy of Testing Data")

plt.xlabel("Value")

plt.ylabel("Accuracy")

plt.legend()


# Plotting prediction

plt.figure(2)

plt.plot(Data_trn[Target_trn == 0,0], Data_trn[Target_trn == 0,1],
         'rs', label = value.target_names[0])

plt.hold

plt.plot(Data_trn[Target_trn == 1,0], Data_trn[Target_trn == 1,1],
         'g.', label = value.target_names[1])

plt.legend()

plt.xlabel(value.feature_names[0])

plt.ylabel(value.feature_names[1])
```

Output:

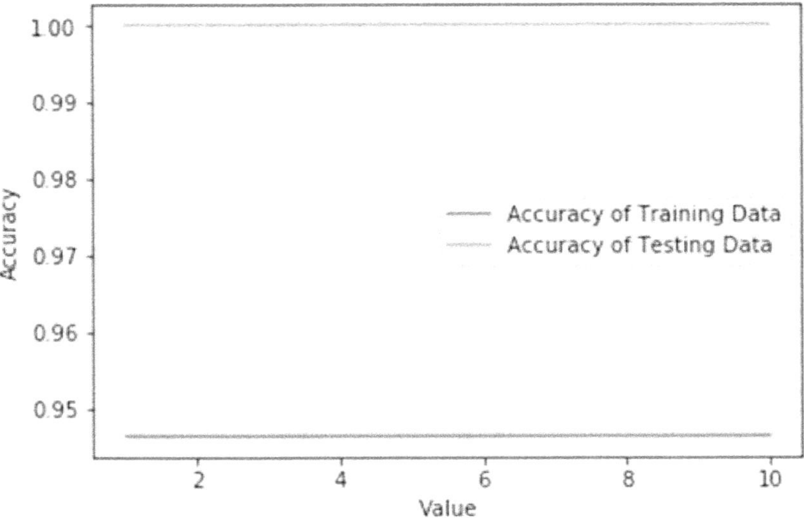

Accuracies of training and testing of Iris dataset using NB

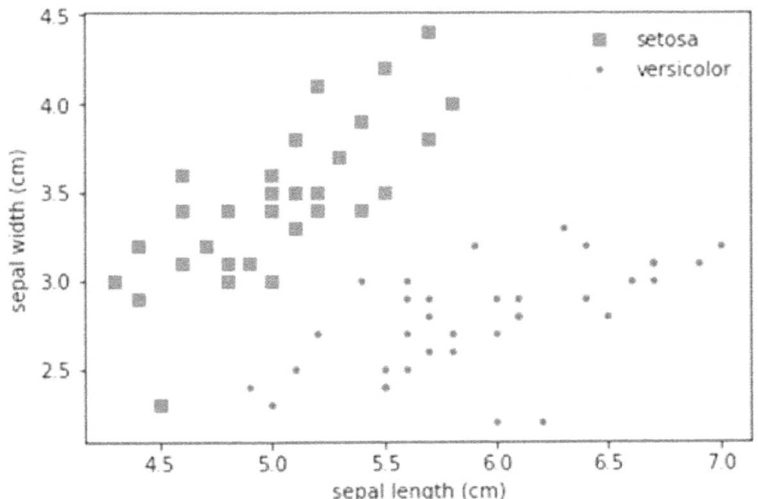

Predictions of iris dataset using NB

Logistic Regression

The logistic regression method is used for classification process as well for machine learning. Although its name suggests that this method may work better for the regression process, but it actually works just for classification process.

This method belongs to the linear classification. It can also be known as binary classification as it assigns zeros and ones to dataset in order to perform the process of classification. This method also works by calculating probabilities of each dataset and then assigns them new values depending on the value of their probabilities. Logistic Regression method will also be applied on both Iris and Breast cancer datasets for classification and then performances will be analyzed.

Applying logistic regression on Breast cancer dataset

Input:

Importing required libraries

from sklearn.linear_model import LogisticRegression as LR

from sklearn.datasets import load_breast_cancer as cancer

from sklearn.model_selection import train_test_split as tss

import matplotlib.pyplot as plt

Loading input data

value = cancer()

```python
# Splitting input data into training and testing data

Data_trn, Data_tst, Target_trn, Target_tst = tss(value.data,
                 value.target, random_state=10)


accuracy_trn = []

accuracy_tst = []


limit = range(1, 11)

for i in limit:


    # Training the model

    lr = LR(tol = 0.01, C = 1.0, max_iter = 100, n_jobs = 1)

    lr.fit(Data_trn, Target_trn)
    # Calculating accuracy of Training Data
    accuracy_trn.append(lr.score(Data_trn, Target_trn))
    # Calculating accuracy of Testing Data
    accuracy_tst.append(lr.score(Data_tst, Target_tst))


# Plotting accuracy of training and testing data
plt.plot(limit, accuracy_trn, label = "Accuracy of Training Data")

plt.plot(limit, accuracy_tst, label = "Accuracy of Testing Data")
```

plt.xlabel("Value")

plt.ylabel("Accuracy")

plt.legend()

Output:

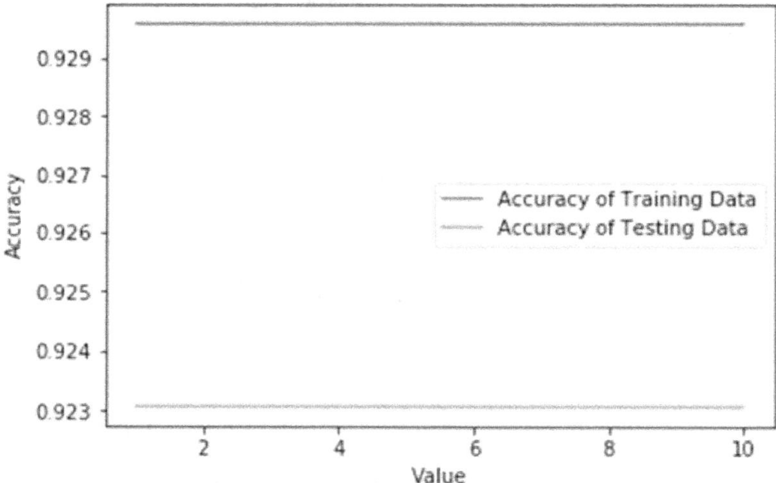

Accuracies of training and testing of Breast cancer dataset using LR
with tolerance of 0.01

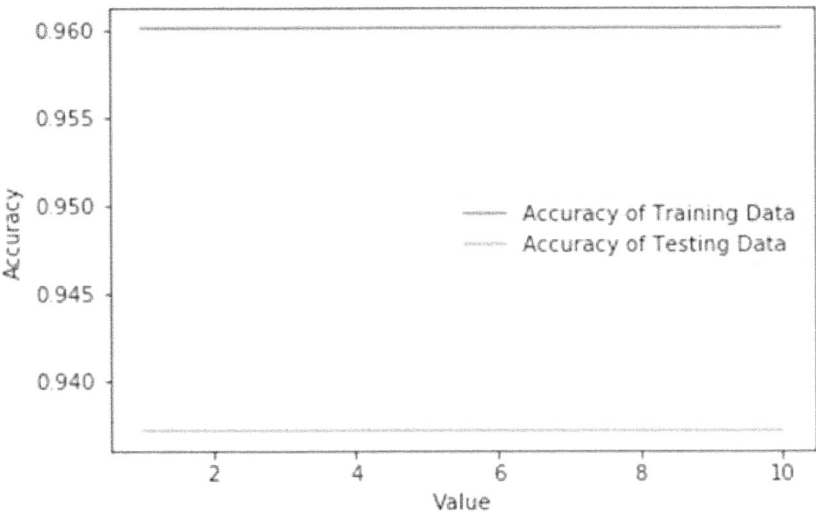

Accuracies of training and testing of Breast cancer dataset using LR
with tolerance of 0.0001

By changing the value of tolerance from 0.01 to 0.0001 through the command shown below, the accuracy of LR algorithm is increased. Accuracy is increased as less tolerance is accepted. With decreasing tolerance, quality output is achieved.

lr = LR(tol = 0.01, C = 1.0, max_iter = 100, n_jobs = 1)

Experiment with the parameters and check how the results vary. You can try and change the value of max_iter as well. However, can the accuracy increase if we reduce the tolerance? That's something for you to check by manipulating the values.

Remember, experiments have lead to great discoveries, we are just trying to gain a bit of an understanding here. Through trial and error, we will soon be able to understand how most of these methods work and how the data output would be like when we change certain values.

Applying logistic regression on Iris dataset

Input:

```python
# Importing required libraries
from sklearn.linear_model import LogisticRegression as LR
from sklearn.datasets import load_iris as iris
from sklearn.model_selection import train_test_split as tss
import matplotlib.pyplot as plt


# Loading input data
value = iris()


# Splitting input data into training and testing data
Data_trn, Data_tst, Target_trn, Target_tst = tss(value.data,
value.target, random_state=10)


accuracy_trn = []

accuracy_tst = []

limit = range(1, 11)

for i in limit:
    # Training the model
    lr = LR(tol = 0.01, C = 10.0, max_iter = 100, n_jobs = 1)
    lr.fit(Data_trn, Target_trn)
```

```python
# Calculating accuracy of Training Data
accuracy_trn.append(lr.score(Data_trn, Target_trn))
# Calculating accuracy of Testing Data
accuracy_tst.append(lr.score(Data_tst, Target_tst))


# Plotting accuracy of training and testing data
plt.plot(limit, accuracy_trn, label = "Accuracy of Training Data")
plt.plot(limit, accuracy_tst, label = "Accuracy of Testing Data")
plt.xlabel("Value")
plt.ylabel("Accuracy")
plt.legend()


# Plotting prediction
plt.figure(2)
plt.plot(Data_trn[Target_trn == 0,0], Data_trn[Target_trn == 0,1],
         'rs', label = value.target_names[0])
plt.hold
plt.plot(Data_trn[Target_trn == 1,0], Data_trn[Target_trn == 1,1],
         'g.', label = value.target_names[1])
plt.legend()
plt.xlabel(value.feature_names[0])
plt.ylabel(value.feature_names[1])
```

Output:

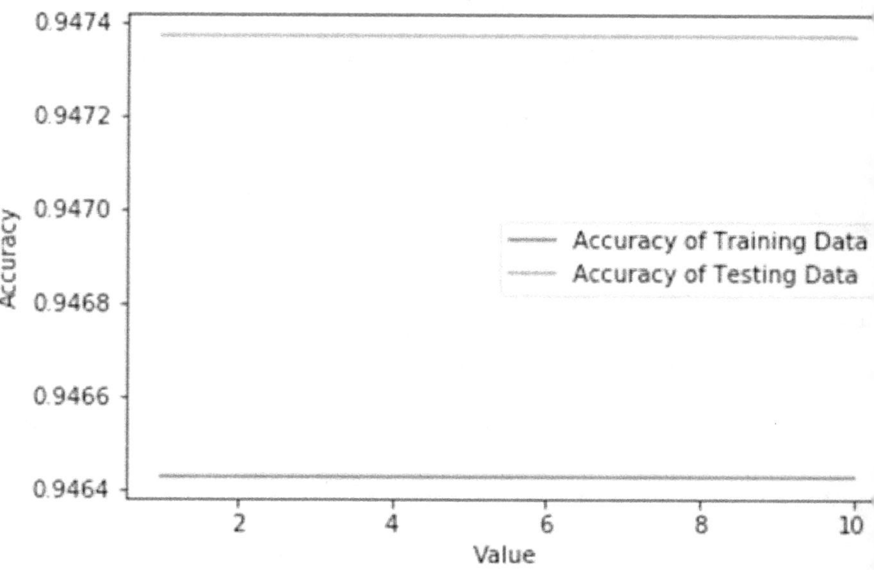

Accuracies of training and testing of Iris dataset using LR with C of 1

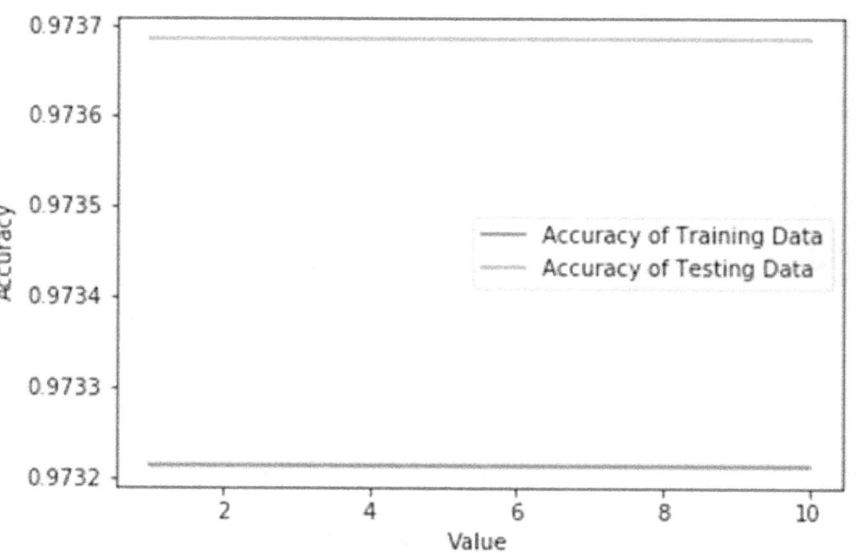

Accuracies of training and testing of Iris dataset using LR with C of

10

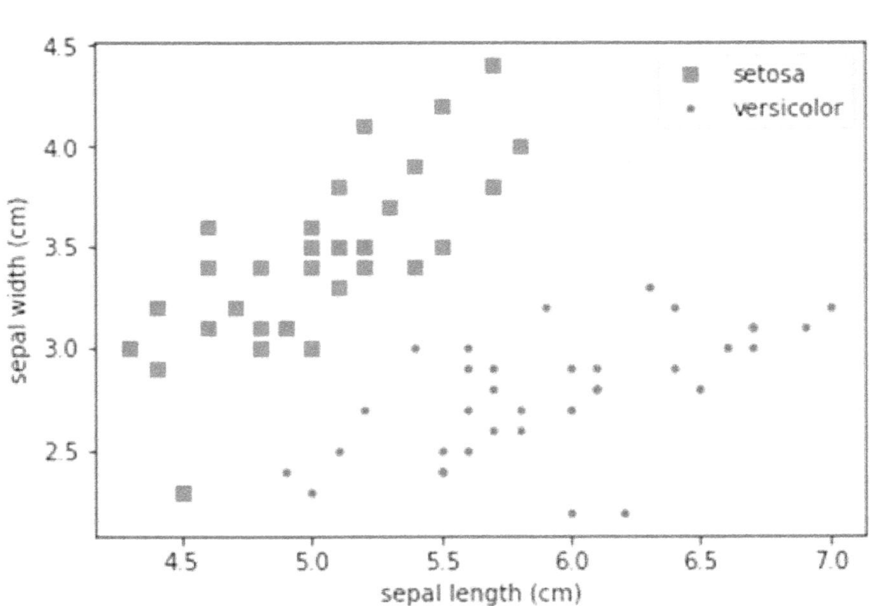

Predictions of iris dataset using LR using LR with C of 1

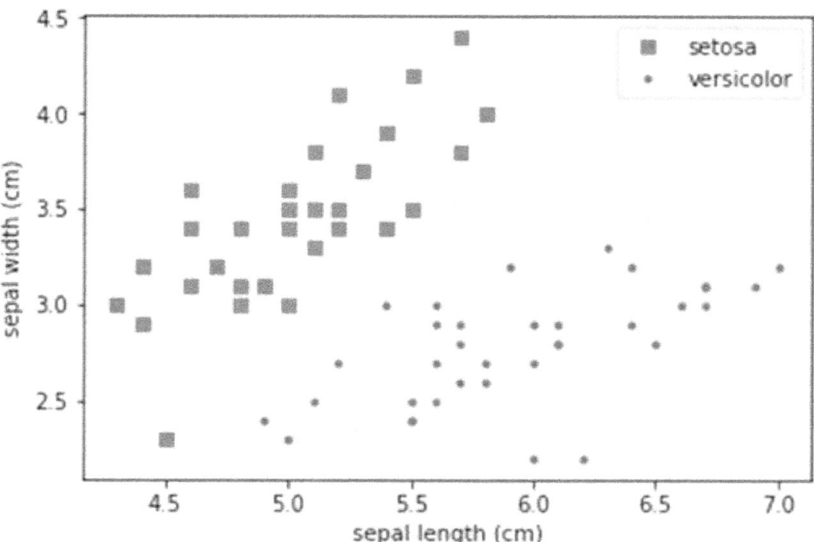

Predictions of iris dataset using LR with value of C of 10

You can observe in this example that by a change in the value of tolerance from 0.01 to 0.0001, no change appeared. We then changed value of C from 1 to 10 which increased the accuracy. Different parameters work differently for different problems. Just like we saw when we looked into Support vector, one example favored linear kernel while other favored rbf kernel. Similarly, change in value of tolerance did not affect the accuracy but C affected the accuracy.

lr = LR(tol = 0.01, C = 1.0, max_iter = 100, n_jobs = 1)

Neural Network

Neural network (NN) is another method of machine learning. It has been used often as a preferred method in machine learning problems. It uses multiple methods, which are modeled much similar to human brain to check patterns for predictions. We will apply NN for classification processes in this chapter. We will apply NN classification to Breast cancer and Iris datasets to validate its working capacity and accuracy.

Applying Neural network on Breast cancer dataset

Input:

```
# Importing required libraries

from keras.models import Sequential as NN

from keras.layers import Dense

from sklearn.datasets import load_breast_cancer as cancer

from sklearn.model_selection import train_test_split as tss

import matplotlib.pyplot as plt

import numpy as np


# Loading input data

value = cancer()


# Splitting input data into training and testing data

Data_trn, Data_tst, Target_trn, Target_tst = tss(value.data,
value.target, random_state=10)
```

```python
accuracy_trn = []

accuracy_tst = []


limit = range(1, 11)

for i in limit:


    # Training the model

    nn = NN()


    nn.add(Dense(1, activation = 'relu'))

    # compile the keras model

    nn.compile(loss = 'binary_crossentropy', optimizer = 'adam',
               metrics = ['accuracy'])

    # fit keras model on dataset

    nn.fit(Data_trn, Target_trn, epochs = 150, batch_size = 10)

    # Calculating accuracy of Training Data

    accuracy_trn.append(nn.evaluate(Data_trn, Target_trn))

    # Calculating accuracy of Testing Data

    accuracy_tst.append(nn.evaluate(Data_tst, Target_tst))


A = np.array([accuracy_trn])

B = np.array([accuracy_tst])
```

```python
AA = A[0, :, 1]

BB = B[0, :, 1]


# Plotting accuracy of training and testing data

plt.plot(limit, AA, label = "Accuracy of Training Data")

plt.plot(limit, BB, label = "Accuracy of Testing Data")

plt.xlabel("Value")

plt.ylabel("Accuracy")

plt.legend()
```

Output:

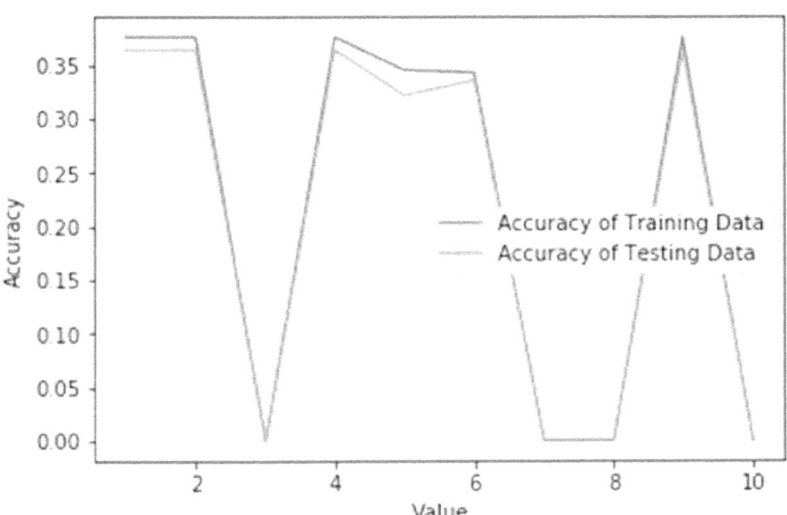

Accuracies of training and testing of Breast cancer dataset using NN with relu activation

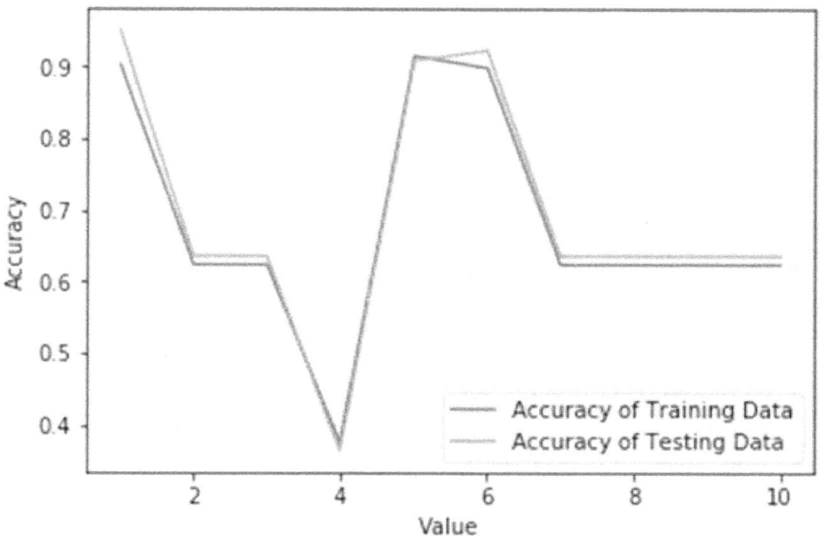

Accuracies of training and testing of Breast cancer dataset using NN with sigmoid activation

Change in the value of activation from 'relu' to 'sigmoid' in the command mentioned below, you can observe the increase in accuracy of **NN** algorithm.

```
nn.add(Dense(1, activation = 'relu'))
```

You can shuffle the activation to check the performance of the NN algorithm as well.

Applying Neural network on Iris dataset

Input:

```
# Importing required libraries

from keras.models import Sequential as NN
```

```python
from keras.layers import Dense

from sklearn.datasets import load_iris as iris

from sklearn.model_selection import train_test_split as tss

import matplotlib.pyplot as plt

import numpy as np


# Loading input data

value = iris()


# Splitting input data into training and testing data

Data_trn, Data_tst, Target_trn, Target_tst = tss(value.data,
                value.target, random_state=10)


accuracy_trn = []

accuracy_tst = []


limit = range(1, 11)

for i in limit:

# Training the model

nn = NN()

nn.add(Dense(1, activation = 'relu'))

# compile the keras model
```

```python
nn.compile(loss = 'binary_crossentropy', optimizer = 'adam',
           metrics = ['accuracy'])

# fit keras model on dataset

nn.fit(Data_trn, Target_trn, epochs = 150, batch_size = 10)

# Calculating accuracy of Training Data

accuracy_trn.append(nn.evaluate(Data_trn, Target_trn))

# Calculating accuracy of Testing Data

accuracy_tst.append(nn.evaluate(Data_tst, Target_tst))


A = np.array([accuracy_trn])

B = np.array([accuracy_tst])

AA = A[0, :, 1]

BB = B[0, :, 1]


# Plotting accuracy of training and testing data

plt.plot(limit, AA, label = "Accuracy of Training Data")

plt.plot(limit, BB, label = "Accuracy of Testing Data")

plt.xlabel("Value")

plt.ylabel("Accuracy")

plt.legend()


# Plotting prediction
```

```
plt.figure(2)

plt.plot(Data_trn[Target_trn == 0,0], Data_trn[Target_trn == 0,1],
         'rs', label = value.target_names[0])

plt.hold

plt.plot(Data_trn[Target_trn == 1,0], Data_trn[Target_trn == 1,1],
         'g.', label = value.target_names[1])

plt.legend()

plt.xlabel(value.feature_names[0])

plt.ylabel(value.feature_names[1])
```

Output:

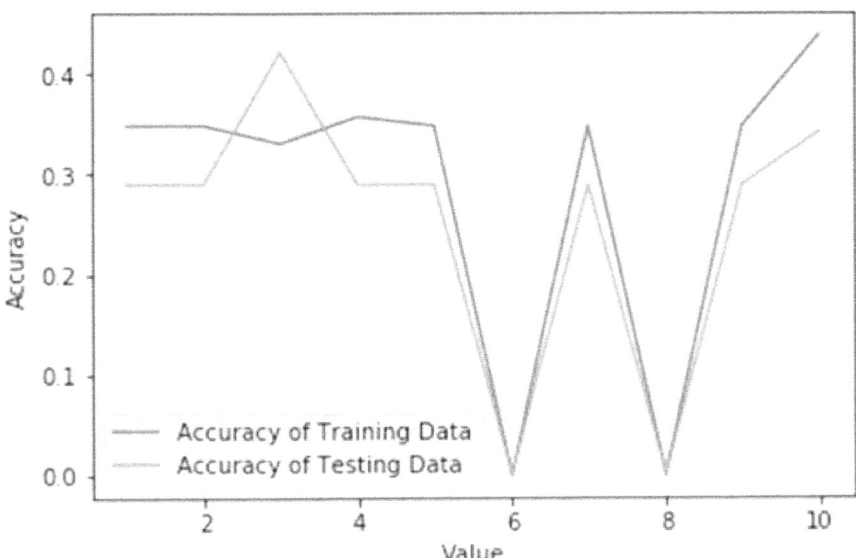

Accuracies of training and testing of Iris dataset using NN with relu activation

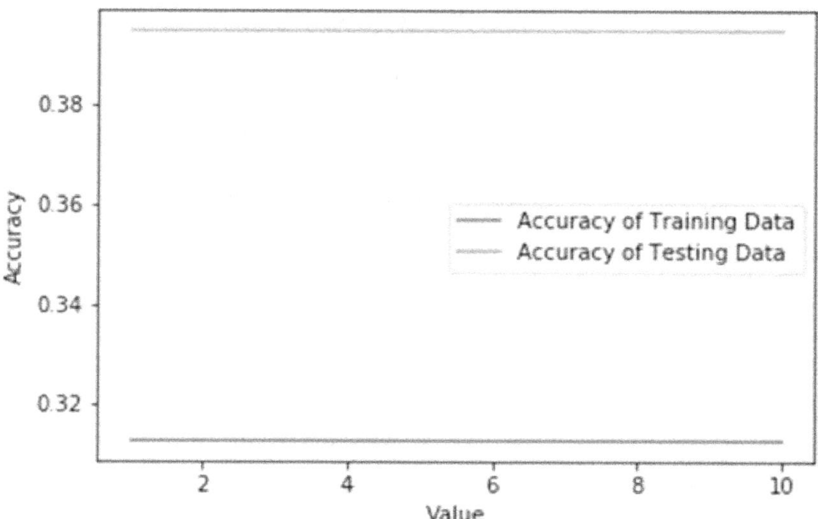

Accuracies of training and testing of Iris dataset using NN with sigmoid activation

By changing the value further, you can observe the increase in accuracy of NN algorithm.

```
nn.add(Dense(1, activation = 'relu'))
```

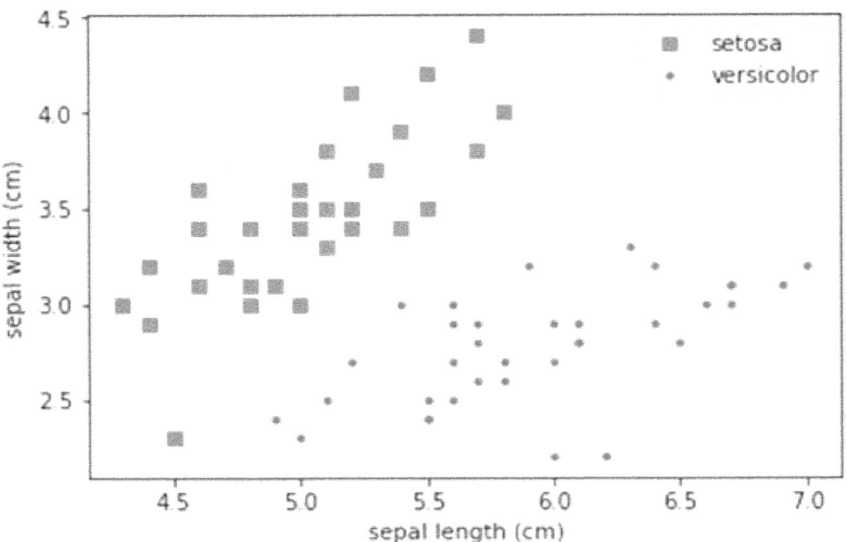

Predictions of iris dataset using NN with relu activation

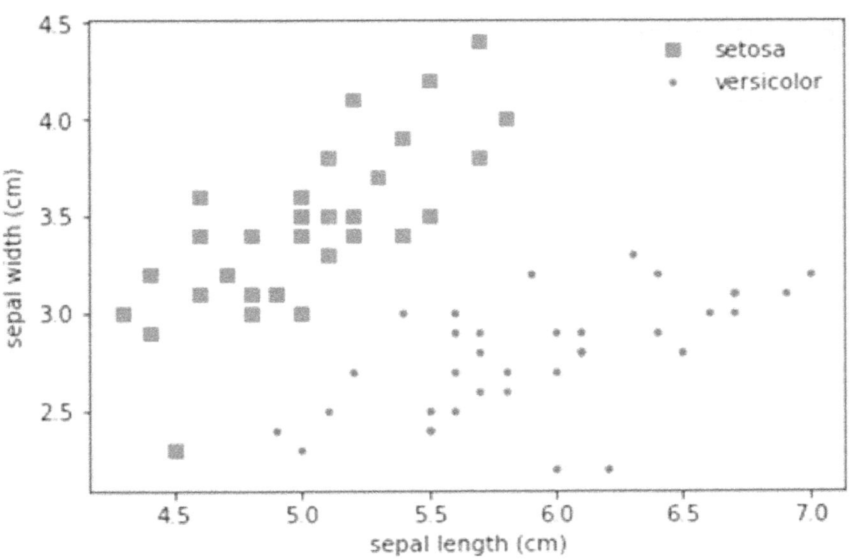

Predictions of iris dataset using NN with sigmoid activation

By changing the value further, you can observe the increase in accuracy of NN algorithm. The prediction achieved through sigmoid activation instead of relu activation is exactly the same, which is why we will not be looking at the plotting of the same.

```
nn.add(Dense(1, activation = 'relu'))
```

Things to remember:

We learned how we apply various classifications using numerous methods and functions. Each one of them has its unique use and application. Their accuracy in mapping and plotting varies, which is why it is ideal to get yourself familiarized with these through practice.

There are hundreds of thousands of datasets available for practice purposes. You can simply browse the internet and download these datasets from various websites. It is recommended that you continue practicing and learning numerous methods to gain the competitive advantage you are looking for. Since this book is targeting advanced learning, we will not continue with practices and move toward our next aspect of learning.

Chapter 3: Supervised Machine Learning for Continuous Class Label

Understanding the Concept of Regression

We already have discussed in the previous chapter that the term Supervised learning originated from the term supervision. Supervised learning takes data as inputs, and it also knows its corresponding outputs as well, and when different inputs are provided to that system, it can predict its output using that trained model.

We also discussed in the previous chapter that supervised machine learning comprises of two types: classification and regression. We discussed classification earlier in detail, which is used to predict discrete label, which means that it provides discrete output of specific input for training.

In this chapter, we will discuss the regression method that is used to predict continuous label which means that provides continuous output of specific input for training.

You can distinguish between two categories of supervised machine learning, classification and regression, by checking whether your output, given by prediction, contains any continuity or not. If the data contains continuity, then it is an example of regression and if it contains discrete output then it can safely be deduced as an example of classification. If you may recall, we already have discussed an example an individual's annual income when we initially touched upon regression.

We can have multiple applications of regression. We can have both sets of data either discrete or continuous. We need to understand both the schemes of machine learning in order to apply these methods in practical problems.

Regression Models

We have discussed the classification versions of KNN, Decision tree, SVM, Naive Bayes, logistic regression and Neural Network in the previous chapter. We applied those classification methods on Iris and Breast cancer datasets. Some of them contained features of regression as well.

There are many regression models that will be used in this chapter to predict continuous labels. We will discuss regression using KNN, Decision tree, SVM, Random forest, linear regression and Neural Network. We will apply these regression methods on Boston and Diabetes datasets; these are pre-defined datasets, available within the Scikit-Learn.

While performing the process of regression, we need to keep the factors of overfitting and underfitting in consideration. We need to know if our training datasets or models will work just on the training, test data and/or with new test data. We also should keep an eye out to know if we need to completely change the model to work for other test data.

K-Nearest Neighbors Regression

As we discussed in the previous chapter, KNN is the simplest machine learning algorithm that is used for both classification and regression processes. We used this method for classification process in the previous chapter, and this time, we will use it for the application of regression process.

The working procedure will remain the same for KNN for regression. This means, as before, it will take k nearest neighbors to calculate a new data point for any given data. If we keep value of k as one, it will be simplest version of KNN regression, which will take only one nearest neighbor as reference to calculate new data point for an input data. It will work exactly the same for calculating new data points for all the given data. We will apply the KNN-based regression to Boston and Diabetes datasets to analyze the accuracy. The value of K can also be varied to observe changes in the prediction.

Applying KNN regression on Boston dataset

Input:

```python
# Importing required libraries
from sklearn.neighbors import KNeighborsRegressor as KNN
from sklearn.datasets import load_boston as boston
from sklearn.model_selection import train_test_split as tss
import matplotlib.pyplot as plt
import pandas as pd


# Loading input data
value = boston()
df = pd.DataFrame(value.data, columns = value.feature_names)
df["MEDV"] = value.target
X = df.drop("MEDV",1)   # Feature Matrix
Y = df["MEDV"]          # Target Vector


# Splitting input data into training and testing data
Data_trn, Data_tst, Target_trn, Target_tst = tss(X, Y, random_state = 10)


# Printing size of training and testing data
print(Data_trn.shape)
```

```python
print(Data_tst.shape)
```

Output:

```
(379, 13)

(127, 13)
```

Input:

```python
accuracy_trn = []
accuracy_tst = []


limit = range(1, 11)

for i in limit:
    # Training the model
    knn = KNN(n_neighbors = 1)
    knn.fit(Data_trn, Target_trn)
    # Calculating accuracy of Training Data
    accuracy_trn.append(knn.score(Data_trn, Target_trn))
    # Calculating accuracy of Testing Data
    accuracy_tst.append(knn.score(Data_tst, Target_tst))


# Plotting accuracy of training and testing data
plt.plot(limit, accuracy_trn, label = "Accuracy of Training Data")
```

plt.plot(limit, accuracy_tst, label = "Accuracy of Testing Data")

plt.xlabel("Value")

plt.ylabel("Accuracy")

plt.legend()

Output:

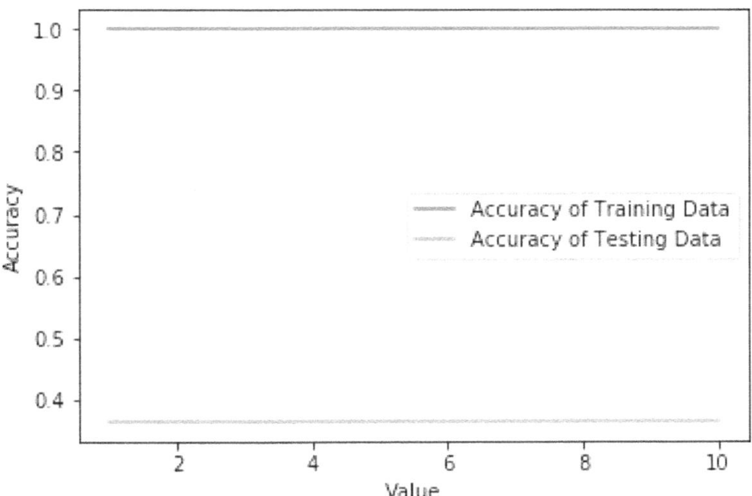

Accuracies of training and testing on Boston dataset using KNN with 2 neighbors

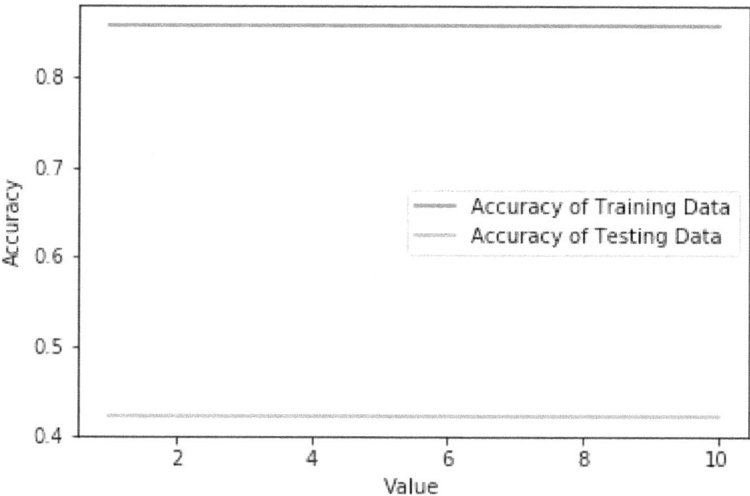

Accuracies of training and testing on Boston dataset using KNN with 3 neighbors

As before, if we change the value of n_neighbors while predicting its output from 1 to 2, we can observe the increase in accuracy of the KNN algorithm. Increasing the value of the nearest neighbors, the accuracy of KNN algorithm also increases. However, by increasing too many nearest neighbors, the complexity and simulation time increases as well.

Similarly, by using a much bigger value of number for neighbors, it can lead to lesser classes. You can further change value of k to check the change in accuracy of the prediction. Try to use different values for the code and analyze the performance of KNN algorithm. You can also apply this code to another dataset as well.

knn = KNN(n_neighbors = 2)

Applying KNN regression on Diabetes dataset

Input:

Importing required libraries

from sklearn.neighbors import KNeighborsRegressor as KNN

```python
from sklearn.datasets import load_diabetes as diabetes

from sklearn.model_selection import train_test_split as tss

import matplotlib.pyplot as plt

import pandas as pd


# Loading input data

value = diabetes()

df = pd.DataFrame(value.data, columns = value.feature_names)

df["MEDV"] = value.target

X = df.drop("MEDV",1)   # Feature Matrix

Y = df["MEDV"]          # Target Vector


# Splitting input data into training and testing data

Data_trn, Data_tst, Target_trn, Target_tst = tss(X, Y, random_state = 10)


# Printing size of training and testing data

print(Data_trn.shape)

print(Data_tst.shape)


Output:
```

```
(331, 10)

(111, 10)
```

Input:

```python
accuracy_trn = []

accuracy_tst = []


limit = range(1, 11)

for i in limit:

    # Training the model

    knn = KNN(n_neighbors = 2)

    knn.fit(Data_trn, Target_trn)

    # Calculating accuracy of Training Data

    accuracy_trn.append(knn.score(Data_trn, Target_trn))

    # Calculating accuracy of Testing Data

    accuracy_tst.append(knn.score(Data_tst, Target_tst))


# Plotting accuracy of training and testing data

plt.plot(limit, accuracy_trn, label = "Accuracy of Training Data")

plt.plot(limit, accuracy_tst, label = "Accuracy of Testing Data")

plt.xlabel("Value")

plt.ylabel("Accuracy")
```

```
plt.legend()
```

Output:

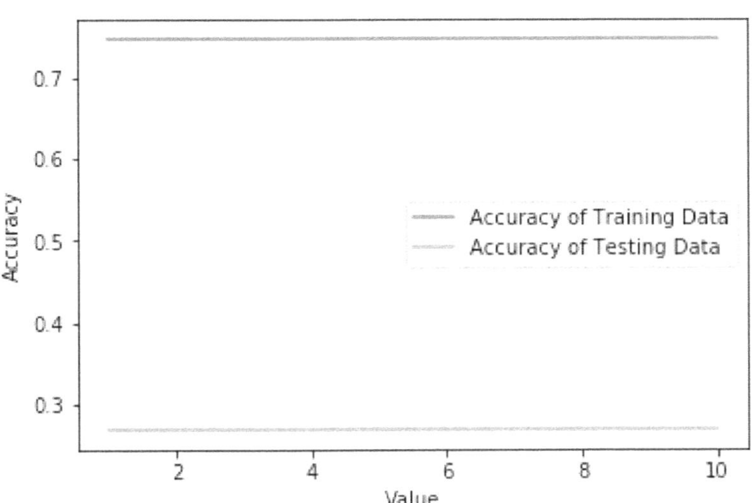

Accuracies of training and testing on Diabetes dataset using KNN
with 2 neighbors

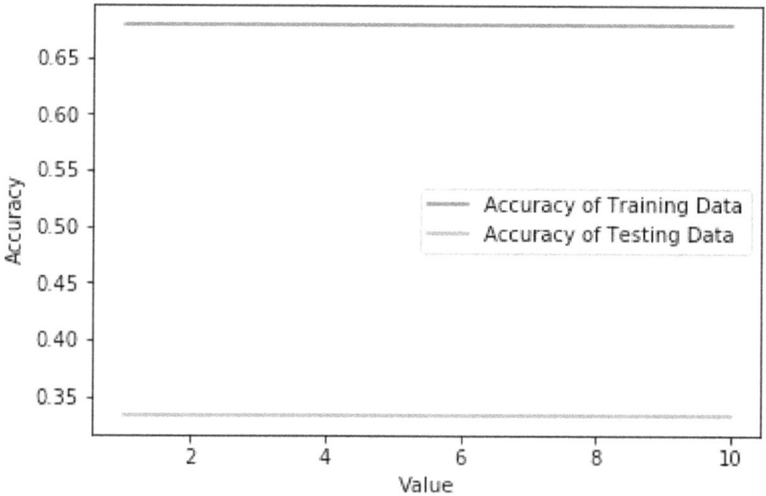

Accuracies of training and testing on Diabetes dataset using KNN
with 3 neighbors

Decision Tree Regression

We have discussed in the previous chapter about usage of Decision Tree method for classification process. We discussed that it makes a tree-based decision in classifying the data sets. We used this method for classification process previously but in this chapter, we will apply regression process using Decision tree regression. We will apply Decision tree to Boston and Diabetes datasets to validate its accuracy.

Applying Decision Tree regression on Boston dataset

Input:

```
# Importing required libraries

from sklearn.tree import DecisionTreeRegressor as DTR

from sklearn.datasets import load_boston as boston

from sklearn.model_selection import train_test_split as tss
```

```python
import matplotlib.pyplot as plt

import pandas as pd


# Loading input data

value = boston()

df = pd.DataFrame(value.data, columns = value.feature_names)

df["MEDV"] = value.target

X = df.drop("MEDV",1)   # Feature Matrix

Y = df["MEDV"]              # Target Vector


# Splitting input data into training and testing data
Data_trn, Data_tst, Target_trn, Target_tst = tss(X, Y, random_state
                            = 10)


accuracy_trn = []

accuracy_tst = []

limit = range(1, 11)

for i in limit:

# Training the model

dtr = DTR(min_samples_split = 50, max_features = 3, max_depth
                            = 2)

dtr.fit(Data_trn, Target_trn)

# Calculating accuracy of Training Data
```

```
accuracy_trn.append(dtr.score(Data_trn, Target_trn))

# Calculating accuracy of Testing Data

accuracy_tst.append(dtr.score(Data_tst, Target_tst))


# Plotting accuracy of training and testing data

plt.plot(limit, accuracy_trn, label = "Accuracy of Training Data")

plt.plot(limit, accuracy_tst, label = "Accuracy of Testing Data")

plt.xlabel("Value")

plt.ylabel("Accuracy")

plt.legend()
```

Output:

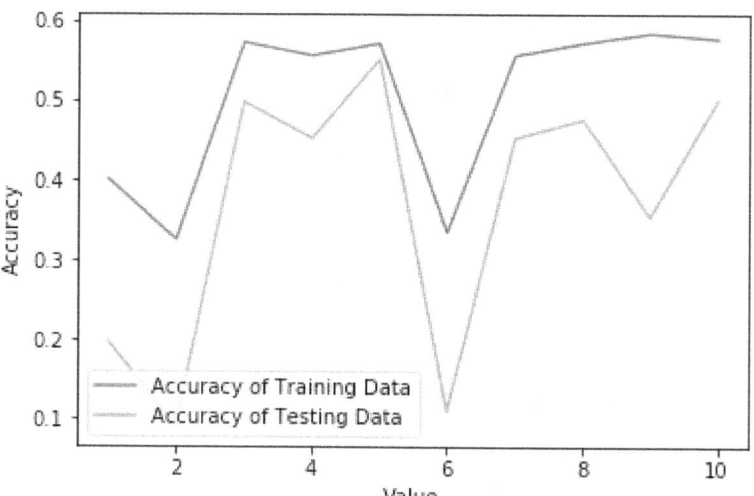

Accuracies accuracy of training and testing of Boston dataset using

DTR with 3 features

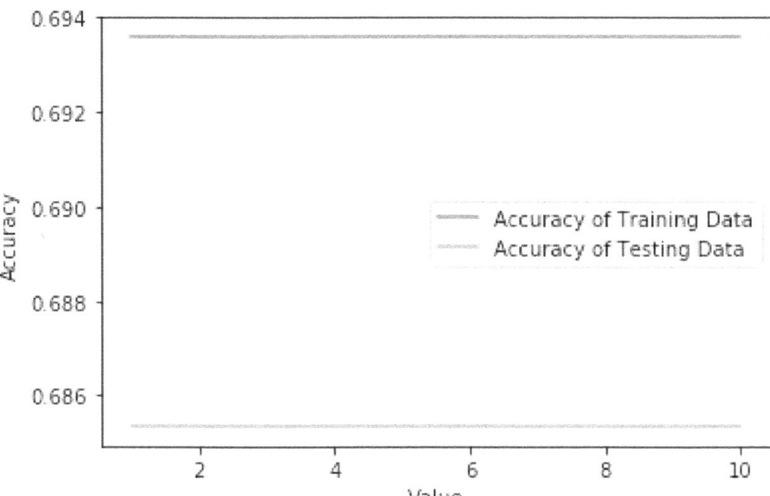

Accuracies of training and testing of Boston cancer dataset using DTR with 13 features

If we change the value of max_features, which represents the maximum features of the algorithm, from 3 to 13 in the below-mentioned command, we can observe that the accuracy of DT algorithm is greatly increased. Accuracy is increased with increase in the number of features because the dataset actually contains all 13 features and when algorithm uses all features, the algorithm is classified effectively and hence the accuracy is spot on.

As with the increase in the value of features, accuracy of DT algorithm increases, along with the complexity and the simulation time. Owing to the nature of this output, we need to strike a healthy balance between accuracy and simulation time.

dtr = DTR(min_samples_split = 50, max_features = 3, max_depth = 2)

You can again change value of max_features to check the change in accuracy of the prediction. Go ahead and change the values to analyze the performance of DTR algorithm. You should apply this code to other dataset as well to see how it performs with them.

Applying Decision Tree regression on Diabetes dataset

Input:

```python
# Importing required libraries

from sklearn.tree import DecisionTreeRegressor as DTR

from sklearn.datasets import load_diabetes as diabetes

from sklearn.model_selection import train_test_split as tss

import matplotlib.pyplot as plt

import pandas as pd


# Loading input data

value = diabetes()

df = pd.DataFrame(value.data, columns = value.feature_names)

df["MEDV"] = value.target

X = df.drop("MEDV",1)   # Feature Matrix

Y = df["MEDV"]          # Target Vector


# Splitting input data into training and testing data

Data_trn, Data_tst, Target_trn, Target_tst = tss(X, Y, random_state = 10)


accuracy_trn = []

accuracy_tst = []
```

```python
limit = range(1, 11)

for i in limit:

    # Training the model

    dtr = DTR(min_samples_split = 50, max_features = 3, max_depth
              = 2)

    dtr.fit(Data_trn, Target_trn)

    # Calculating accuracy of Training Data

    accuracy_trn.append(dtr.score(Data_trn, Target_trn))

    # Calculating accuracy of Testing Data

    accuracy_tst.append(dtr.score(Data_tst, Target_tst))


# Plotting accuracy of training and testing data

plt.plot(limit, accuracy_trn, label = "Accuracy of Training Data")

plt.plot(limit, accuracy_tst, label = "Accuracy of Testing Data")

plt.xlabel("Value")

plt.ylabel("Accuracy")

plt.legend()
```

Output:

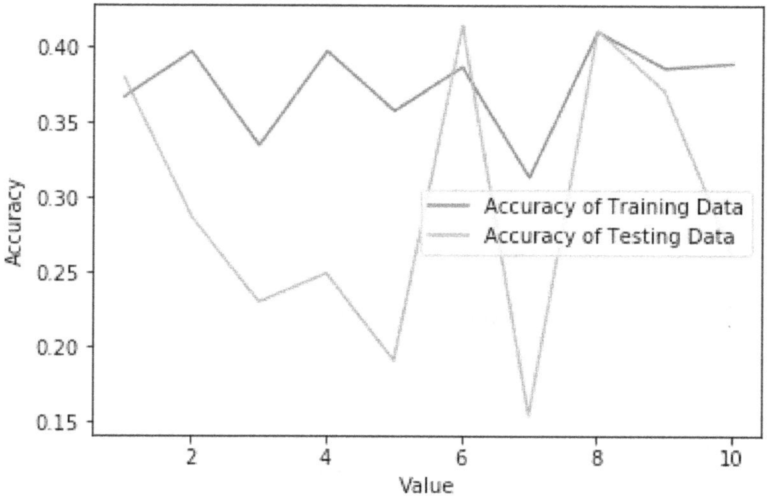

Accuracies of training and testing of iris dataset using DTR with 3 features

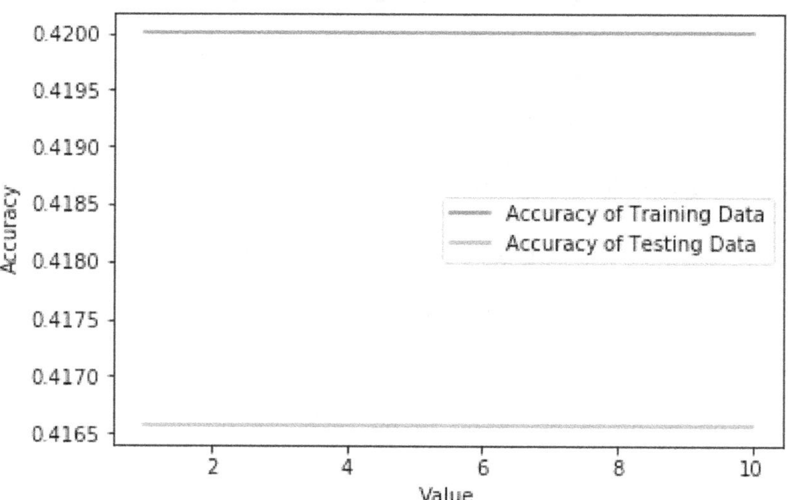

Accuracies of training and testing of iris dataset using DTR with 10 features

Support Vector Regression

We have discussed Support vector machines in a previous chapter. We have discussed its classification method in that chapter, and we will apply SVM for regression process in this chapter. We will apply SVM to Boston and Diabetes datasets to validate its accuracy. As it belongs to supervised machine learning, labeled training data are given to that model, and that model assigns new values to these datasets. It creates categories separated by clear gap. The data belongs to class which is near to that line representing specific class. This process proceeds until each data set gets assigned.

Applying support vector regression on Boston dataset

Input:

```
# Importing required libraries

from sklearn.svm import SVR

from sklearn.datasets import load_boston as boston

from sklearn.model_selection import train_test_split as tss

import matplotlib.pyplot as plt

import pandas as pd


# Loading input data

value = boston()

df = pd.DataFrame(value.data, columns = value.feature_names)

df["MEDV"] = value.target

X = df.drop("MEDV",1)   # Feature Matrix

Y = df["MEDV"]          # Target Vector
```

```python
# Splitting input data into training and testing data
Data_trn, Data_tst, Target_trn, Target_tst = tss(X, Y, random_state = 10)


accuracy_trn = []

accuracy_tst = []


limit = range(1, 11)

for i in limit:

    # Training the model

    svr = SVR(C = 1.0, gamma = 'auto', kernel = 'rbf')

    svr.fit(Data_trn, Target_trn)

    # Calculating accuracy of Training Data

    accuracy_trn.append(svr.score(Data_trn, Target_trn))

    # Calculating accuracy of Testing Data

    accuracy_tst.append(svr.score(Data_tst, Target_tst))


# Plotting accuracy of training and testing data

plt.plot(limit, accuracy_trn, label = "Accuracy of Training Data")

plt.plot(limit, accuracy_tst, label = "Accuracy of Testing Data")

plt.xlabel("Value")

plt.ylabel("Accuracy")
```

```python
plt.legend()
```

Output:

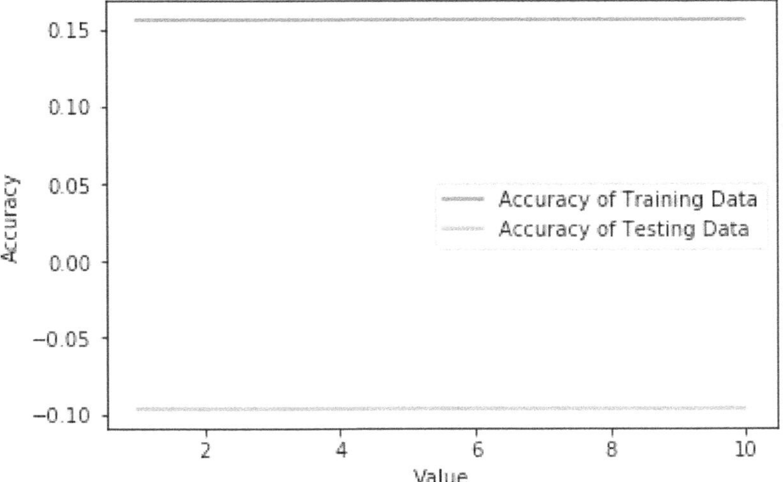

Accuracies of training and testing of Boston dataset using SVR with rbf kernel

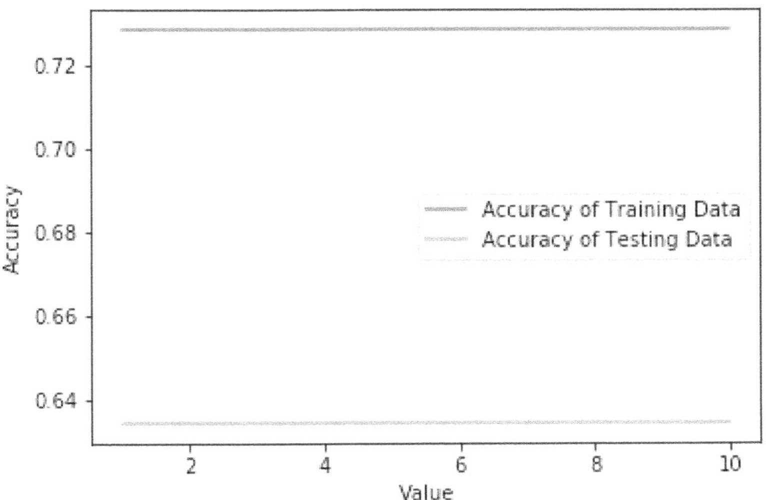

Accuracies of training and testing of Boston dataset using SVR with linear kernel

```
svr = SVR(C = 1.0, gamma = 'auto', kernel = 'rbf')
```

You can change the kernel value above to linear, as the above case is linear in nature, to improve the accuracy. Remember, had this been a nonlinear version, we would have preferred the 'RBF' instead.

Changing values of kernel is a great way to check the change in accuracy of the prediction. You can change the value of C as well. In many cases, C plays a vital role; however, will it play its role in this algorithm? Try it out yourself and see what happens when you change the value of C to anything else than 1.0.

While you practice using these methods and codes, try to change the value of gamma as well. Sometimes, you may need to fine tune your adjustments and values in order to bring out the best results and accuracy possible. If you are presented with an error, you would immediately know that the program is unable to compute using the given values and hence you can find out about their minimum and maximum values as well.

Applying support vector regression on Diabetes dataset

Input:

```
# Importing required libraries

from sklearn.svm import SVR

from sklearn.datasets import load_diabetes as diabetes

from sklearn.model_selection import train_test_split as tss

import matplotlib.pyplot as plt
```

```python
import pandas as pd

# Loading input data

value = diabetes()

df = pd.DataFrame(value.data, columns = value.feature_names)

df["MEDV"] = value.target

X = df.drop("MEDV",1)   # Feature Matrix

Y = df["MEDV"]          # Target Vector


# Splitting input data into training and testing data

Data_trn, Data_tst, Target_trn, Target_tst = tss(X, Y, random_state
                                                 = 10)


accuracy_trn = []

accuracy_tst = []


limit = range(1, 11)

for i in limit:

# Training the model

svr = SVR(C = 1000.0, gamma = 'auto', kernel = 'rbf')

svr.fit(Data_trn, Target_trn)

# Calculating accuracy of Training Data
```

```python
accuracy_trn.append(svr.score(Data_trn, Target_trn))

# Calculating accuracy of Testing Data

accuracy_tst.append(svr.score(Data_tst, Target_tst))


# Plotting accuracy of training and testing data

plt.plot(limit, accuracy_trn, label = "Accuracy of Training Data")

plt.plot(limit, accuracy_tst, label = "Accuracy of Testing Data")

plt.xlabel("Value")

plt.ylabel("Accuracy")

plt.legend()
```

Output:

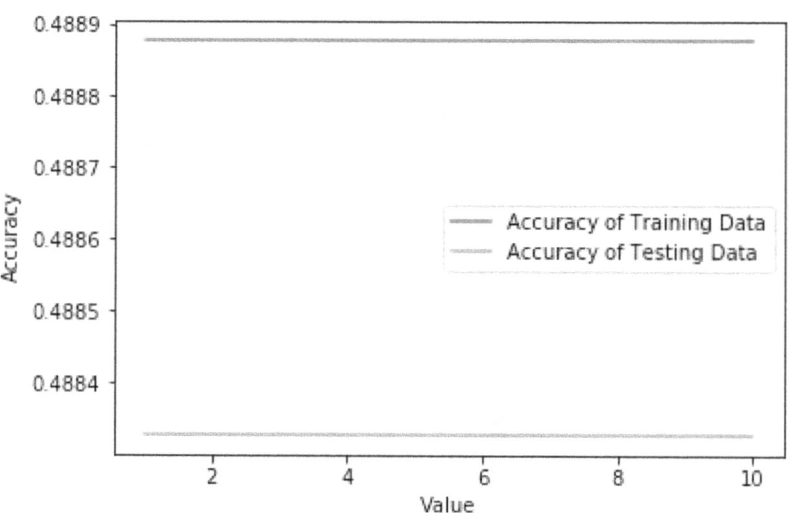

Accuracies of training and testing of Diabetes dataset using SVR

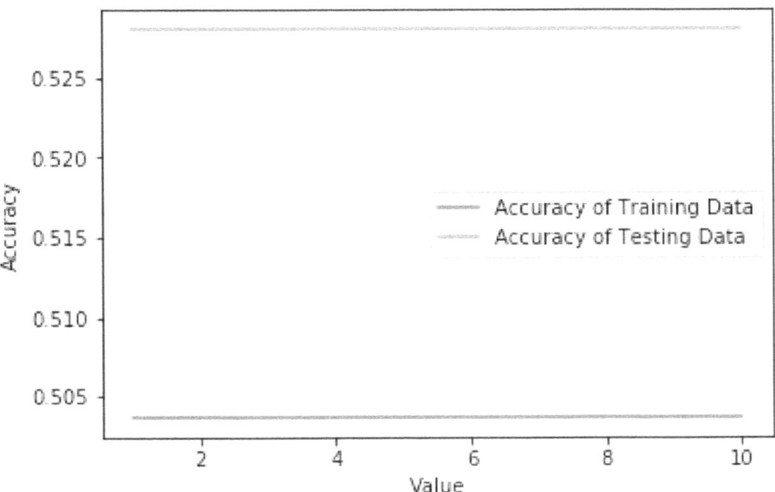

Accuracies of training and testing of Diabetes dataset using SVR with linear kernel

Random Forest Regression

Random forest method is another example of machine learning that is mainly used for regression process. This also work same as decision tree to some extent as it calculates probabilities of each data set and assign them new values depending on the value of their probabilities. It is used to take mode of classes or mean of trees in order to predict new value of data. This process proceeds until each data set get assigned. We will apply Random forest regression to Boston and Diabetes datasets to analyze its working and accuracy.

Applying Random Forest Regression on Boston dataset

Input:

```python
# Importing required libraries

from sklearn.ensemble import RandomForestRegressor as RFR

from sklearn.datasets import load_boston as boston

from sklearn.model_selection import train_test_split as tss

import matplotlib.pyplot as plt

import pandas as pd


# Loading input data

value = diabetes()

df = pd.DataFrame(value.data, columns = value.feature_names)

df["MEDV"] = value.target

X = df.drop("MEDV",1)   # Feature Matrix

Y = df["MEDV"]          # Target Vector


# Splitting input data into training and testing data

Data_trn, Data_tst, Target_trn, Target_tst = tss(X, Y, random_state
                                             = 10)


accuracy_trn = []

accuracy_tst = []


limit = range(1, 11)
```

```python
for i in limit:
    # Training the model
    rfr = RFR(n_estimators = 10, random_state = 0)
    rfr.fit(Data_trn, Target_trn)
    # Calculating accuracy of Training Data
    accuracy_trn.append(rfr.score(Data_trn, Target_trn))
    # Calculating accuracy of Testing Data
    accuracy_tst.append(rfr.score(Data_tst, Target_tst))
# Plotting accuracy of training and testing data
plt.plot(limit, accuracy_trn, label = "Accuracy of Training Data")
plt.plot(limit, accuracy_tst, label = "Accuracy of Testing Data")
plt.xlabel("Value")
plt.ylabel("Accuracy")
plt.legend()
```

Output:

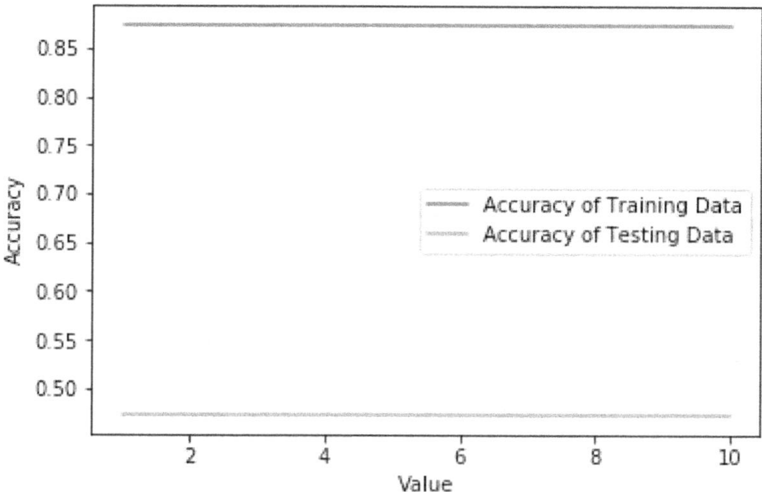

Accuracies of training and testing of Boston dataset using RFR with
n_estimators of 10

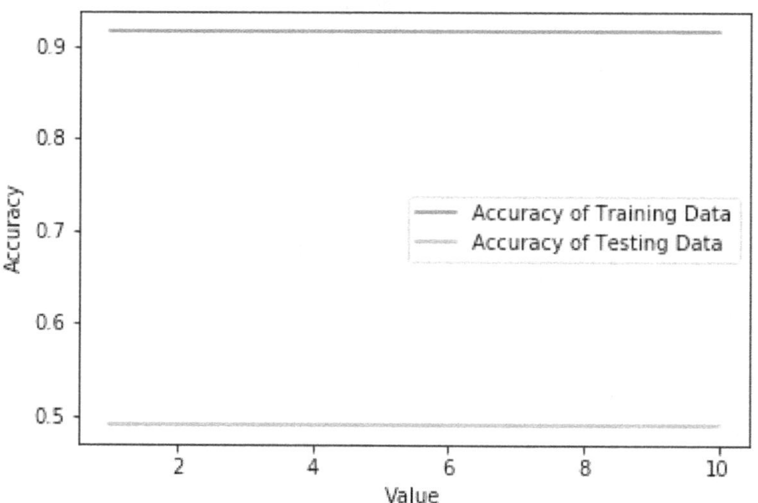

Accuracies of training and testing cf Boston dataset using RFR with
n_estimators of 100

Applying Random Forest Regression on Diabetes dataset

Input:

```python
# Importing required libraries

from sklearn.ensemble import RandomForestRegressor as RFR

from sklearn.datasets import load_diabetes as diabetes

from sklearn.model_selection import train_test_split as tss

import matplotlib.pyplot as plt

import pandas as pd


# Loading input data

value = diabetes()

df = pd.DataFrame(value.data, columns = value.feature_names)

df["MEDV"] = value.target

X = df.drop("MEDV",1)   # Feature Matrix

Y = df["MEDV"]          # Target Vector


# Splitting input data into training and testing data

Data_trn, Data_tst, Target_trn, Target_tst = tss(X, Y, random_state = 10)


accuracy_trn = []

accuracy_tst = []
```

```python
limit = range(1, 11)

for i in limit:
    # Training the model
    rfr = RFR(n_estimators = 10, random_state = 0)
    rfr.fit(Data_trn, Target_trn)
    # Calculating accuracy of Training Data
    accuracy_trn.append(rfr.score(Data_trn, Target_trn))
    # Calculating accuracy of Testing Data
    accuracy_tst.append(rfr.score(Data_tst, Target_tst))


# Plotting accuracy of training and testing data
plt.plot(limit, accuracy_trn, label = "Accuracy of Training Data")
plt.plot(limit, accuracy_tst, label = "Accuracy of Testing Data")
plt.xlabel("Value")
plt.ylabel("Accuracy")
plt.legend()
```

Output:

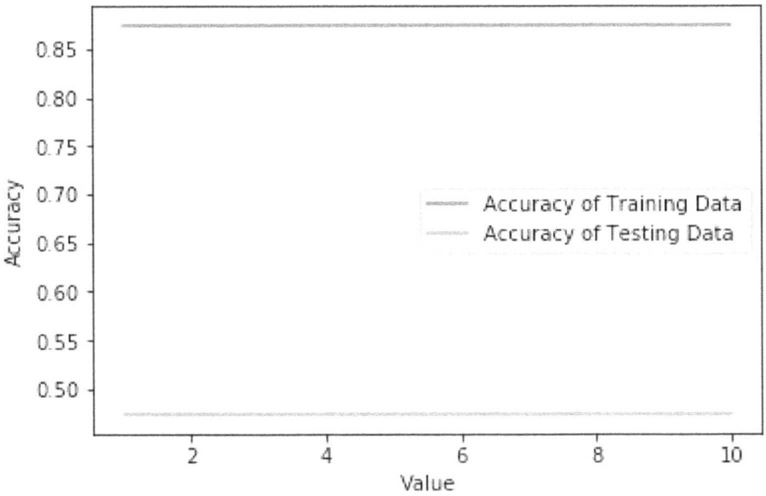

Accuracies of training and testing of Diabetes dataset using RFR
with n_estimators of 10

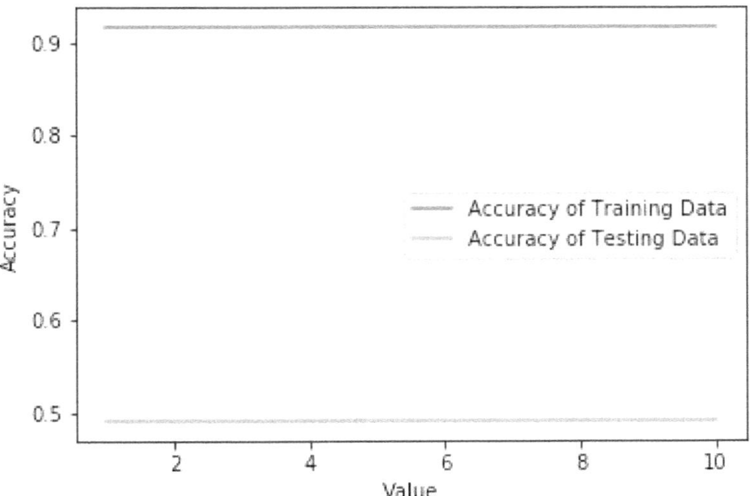

Accuracies of training and testing of Diabetes dataset using RFR
with n_estimators of 100

In both the examples here and above, one parameter is playing a vital part. Changing that will alter the rate of accuracy. This is represented as:

rfr = RFR(n_estimators = 10, random_state = 0)

You can try to modify the value of n_estimators, which denotes the number of estimators. You can vary the numeric value from 10 to 100 and see how the accuracy is affected. Alternatively, you can also try to change the value of the random_state variable to anything other than zero.

Linear Regression

Linear regression method is another basic method of machine learning that is just used for regression process. This method belongs to linear classification. As its name suggests, once the model is trained, it uses linear functions to predict the output value of given data. These models are also known as linear models. This method is being used much as compare to other predictive methods. The reason behind its success is that the models that rely linearly on unknown parameters can fit better than those models who rely nonlinearly on unknown parameters. This process proceeds until each data set get assigned. We will apply linear regression to Boston and Diabetes datasets to validate its working and accuracy.

Applying linear regression on Boston dataset

Input:

Importing required libraries

from sklearn.linear_model import LinearRegression as LR

from sklearn.datasets import load_boston as boston

from sklearn.model_selection import train_test_split as tss

import matplotlib.pyplot as plt

import pandas as pd

```python
# Loading input data

value = boston()

df = pd.DataFrame(value.data, columns = value.feature_names)

df["MEDV"] = value.target

X = df.drop("MEDV",1)   # Feature Matrix

Y = df["MEDV"]          # Target Vector


# Splitting input data into training and testing data

Data_trn, Data_tst, Target_trn, Target_tst = tss(X, Y, random_state
                                                 = 10)


accuracy_trn = []

accuracy_tst = []


limit = range(1, 11)

for i in limit:

# Training the model

rf = LR(n_jobs = 1)

rf.fit(Data_trn, Target_trn)

# Calculating accuracy of Training Data

accuracy_trn.append(rf.score(Data_trn, Target_trn))
```

Calculating accuracy of Testing Data

accuracy_tst.append(rf.score(Data_tst, Target_tst))

Plotting accuracy of training and testing data

plt.plot(limit, accuracy_trn, label = "Accuracy of Training Data")

plt.plot(limit, accuracy_tst, label = "Accuracy of Testing Data")

plt.xlabel("Value")

plt.ylabel("Accuracy")

plt.legend()

Output:

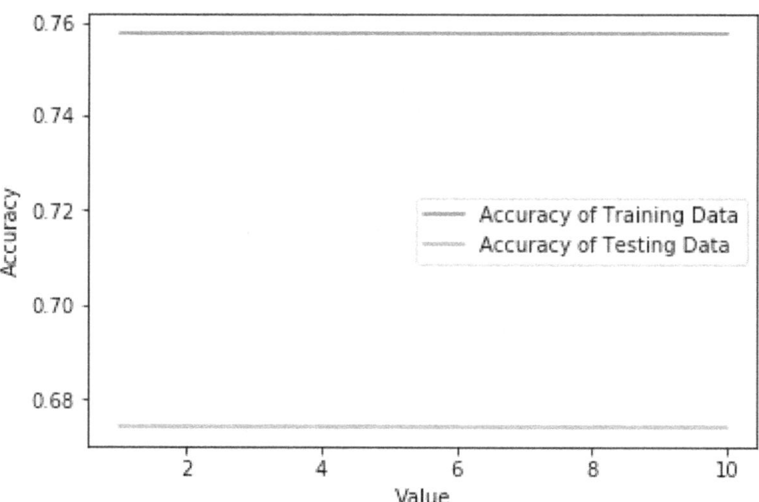

Accuracies of training and testing of Boston dataset using LR

Have a look at the command highlighted below. We can see that once again a single parameter plays a vital role to run this method.

rf = LR(n_jobs = 1)

Change value of n_jobs and check the result. Try to find out how large can you set its value.

Applying linear regression on Diabetes dataset

Input:

```python
# Importing required libraries

from sklearn.linear_model import LinearRegression as LR

from sklearn.datasets import load_diabetes as diabetes

from sklearn.model_selection import train_test_split as tss

import matplotlib.pyplot as plt

import pandas as pd


# Loading input data

value = diabetes()

df = pd.DataFrame(value.data, columns = value.feature_names)

df["MEDV"] = value.target

X = df.drop("MEDV",1)   # Feature Matrix

Y = df["MEDV"]          # Target Vector


# Splitting input data into training and testing data

Data_trn, Data_tst, Target_trn, Target_tst = tss(X, Y, random_state = 10)
```

```python
accuracy_trn = []
accuracy_tst = []


limit = range(1, 11)
for i in limit:
    # Training the model
    rf = LR(n_jobs = 1)
    rf.fit(Data_trn, Target_trn)
    # Calculating accuracy of Training Data
    accuracy_trn.append(rf.score(Data_trn, Target_trn))
    # Calculating accuracy of Testing Data
    accuracy_tst.append(rf.score(Data_tst, Target_tst))


# Plotting accuracy of training and testing data
plt.plot(limit, accuracy_trn, label = "Accuracy of Training Data")
plt.plot(limit, accuracy_tst, label = "Accuracy of Testing Data")
plt.xlabel("Value")
plt.ylabel("Accuracy")
plt.legend()
```

Output:

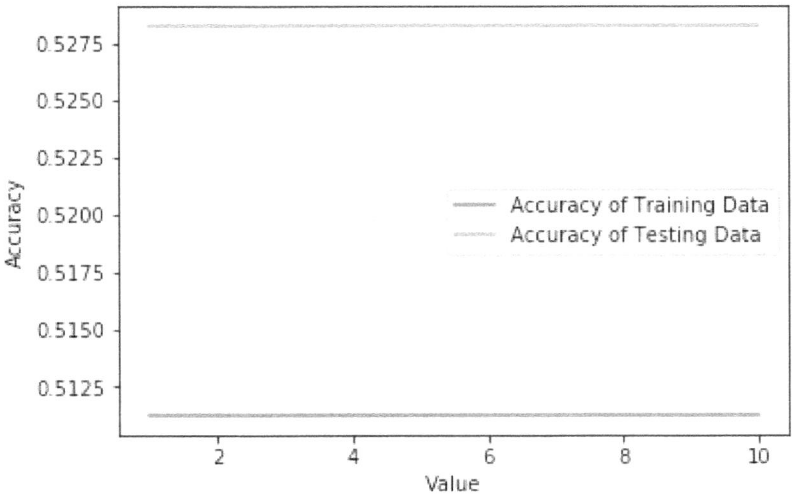

Accuracies of training and testing of Diabetes dataset using LR

By applying various methods to the same datasets, we can see how the variations occur and how much accuracy we can obtain. While the charts may seemingly appear the same, the finer details are being changed to either provide a greater accuracy or otherwise.

Neural Network Regression

We have discussed the application of NN in terms of classification in a previous chapter. Now, we shall apply the NN for regression process. We will apply NN regression to Boston and Diabetes datasets to validate its working and accuracy.

Applying neural network regression on Boston dataset

Input:

```python
# Importing required libraries
from sklearn.neural_network import MLPRegressor as MLPR
from sklearn.datasets import load_boston as boston
from sklearn.model_selection import train_test_split as tss
import matplotlib.pyplot as plt
import pandas as pd


# Loading input data
value = boston()
df = pd.DataFrame(value.data, columns = value.feature_names)
df["MEDV"] = value.target
X = df.drop("MEDV",1)   # Feature Matrix
Y = df["MEDV"]          # Target Vector


# Splitting input data into training and testing data
Data_trn, Data_tst, Target_trn, Target_tst = tss(X, Y, random_state = 10)


accuracy_trn = []
accuracy_tst = []
```

```python
limit = range(1, 11)

for i in limit:

    # Training the model

    mlpr = MLPR(activation = 'tanh',max_iter = 1000, random_state = 0)

    mlpr.fit(Data_trn, Target_trn)

    # Calculating accuracy of Training Data

    accuracy_trn.append(mlpr.score(Data_trn, Target_trn))

    # Calculating accuracy of Testing Data

    accuracy_tst.append(mlpr.score(Data_tst, Target_tst))


# Plotting accuracy of training and testing data
plt.plot(limit, accuracy_trn, label = "Accuracy of Training Data")

plt.plot(limit, accuracy_tst, label = "Accuracy of Testing Data")

plt.xlabel("Value")

plt.ylabel("Accuracy")

plt.legend()
```

Output:

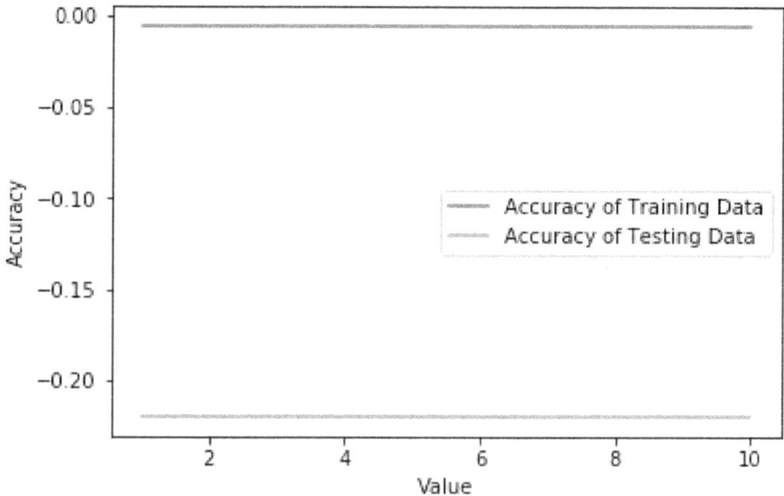

Accuracies of training and testing of Boston dataset using NN with max_iters of 100

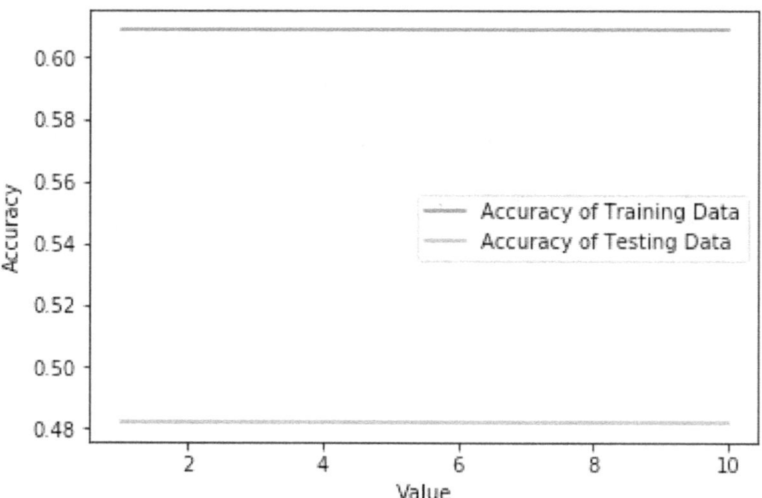

Accuracies of training and testing of Boston dataset using NN with max_iters of 1000

We can observe that NN algorithm is using 'tanh' as activation. If we change the value of max_iter, which represents the maximum iterations from 100 to 1000, we can observe the increase in accuracy of the NN algorithm. It is obvious that accuracy of any algorithm increases with the increase in number of iterations. It takes quite a bit of processing to perform any task. It might consume more time, but it will come up with a better accuracy.

```python
mlpr = MLPR(activation = 'tanh',max_iter = 1000, random_state = 0)
```

Applying neural network regression on Diabetes dataset

Input:

```python
# Importing required libraries

from sklearn.neural_network import MLPRegressor as MLPR

from sklearn.datasets import load_diabetes as diabetes

from sklearn.model_selection import train_test_split as tss

import matplotlib.pyplot as plt

import pandas as pd


# Loading input data

value = diabetes()

df = pd.DataFrame(value.data, columns = value.feature_names)

df["MEDV"] = value.target

X = df.drop("MEDV",1)   # Feature Matrix

Y = df["MEDV"]          # Target Vector
```

```python
# Splitting input data into training and testing data
Data_trn, Data_tst, Target_trn, Target_tst = tss(X, Y, random_state = 10)


accuracy_trn = []

accuracy_tst = []


limit = range(1, 11)

for i in limit:

    # Training the model

    mlpr = MLPR(activation = 'tanh',max_iter = 1000, random_state = 0)

    mlpr.fit(Data_trn, Target_trn)

    # Calculating accuracy of Training Data

    accuracy_trn.append(mlpr.score(Data_trn, Target_trn))

    # Calculating accuracy of Testing Data

    accuracy_tst.append(mlpr.score(Data_tst, Target_tst))


# Plotting accuracy of training and testing data

plt.plot(limit, accuracy_trn, label = "Accuracy of Training Data")

plt.plot(limit, accuracy_tst, label = "Accuracy of Testing Data")

plt.xlabel("Value")

plt.ylabel("Accuracy")
```

plt.legend()

Output:

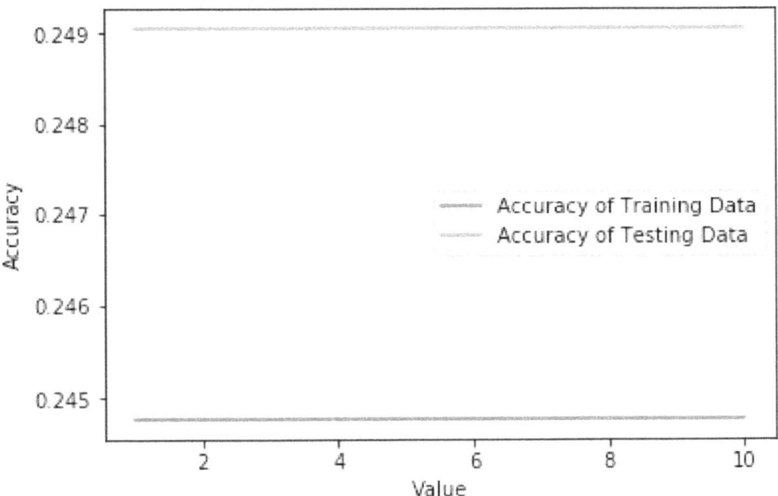

Accuracies of training and testing of Diabetes dataset using NN with max_iters of 1000

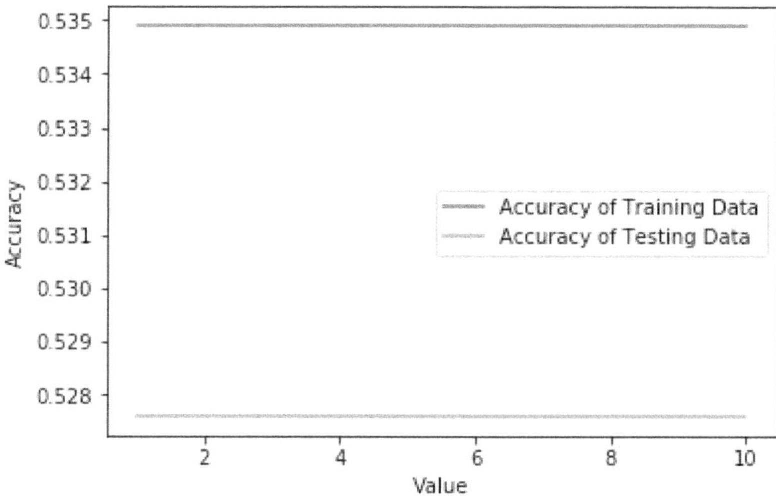

Accuracies of training and testing of Diabetes dataset using NN with max_iters of 10000

Once again, the NN algorithm is using tanh as activation. If we change the value of max_iter from 1000 to 10000, it will increase the accuracy of the NN algorithm. It is therefore understandable that accuracy of any algorithm increases with the increase in number of iterations.

In the previous chapter, we learned about discrete class labels and classification methods; however, this chapter introduced us to continuous class label classification methods. We went through a few examples and used Boston and Diabetes datasets to draw outputs from.

In the next chapter, we will be diving into the world of unsupervised learning to see just why it is slightly difficult to get a grasp on things. We will look into the concept of clustering and map out a few examples and codes to see how we can use unsupervised learning to bring out results that we require.

It is of the utmost importance that you continue practicing the codes to develop a firm understanding of the matter. Learning "Machine Learning" within a matter of days is not possible without ample practice, clarification of concepts and the usage of the right

tools, libraries and understanding of Python as a programming
language.

Chapter 4: Unsupervised Machine Learning

Earlier, at the start of the first chapter, we discussed how unsupervised learning is a method of machine learning that is used to gather information from the datasets. However, unlike supervised learning, it does not know the outputs to specific inputs, and when other inputs are given to it, it can just categorize outputs on the basis of some parameters such as Euclidean distance, etc. In short, unsupervised learning does not create datasets to be used for training the model for prediction of outputs.

Understanding the Concept of Clustering

Clustering can easily be defined as a method that partitions or divides the given data into sets of groups. These groups are called clusters. Each cluster contains data that is specific and contains items, components or data that matches. Think of two clusters named 'even' and 'odd,' One of these will contain numbers that are even, while the other would contain numbers that are odd.

There are two main types of unsupervised learning: transformation and clustering. The transformation method can relate with dimension reduction. It takes a high dimensional data, containing many samples of each features or many features, and converts it into low dimensional data. It removes less impactful samples or features.

In many cases, dimension reduction methods reduce to two dimensions. It is very important to apply dimension reduction methods as it can save processing time and avoid confusion, which is usually created when seeing high dimensional data. The dimension reduction methods provide a much-needed motivation to the programmer to dive deep into the data and visualize it better.

The other method of unsupervised learning is clustering. It is used to divide the data on the basis of similarities. If you want to deal with big data, you need it to be divided into multiple groups so that you can carry out efficient and effective analysis. For example, if you want to upload multiple photos to any social media site, you would like to add those photos in groups so that you can keep track of those pictures easily, if and when required. One way would be to add pictures of a similar person in one group. Although the sites don't know about you personally and don't know which picture represents whom, but the site still wants us to divide those pictures into groups as it is a sensible way of managing data.

Challenges in Unsupervised Learning

Unsupervised learning does not contain any information of label, which means we do not know the right output for the corresponding input. The model cannot come to a conclusion whether it went well or not. In such a case, algorithms will divide data on the basis of similarity of some of their features, and while doing so, it does not ensure the output of our choices.

For example, the model can group pictures in a way that one group will contain picture with various people in it, which does not necessarily fulfill the requirement of one who wants to have a group on the basis of individuals (each group containing pictures of a specific person).

Unsupervised learning can be used in cases where a programmer just wishes to understand the data instead of using it for any automation solution. Similarly, unsupervised learning can be used as a preprocessing step for supervised learning. In some cases, it might help to get better accuracy from supervised learning, and it can get less memory data and might be able to save time as well.

Preprocessing and Scaling

Many classification and regression methods have been discussed in previous chapters. We have observed that some of these methods require some work as their accuracies are not up to the mark. Some unsupervised-based preprocessing steps and scaling is performed before applying supervised methods.

Types of Preprocessing

There are different types of preprocessing. StandardScalar is one of the libraries used for preprocessing. It makes sure that each feature of dataset has a mean of zero and variance of one. It is used to keep all features to the same level. Although it does not have any specific minimum or maximum values for features, but it still works fine as it contains features of maintaining required mean and variance.

RobustScaler is another library that is used for preprocessing. It is also used to keep all features to the same level. It uses median and quartiles instead of mean and variance. Due to using different parameters, it ignores the data points which are far away from others. These data points are often known as outliers, which create complications for other scaling methods. Hence, RobustScaler is better in use than StandardScalar.

Then we have the MinMaxScaler library, which is used for preprocessing. It is used to keep the data between 0 and 1 by shifting the data. That means that if the data is plotted, then the scale of the x-axis and y-axis will be between 0 and 1. It can also produce acceptable results.

Normalizer is the last library to be discussed for preprocessing. It scales data points in a way that keeps the distance between the feature vectors of unity. Every data point is scaled at a different value. It is normally used when direction does matter.

Effects of Preprocessing on Supervised Learning

Preprocessing plays a very important role, especially for methods that are sensitive to these scalers. As mentioned earlier, many preprocessing scales can be used. Below is an example of preprocessing using MinMaxScaler.

Input:

```
# Importing required libraries

from sklearn.svm import SVC

from sklearn.datasets import load_breast_cancer as cancer

from sklearn.model_selection import train_test_split as tss

import matplotlib.pyplot as plt

from sklearn.preprocessing import MinMaxScaler as MMS


# Loading input data
```

```python
value = cancer()


# Splitting input data into training and testing data

Data_trn, Data_tst, Target_trn, Target_tst = tss(value.data,
                                                  value.target,

                                                  random_state
                                                  = 10)

accuracy_trn = []

accuracy_tst = []

Data_trn_scld = []

Data_tst_scld = []


mms = MMS()

mms.fit(Data_trn)


Data_trn_scld = mms.transform(Data_trn)

Data_tst_scld = mms.transform(Data_tst)


limit = range(1, 11)

for i in limit:

    # Training the model

    svc = SVC(C = 1.0, gamma = 'auto', kernel = 'rbf')

    svc.fit(Data_trn_scld, Target_trn)
```

```
# Calculating accuracy of Training Data

accuracy_trn.append(svc.score(Data_trn_scld, Target_trn))

# Calculating accuracy of Testing Data

accuracy_tst.append(svc.score(Data_tst_scld, Target_tst))


# Plotting accuracy of training and testing data

plt.plot(limit, accuracy_trn, label = "Accuracy of Training Data")

plt.plot(limit, accuracy_tst, label = "Accuracy of Testing Data")

plt.xlabel("Value")

plt.ylabel("Accuracy")

plt.legend()
```

Output:

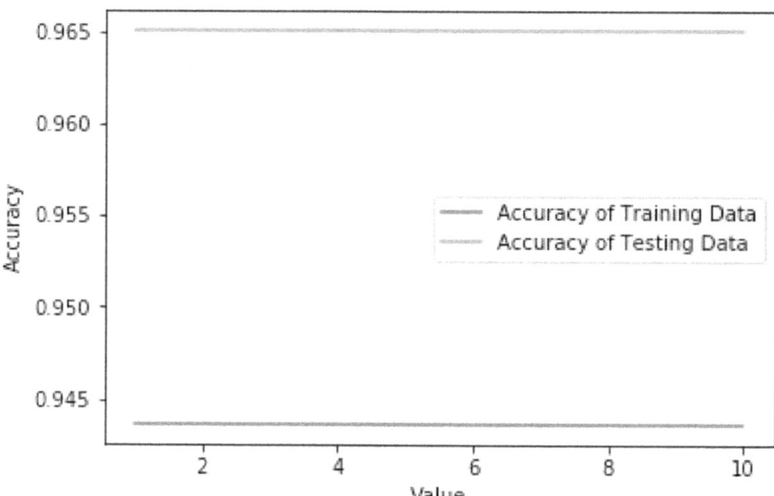

Accuracies of training and testing of Breast cancer dataset using SVC with MinMaxScaler

Let us look at an example of preprocessing using the StandardScaler.

Input:

```python
# Importing required libraries

from sklearn.svm import SVC

from sklearn.datasets import load_breast_cancer as cancer

from sklearn.model_selection import train_test_split as tss

import matplotlib.pyplot as plt

from sklearn.preprocessing import StandardScaler as SS


# Loading input data

value = cancer()


# Splitting input data into training and testing data

Data_trn, Data_tst, Target_trn, Target_tst = tss(value.data, value.target,

                                                  random_state = 10)

accuracy_trn = []

accuracy_tst = []

Data_trn_scld = []

Data_tst_scld = []
```

```python
ss = SS()

ss.fit(Data_trn)


Data_trn_scld = ss.transform(Data_trn)

Data_tst_scld = ss.transform(Data_tst)


limit = range(1, 11)

for i in limit:

    # Training the model

    svc = SVC(C = 1.0, gamma = 'auto', kernel = 'rbf')

    svc.fit(Data_trn_scld, Target_trn)

    # Calculating accuracy of Training Data

    accuracy_trn.append(svc.score(Data_trn_scld, Target_trn))

    # Calculating accuracy of Testing Data

    accuracy_tst.append(svc.score(Data_tst_scld, Target_tst))


# Plotting accuracy of training and testing data

plt.plot(limit, accuracy_trn, label = "Accuracy of Training Data")

plt.plot(limit, accuracy_tst, label = "Accuracy of Testing Data")

plt.xlabel("Value")

plt.ylabel("Accuracy")
```

```
plt.legend()
```

Output:

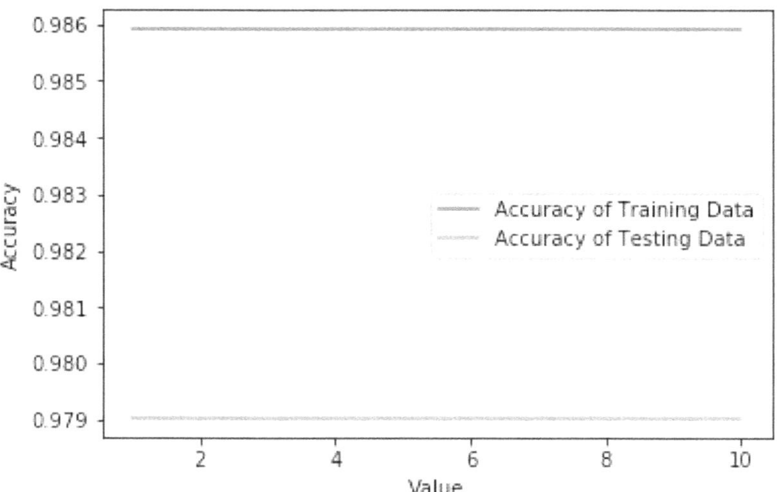

Accuracies of training and testing of Breast cancer dataset using SVC with StandardScaler

You can observe that SVM based classification provided an accuracy of around 0.64, but when we applied the MinMaxScaler based scaling and then applied classification using SVM, an accuracy of around 0.97 is achieved. Similarly, when we applied the StandardScaler based scaling and then applied classification using SVM, an accuracy of around 0.98 was achieved. Results can show that preprocessing is required, and MinMaxScaler and StandardScaler based preprocessing perform well.

Dimension Reduction

Many datasets contain high dimensions, which take long processing times. Along with processing problems, these datasets become difficult to visualize. Dimension reduction is required to reduce the dimensions of high dimensional datasets. It is also very important to retain maximum information even after reducing dimensions of the datasets. There are many methods that are used for dimension reduction.

Principal Component Analysis is famous for dimension reduction. It provides the principal components of the datasets. It removes the least impactful features and retains the highest impactful ones. This way, the datasets will not lose much information and will still be able to represent all the data.

Principal Component Analysis

Principal Component Analysis is a statistical method that works on orthogonal transformation to measure the correlation between variables. It finds out the principal components of datasets. An example of Dimension reduction using PCA is given below.

Applying Principal Component Analysis on Breast cancer dataset

Input [1]:

```
# Importing required libraries

from sklearn.decomposition import PCA

from sklearn.datasets import load_breast_cancer as cancer

from sklearn.model_selection import train_test_split as tss

import matplotlib.pyplot as plt

from sklearn.preprocessing import StandardScaler as SS

# Loading input data

value = cancer()
```

```python
# Splitting input data into training and testing data

Data_trn, Data_tst, Target_trn, Target_tst = tss(value.data,
                value.target, random_state = 10)

Data_trn_scld = []

Data_tst_scld = []


ss = SS()

ss.fit(Data_trn)


Data_trn_scld = ss.transform(Data_trn)

Data_tst_scld = ss.transform(Data_tst)


# Training the model with Principal components of 2
pca = PCA(n_components = 2)

pca.fit(Data_trn_scld)

X_pca = pca.transform(Data_trn_scld)


print("Original Dimension: {}".format(str(Data_trn_scld.shape)))

print("Reduced Dimension: {}".format(str(X_pca.shape)))


Output [1]:
```

Original Dimension: (426, 30)

Reduced Dimension: (426, 2)

Input [2]:

```
# plotting First versus second principal component

plt.plot(X_pca[Target_trn == 0,0], X_pca[Target_trn == 0,1], 'rs',
         label = value.target_names[0])

plt.hold

plt.plot(X_pca[Target_trn == 1,0], X_pca[Target_trn == 1,1], 'g.',
         label = value.target_names[1])

plt.legend()

plt.xlabel("First principal component")

plt.ylabel("Second principal component")
```

Output [2]:

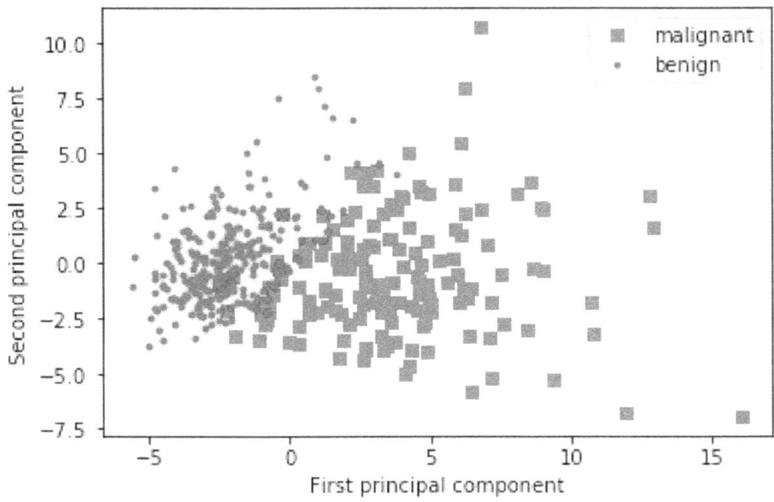

First Principal component versus Second Principal component of
Breast cancer dataset using PCA and StandardScaler

Input [2]:

```
print("Dimension of PCA components: {}".format(pca.components_.shape))
```

Output [2]:

Dimension of PCA components: (2, 30)

Input [3]:

```
print("Components of PCA:\n{}".format(pca.components_))
```

Output [3]:

Components of PCA:

```
[[ 0.22497118  0.10209091  0.23305712  0.22669916  0.13095741
   0.23777761

   0.26054451  0.26113228  0.11857964  0.04990416  0.20451814
   0.01547142

   0.21189041  0.2032527   0.00835308  0.17314863  0.18095912
   0.18353095

   0.03353539  0.10045326  0.23188534  0.09793079  0.24072506
   0.22923198

   0.11457974  0.20876477  0.22872514  0.2501444   0.10389674
   0.12133481]

 [-0.22383928 -0.06901511 -0.20453941 -0.22094646  0.20201801
   0.16857578

   0.04865932 -0.02438319  0.19604069  0.37928075 -0.09722973
   0.0862208

  -0.07797413 -0.13996098  0.20813873  0.237834    0.17790854
   0.12701146

   0.18413975  0.28625985 -0.21230329 -0.06003402 -0.1898874  -
   0.21147895

   0.18822065  0.14823507  0.08302158 -0.00246167  0.13405653
   0.28669719]]
```

Applying Principal Component Analysis on Digits dataset

Input [1]:

```python
# Importing required libraries

from sklearn.decomposition import PCA

from sklearn.datasets import load_digits as Value

import matplotlib.pyplot as plt


# Plotting Digits Dataset

value = Value()

fig, axes = plt.subplots(2, 5, figsize=(10, 5),

    subplot_kw={'xticks':(), 'yticks': ()})

for ax, img in zip(axes.ravel(), value.images):

    ax.imshow(img)


# Training the model with Principal components of 2

pca = PCA(n_components = 2)

pca.fit(value.data)


# PCA Transform

value_pca = pca.transform(value.data)

colors = ["#A83683", "#4E655E", "#853541", "#3A3120",
          "#535D8E",
```

"#476A2A", "#7851B8", "#BD3430", "#4A2D4E", "#875525"]

Output [1]:

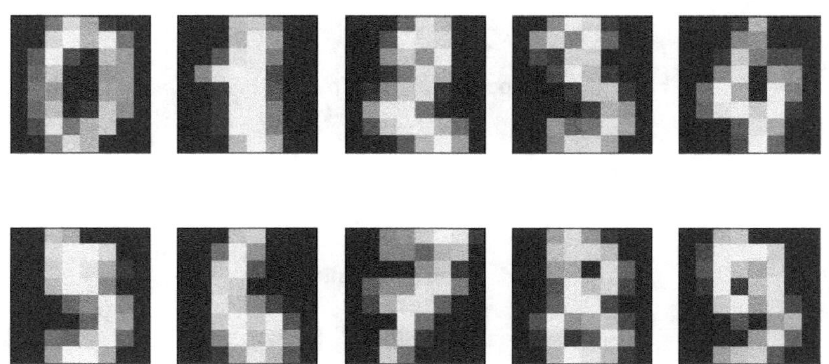

Digits dataset

Input [2]:

```
# Plotting Principal components

plt.figure(figsize = (10, 10))

plt.xlim(value_pca[:, 0].min(), value_pca[:, 0].max())

plt.ylim(value_pca[:, 1].min(), value_pca[:, 1].max())


for i in range(len(value.data)):
plt.text(value_pca[i, 0], value_pca[i, 1], str(value.target[i]), color =
colors[value.target[i]], fontdict = {'weight': 'bold', 'size':
9})

plt.xlabel("First principal component")
```

```
plt.ylabel("Second principal component")
```

Output [2]:

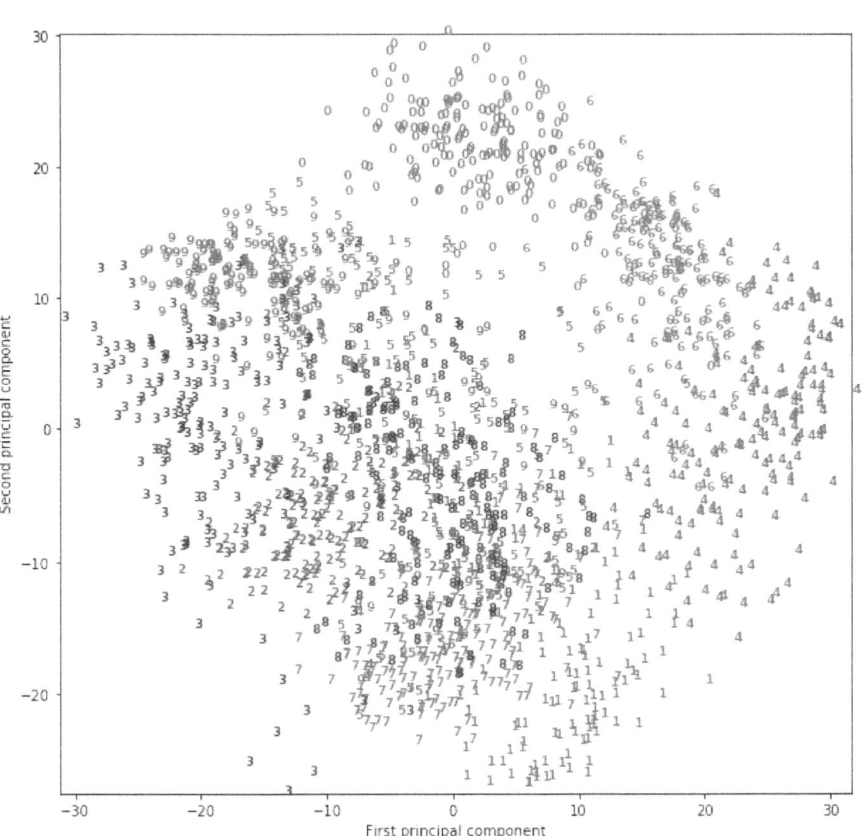

First Principal component versus Second Principal component of
Digits dataset using PCA

Manifold Learning with t-SNE

We have discussed PCA for dimension reduction and data visualization. t-SNE is another method that is used to visualize data. It provides a better visualization of data as compared to PCA. An example of visualization of data using t-SNE method is given below.

Applying t-SNE on Digits dataset

Input:

```python
# Importing required libraries

from sklearn.manifold import TSNE

from sklearn.datasets import load_digits as Value

import matplotlib.pyplot as plt


value = Value()

tsne = TSNE(random_state = 42)



# TSNE Transform

value_tsne = tsne.fit_transform(value.data)

colors = ["#A83683", "#4E655E", "#853541", "#3A3120",
          "#535D8E",

"#476A2A", "#7851B8", "#BD3430", "#4A2D4E", "#875525"]



# Plotting Feature components

plt.figure(figsize = (10, 10))

plt.xlim(value_tsne[:, 0].min(), value_tsne[:, 0].max() + 1)

plt.ylim(value_tsne[:, 1].min(), value_tsne[:, 1].max() + 1)
```

```
for i in range(len(value.data)):

plt.text(value_tsne[i, 0], value_tsne[i, 1], str(value.target[i]),color
    = colors[value.target[i]],fontdict = {'weight': 'bold', 'size': 9})

plt.xlabel("First Feature of t-SNE")

plt.xlabel("Second Feature of t-SNE")
```

Output :

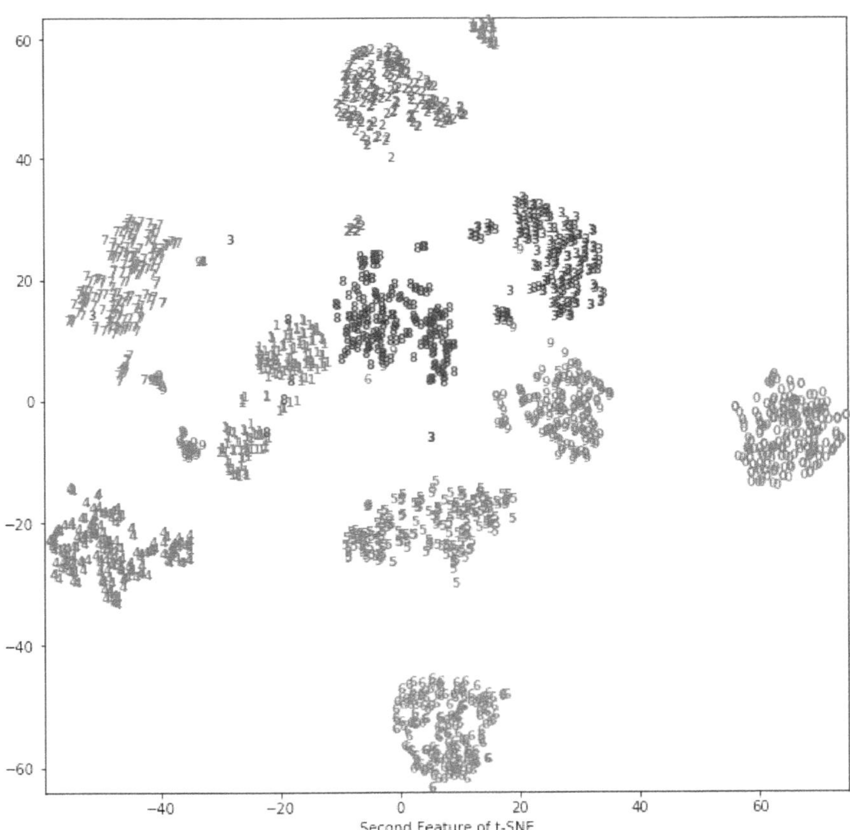

First Feature component versus Second Feature component of Digits
dataset using t-SNE

You can observe through the result that t-SNE method is far better than PCA in terms of visualization of data. It divided classes better than PCA method. There are other methods as well for visualization of data.

Clustering Models

We already know that clustering is used to divide the dataset into groups known as clusters. As it belongs to unsupervised machine learning, it deals without the knowledge of labels. There are many methods for clustering process. We will discuss K-Means clustering, Agglomerative clustering, and DBSCAN methods.

K-Means Clustering

K-means clustering is a commonly used method due to it being the simplest method of clustering. It finds the center of clusters that belong to certain regions of dataset. The user gives an input to the method by providing the required number of clusters, and by using that information, it starts with random centers of those number of clusters, takes the mean of these cluster centers with each data point, and then finds the updated cluster center. It keeps on doing this process in multiple iterations until no further change is detected. The result can be contradictory as method does not have the knowledge of labels, so it just makes the clusters by using specific techniques.

Applying K-Means Clustering on Blobs dataset

Input [1]:

```
# Importing required libraries

from sklearn.datasets import make_blobs as blobs

from sklearn.cluster import KMeans

import matplotlib.pyplot as plt


# Reading input data

Data, Target = blobs(random_state = 1)

# Making clustering model

kmeans = KMeans(n_clusters = 3)
```

```python
kmeans.fit(Data)

print("Clusters:\n{}".format(kmeans.labels_))
```

Output [1]:

```
Clusters:

[0 2 2 2 1 1 1 2 0 0 2 2 1 0 1 1 1 0 2 2 1 2 1 0 2 1 1 0 0 1 0 0 1 0 0 1 0 2
 1 2

 2 2 1 1 2 0 2 2 1 0 0 0 0 2 1 1 1 0 1 2 2 0 0 2 1 1 2 2 1 0 1 0 2 2 2
 1 0

 0 2 1 1 0 2 0 2 2 1 0 0 0 0 2 0 1 0 0 2 2 1 1 0 1 0]
```

Input [2]:

```python
print("Predictions:\n{}".format(kmeans.predict(Data)))
```

Output [2]:

```
Predictions:

[0 2 2 2 1 1 1 2 0 0 2 2 1 0 1 1 1 0 2 2 1 2 1 0 2 1 1 0 0 1 0 0 1 0 0 1 0 2
 1 2

 2 2 1 1 2 0 2 2 1 0 0 0 0 2 1 1 1 0 1 2 2 0 0 2 1 1 2 2 1 0 1 0 2 2 2
 1 0

 0 2 1 1 0 2 0 2 2 1 0 0 0 0 2 0 1 0 0 2 2 1 1 0 1 0]
```

Input [3]:

```python
plt.scatter(X[: , 0], X[: , 1], c = kmeans.labels_)
```

```
plt.legend()

plt.xlabel(kmeans.labels_[0])

plt.ylabel(kmeans.labels_[1])

plt.hold

plt.show
```

Output [3]:

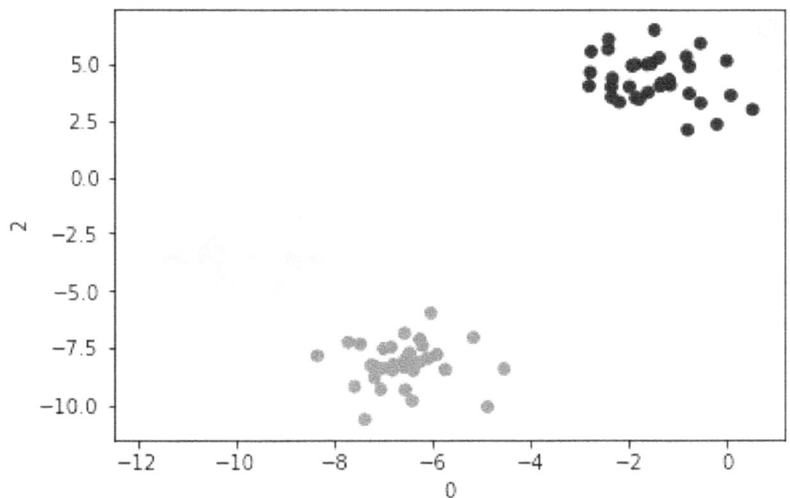

Prediction of Blobs Dataset using K-Means

Applying K-Means Clustering on Dense Blobs dataset

Input [1]:

```
# Importing required libraries

from sklearn.datasets import make_blobs as blobs

from sklearn.cluster import KMeans
```

```python
import matplotlib.pyplot as plt

# Reading input data
Data, Target = blobs(n_samples = 200,cluster_std = [1.0, 2.5, 0.5],random_state = 170)

# Making clustering model
kmeans = KMeans(n_clusters = 3, random_state = 0)

kmeans.fit(Data)

print("Clusters:\n{}".format(kmeans.labels_))
```

Output [1]:

Clusters:

```
[1 2 2 0 0 1 2 0 1 0 2 1 1 0 1 2 0 0 1 0 1 0 0 1 0 0 0 0 2 1 2 0 1 1 0
 1 2
 2 1 1 2 0 1 0 2 0 2 2 0 2 2 1 1 2 1 0 2 2 0 2 2 0 1 1 2 1 2 0 1 1 2 2
 1 1
 2 2 0 2 1 2 2 0 1 1 0 0 0 1 0 2 0 0 0 0 2 0 0 0 2 2 1 1 2 0 1 1 2 1 1
 2 2
 1 0 1 1 2 2 0 0 0 0 1 1 2 1 0 1 1 1 1 2 0 1 0 0 1 0 0 1 1 1 2 1 0 0 2
 0 1
 1 0 2 1 0 1 1 1 2 1 2 2 0 1 1 0 0 0 1 0 1 1 1 0 0 0 2 0 0 0 0 0 0 2 0
 2 2
 1 0 2 0 1 0 1 2 1 2 0 0 0 0 2]
```

Input [2]:

```python
print("Predictions:\n{}".format(kmeans.predict(Data)))
```

Output [2]:

Predictions:

[1 2 2 0 0 1 2 0 1 0 2 1 1 0 1 2 0 0 1 0 1 0 0 1 0 0 0 0 2 1 2 0 1 1 0
 1 2

 2 1 1 2 0 1 0 2 0 2 2 0 2 2 1 1 2 1 0 2 2 0 2 2 0 1 1 2 1 2 0 1 1 2 2
 1 1

 2 2 0 2 1 2 2 0 1 1 0 0 0 1 0 2 0 0 0 0 2 0 0 0 2 2 1 1 2 0 1 1 2 1 1
 2 2

 1 0 1 1 2 2 0 0 0 0 1 1 2 1 0 1 1 1 1 2 0 1 0 0 1 0 0 1 1 1 2 1 0 0 2
 0 1

 1 0 2 1 0 1 1 1 2 1 2 2 0 1 1 0 0 0 1 0 1 1 1 0 0 0 2 0 0 0 0 0 0 0 2 0
 2 2

 1 0 2 0 1 0 1 2 1 2 0 0 0 0 2]

Input [3]:

```python
plt.scatter(Data[: , 0], Data[: , 1], c = kmeans.labels_)

plt.xlabel(kmeans.labels_[0])

plt.ylabel(kmeans.labels_[1])

plt.hold

plt.show
```

Output [3]:

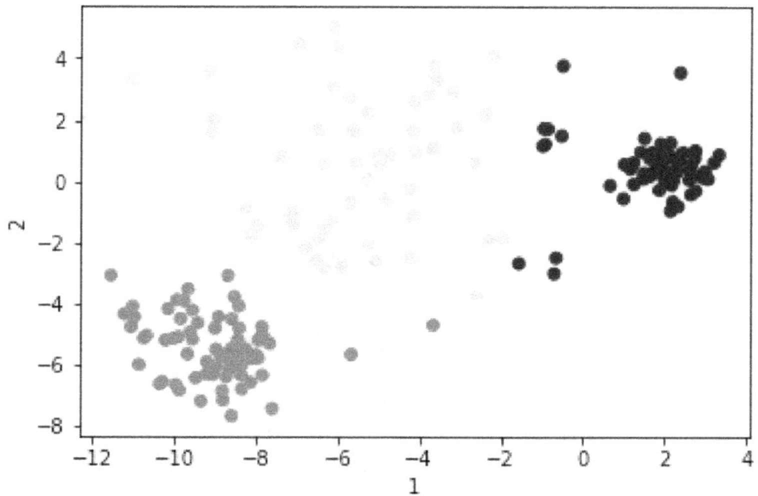

Prediction of Dense Blobs Dataset using K-Means

Applying K-Means Clustering on Stretched Blobs dataset

Input [1]:

```python
# Importing required libraries
from sklearn.datasets import make_blobs as blobs
from sklearn.cluster import KMeans
import matplotlib.pyplot as plt
import numpy as np


# Reading input data
Data, Target = blobs(random_state = 170, n_samples = 600)
rnd = np.random.RandomState(74)
```

```python
# Data stretching through transformation

transformation = rnd.normal(size = (2, 2))

Data = np.dot(Data, transformation)


# Making clustering model

kmeans = KMeans(n_clusters = 3)

kmeans.fit(Data)


plt.scatter(Data[: , 0], Data[: , 1], c = kmeans.labels_)

plt.xlabel(kmeans.labels_[0])

plt.ylabel(kmeans.labels_[1])

plt.hold

plt.show
```

Output:

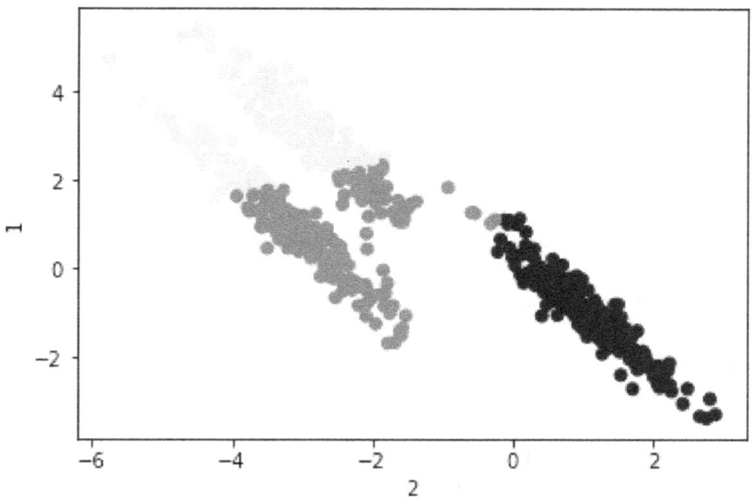

Prediction of Stretched Blobs Dataset using K-Means

You can observe that as long as we are making complex data, the performance of k-means method is decreasing. We are trying more complex data to further validate its performance.

Applying K-Means Clustering on Moons dataset

Input [1]:

Importing required libraries

from sklearn.datasets import make_moons as moons

from sklearn.cluster import KMeans

import matplotlib.pyplot as plt

Reading input data

```python
Data, Target = moons(n_samples = 200, noise = 0.05,
                     random_state = 0)


# Making clustering model

kmeans = KMeans(n_clusters = 2)

kmeans.fit(Data)

plt.scatter(Data[: , 0], Data[: , 1], c = kmeans.labels_)

plt.xlabel(kmeans.labels_[0])

plt.ylabel(kmeans.labels_[1])

plt.hold

plt.show
```

Output:

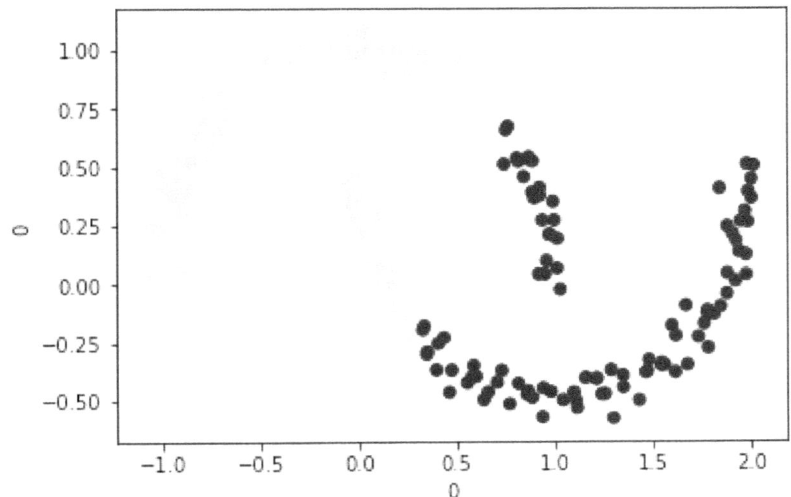

Prediction of Moons Dataset using K-Means

Here, we can evidently see that K-means was performing well on simple data, but when we moved to the Moons dataset, which is comparatively complex than Blobs dataset, K-means failed to make proper clusters. Both predicted classes contain members of other classes. We can analyze that k-Means does not work on complex datasets. For these problems, we need to look for other clustering methods.

Agglomerative Clustering

Agglomerative clustering is another method of clustering, which is somehow similar to the K-means clustering method as it also starts with random cluster. It then merges those clusters into similar clusters until no change occurs. We will apply Agglomerative clustering on blobs dataset to compare its performance with k-means.

Applying Agglomerative Clustering on Blobs dataset

Input:

```
# Importing required libraries

from sklearn.datasets import make_blobs as blobs

from sklearn.cluster import AgglomerativeClustering as Agg

import matplotlib.pyplot as plt


# Reading input data

Data, Target = blobs(random_state = 1)

# Making clustering model

agg = Agg(n_clusters = 3)

agg.fit_predict(Data)
```

plt.scatter(Data[: , 0], Data[: , 1], c = agg.labels_)

plt.legend()

plt.xlabel(agg.labels_[0])

plt.ylabel(agg.labels_[1])

plt.hold

plt.show

Output:

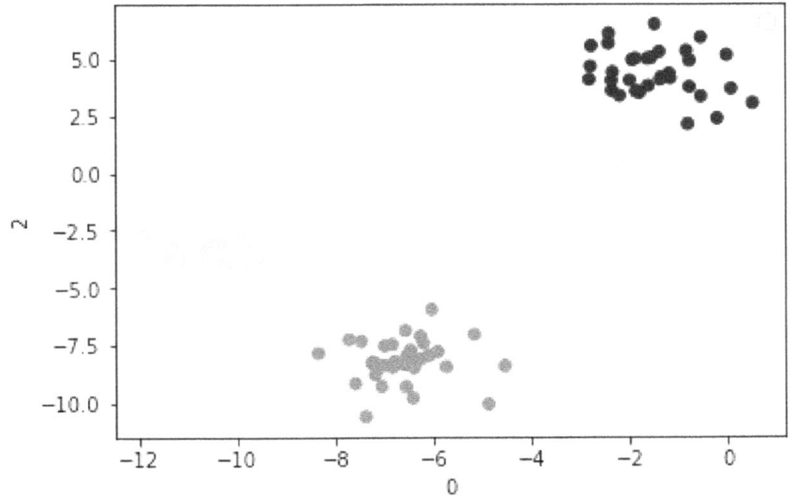

Prediction of Blobs Dataset using Agglomerative Clustering

You can observe that the performance of the Agglomerative clustering is much better than that of K-means clustering as it made clusters effectively. It has made clear clusters as compared to the ones K-means clustering came up with.

Applying Agglomerative Clustering on Moons dataset

Input:

```
# Importing required libraries

from sklearn.datasets import make_moons as moons

from sklearn.cluster import AgglomerativeClustering as Agg

import matplotlib.pyplot as plt


# Reading input data

Data, Target = moons(random_state = 1)


# Making clustering model

agg = Agg(n_clusters = 3)

agg.fit_predict(Data)


plt.scatter(Data[:,0], Data[:,1], c = agg.labels_)

plt.legend()

plt.xlabel(agg.labels_[0])

plt.ylabel(agg.labels_[1])

plt.hold

plt.show
```

Output:

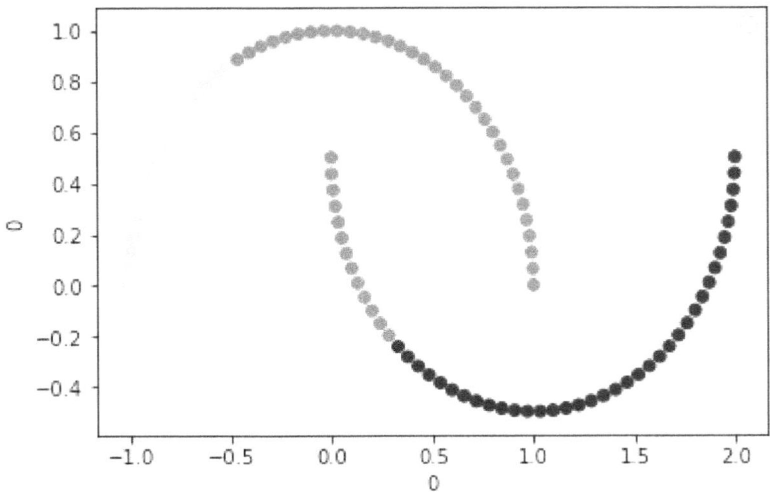

Prediction of Moons Dataset using Agglomerative Clustering

You can again observe that although the Agglomerative clustering method could not perform perfectly in prediction of the Moons dataset, its performance is still much better than K-means clustering.

DBSCAN

DBSCAN is yet another clustering method that is different from previous clustering methods we have looked upon so far. It works on points that are situated in the crowd region. Those crowd regions are also known as dense regions. It performs slower than Agglomerative clustering but gives better results than K-means clustering and Agglomerative clustering. Let us look at how this fares by applying the DBSCAN on moons dataset.

Applying DBSCAN Clustering on Blobs dataset

Input:

Importing required libraries

```python
from sklearn.datasets import make_blobs as blobs

from sklearn.cluster import DBSCAN as DB

import matplotlib.pyplot as plt


# Reading input data

Data, Target = blobs(random_state = 0, n_samples = 12)


# Making clustering model

db = DB()

dd = db.fit_predict(Data)


print("Cluster:\n{}".format(dd))
```

Output:

Cluster:

[-1 -1 -1 -1 -1 -1 -1 -1 -1 -1 -1 -1]

Applying DBSCAN Clustering on Moons dataset

Input [1]:

```python
# Importing required libraries

from sklearn.datasets import make_moons as moons
```

```python
from sklearn.preprocessing import StandardScaler as SS

from sklearn.cluster import DBSCAN as DB

import matplotlib.pyplot as plt


# Reading input data

Data, Target = moons(n_samples = 200, noise = 0.05,
                     random_state = 0)

ss = SS()

ss.fit(Data)

Data_scaled = ss.transform(Data)


# Making clustering model

db = DB()

dd = db.fit_predict(Data_scaled)


print("Cluster:\n{}".format(dd))
```

Output [1]:

Cluster:

```
[0 1 1 0 1 1 0 1 0 1 0 1 0 1 1 1 0 0 0 1 0 0 1 1 0 1 0 1 1 1 1 0 0 0 1 1 0
 1 1

 0 0 1 1 0 0 1 1 0 0 0 1 1 0 1 1 0 1 0 0 1 0 0 1 0 0 1 0 1 0 1 0 0 1 0 0 1 0
 1 1
```

```
 1 0 1 0 0 1 1 0 1 1 1 0 0 0 1 1 0 0 1 0 1 1 1 1 0 1 1 1 0 0 0 1 0 0 1
 0 0

 0 0 0 0 1 0 1 1 0 0 0 1 0 1 0 0 1 1 1 0 0 0 1 1 1 1 0 1 0 1 1 0 0 0 0
 1 1

 0 1 1 1 0 0 1 0 1 1 0 0 1 1 0 1 1 1 0 1 1 1 0 0 0 0 1 1 1 0 0 0 1 0 1
 1 1

 0 0 1 0 0 0 0 0 0 1 0 1 1 0 1]
```

Input [2]:

```python
plt.scatter(Data[:,0], Data[:,1], c = db.labels_)

plt.xlabel(db.labels_[0])

plt.ylabel(db.labels_[1])

plt.hold

plt.show
```

Output [2]:

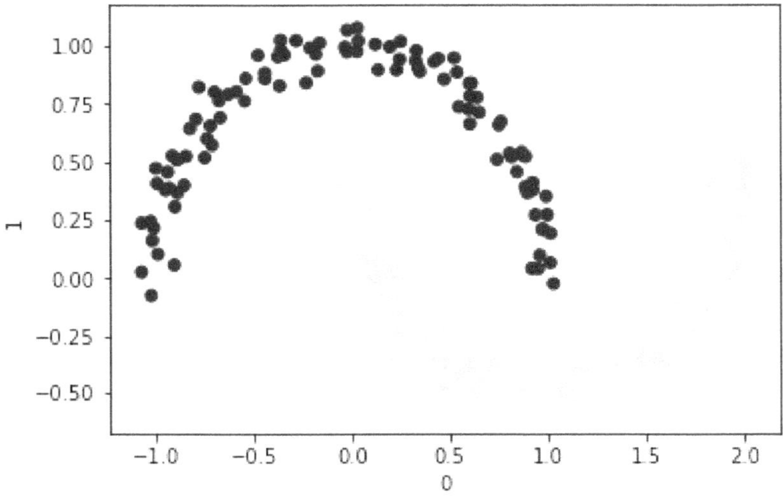

Prediction of Moons Dataset using DBSCAN

Sure enough, the performance of the DBSCAN clustering is best among all clustering algorithms. It has made many clear clusters as compared to K-means clustering and Agglomerative clustering. Although it has used StandardScaler, it has still performed well in dividing the classes.

Rounding off clustering:

We have seen various methods of clustering and how these can help us achieve significant results. Some of these have are quicker while others are more accurate. We have gone through a few visual representations to see exactly how each of these work and how they produce results accordingly.

In the next chapter, we will be looking at how we can work with data that contains text. We will go through sentiment analysis with appropriate examples, we will look at what 'stopwords' are and how we can use methods to analyze the text to fetch desired results.

Chapter 5: Working with Text Data

We have discussed two types of features to represent our dataset. One type comprises a continuous feature that describes the quantity, and the other one is a categorical feature that represents items from fixed list. There is another type of data, which is text. Text data has many applications all over the world.

We have discussed one example of the email message in the 2nd chapter, in which we discussed that email messages could be an example of classification in which one has to classify the email as genuine or spam. The classification will be performed using the provided data. In fact, that email message might contain textual data, which is represented as strings. Similarly, if someone wants to learn about the opinion of any politician on any specific topic, we can take help from his/her speeches or tweets related to that topic to come to a conclusion. That speech or tweets will also contain some textual data that can further help us acquire a better understanding.

In a similar way, in case of customer services, a company needs to check whether the customer has lodged a complaint or an inquiry. This can be done by the representative of the company after checking the subject line of the email that has been sent by the customer. The subject line alone should provide a clue as to what nature of email the customer has sent. One can easily classify it as a complaint or inquiry. That email or document will also contain some textual data.

There are many scenarios in which we deal with textual data, and therefore we need to understand how to deal with textual data. We can perform some machine learning methods to perform classification, clustering or regression depending on these specific problems.

Types of Data Represented as Strings

Text in any dataset consists of strings, but it does not mean that all string features will be assumed as text data. A feature containing strings can represent categorical features as well, which is why we first need to check the data to analyze the constituents of datasets. The string can be comprised of four types, such as text data, categorical data, structured string data and free strings that can be semantically mapped to categories.

Categorical data comes from a fixed list. For example, you have a list of colors such as 'red,' 'green,' 'pink,' 'purple,' 'orange,' 'brown,' 'yellow' and 'black' and you ask someone to select his favorite color from specific list. The person will then select his/her favorite color present within the specific list. Each color will be represented by a categorical variable. As there are eight colors, there should be eight categorical variables. If he/she sees more than eight variables, it will no longer be an example of Categorical data.

This can happen as any color like black was misspelled as blak or blac, and that will lead to the creation of two or more variables for a specific color. As these different variables are representing the same color, these variables can be mapped to the same category.

If the person's favorite color is not present in that specific list, it is either because the person is looking for an unusual color, or that person is confused between 'gray' or 'grey,' or the person can come up with names like 'midnight blue,' which are difficult to be mapped into any color. Depending on the response you get, if the said response does not belong to the primary list, it is considered to be a part of a secondary list. It will then be referred as free strings that can be semantically mapped to categories.

The other type is structured string data. It does not come from fixed categories. It contains structures such as names and addresses of people, telephone numbers, and dates. These types of data demand more effort to deal with.

Text data is the last type of string data that consists of phrases or sentences. This type contains examples of tweets, chats, and reviews. For text analysis, natural language processing (NLP) plays a vital role here.

Sentiment Analysis of Movie Reviews

Sentiment analysis has become a very popular field these days. We will apply sentiment analysis to movie reviews. Reviews comprise of either positive or negative feedback from the audience. The dataset is collected from the Internet Movie Database website. It contains text-based movie reviews.

You will need to download this dataset and then load it in Python. This dataset contains two folders, one is for training data, and the other one is the test data. Both of these folders are further divided into subfolders where one is 'pos' and the other one is 'neg'. The 'pos' folder contains positive reviews while the 'neg' folder contains negative reviews. The dataset is available at http://ai.stanford.edu/~amaas/data/sentiment/.

Input [1]:

```python
# Importing required libraries

from sklearn.datasets import load_files

import matplotlib.pyplot as plt

import numpy as np


# Reading input Training data

reviews_trn = load_files("aclImdb/train/")


# Extracting data and target values from Training data

Data_trn = reviews_trn.data

Target_trn = reviews_trn.target


print("Type of Data_trn: {}".format(type(Data_trn)))
```

Output [1]:

```
Type of Data_trn: <class 'list'>
```

Input [3]:

```python
print("Length of Data_trn: {}".format(len(Data_trn)))
```

Output [2]:

Length of Data_trn: 75000

Input [3]:

```python
print("Data_trn [1]:\n{}".format(Data_trn[1]))
```

Output [3]:

Data_trn [1]:

b"Amount of disappointment I am getting these days seeing movies like Partner, Jhoom Barabar and now, Heyy Babyy is gonna end my habit of seeing first day shows.

The movie is an utter disappointment because it had the potential to become a laugh riot only if the d\xc3\xa9butant director, Sajid Khan hadn't tried too many things. Only saving grace in the movie were the last thirty minutes, which were seriously funny elsewhere the movie fails miserably. First half was desperately been tried to look funny but wasn't. Next 45 minutes were emotional and looked totally artificial and illogical.

OK, when you are out for a movie like this you don't expect much logic but all the flaws tend to appear when you don't enjoy the movie and thats the case with Heyy Babyy. Acting is good but thats not enough to keep one interested.

For the positives, you can take hot actresses, last 30 minutes, some comic scenes, good acting by the lead cast and the baby. Only problem is that these things do not come together properly to make a good movie.

Anyways, I read somewhere that It isn't a copy of Three men and a baby but I think it would have been better if it was."

Input [4]:

```python
Data_trn = [doc.replace(b"<br />", b" ") for doc in Data_trn]

print("Samples per class: {}".format(np.bincount(Target_trn)))
```

Output [4]:

Samples per class: [12500 12500 50000]

Input [5]:

```python
# Reading input Test data

reviews_tst = load_files("data/aclImdb/test/")

# Extracting data and target values from Test data

Data_tst = reviews_tst.data

Target_tst = reviews_tst.target


print("Number of documents in test data: {}".format(len(Data_tst)))
```

Output [5]:

Number of documents in test data: 25000

Input [6]:

```python
Data_tst = [doc.replace(b"<br />", b" ") for doc in Data_tst]

print("Samples per class (test): {}".format(np.bincount(Target_tst)))
```

Output [6]:

Samples per class (test): [12500 12500]

Representing Text Data as Bags of Words

We already have discussed the importance of text data. The usage of bags of words for machine learning methods has become very popular. While dealing with this representation, we usually remove some of the structures, such as words, sentences, paragraphs, chapters, and formatting. It only counts words that appear in each text. By removing structure and counting just word, it provides a representation of text in the form of a 'bag.'

While carrying out a representation of bags of words, the steps required are as follows;

- Splitting each document into words that are known as tokens and the process, that is known as tokenization.

- The collection of vocabulary of all words appearing in each document and numbering them is known as vocabulary building.

- Counting words in vocabulary is known as encoding.

Applying Bag of Words on a Toy dataset

Bag of words is applied in CountVectorizor, which is used to perform transformation. We are applying bag of words to the toy dataset.

Input [1]:

```python
# Initializing words

words = ["Every one is not wise,","Every one can not be wise,"]
```

```python
# Importing required libraries

from sklearn.feature_extraction.text import CountVectorizer

Cvect = CountVectorizer()

Cvect.fit(words)
```

Output [1]:

```
CountVectorizer(analyzer='word', binary=False, decode_error='strict',
        dtype=<class 'numpy.int64'>, encoding='utf-8', input='content',
        lowercase=True, max_df=1.0, max_features=None, min_df=1,
        ngram_range=(1, 1), preprocessor=None, stop_words=None,
        strip_accents=None, token_pattern='(?u)\\b\\w\\w+\\b',
        tokenizer=None, vocabulary=None)
```

Input [2]:

```python
print("Size of Vocabulary: {}".format(len(Cvect.vocabulary_)))
```

Output [2]:

Size of Vocabulary: 7

Input [3]:

```python
print("Content of Vocabulary:\n {}".format(Cvect.vocabulary_))
```

Output [3]:

Content of Vocabulary:

{'every': 2, 'one': 5, 'is': 3, 'not': 4, 'wise': 6, 'can': 1, 'be': 0}

You can observe the size of vocabulary and counts of each word in the list of words. It is showing the number of occurrences for each word.

If you want to get the bag of words representation of training data, you can use 'transform'.

Input [1]:

```python
bag_of_words = Cvect.transform(words)

print("bag_of_words: {}".format(repr(bag_of_words)))
```

Output [1]:

bag_of_words: <2x7 sparse matrix of type '<class 'numpy.int64'>'

with 11 stored elements in Compressed Sparse Row format>

You can observe the bag of words representation of training data. Bag of words representation is stored in SciPy sparse matrix which only stores non-zero entries. If you want to mapping of words you can perform below steps.

Input [2]:

```python
print("Dense Representation of bag of words:\n{}".format(bag_of_words.toarray()))
```

Output [2]:

Dense Representation of bag of words:

[[0 0 1 1 1 1 1]

[1 1 1 0 1 1 1]]

You can see that words have been mapped to either 0 or 1.

Applying Bag of Words on Movie Reviews

Input [1]:

```python
# Importing required libraries

from sklearn.datasets import load_files

from sklearn.feature_extraction.text import CountVectorizer

import matplotlib.pyplot as plt

import numpy as np


# Reading input data
```

```python
reviews_trn = load_files("aclImdb/train/")

reviews_tst = load_files("aclImdb/test/")


# Extracting data and target values from Training data

Data_trn = reviews_trn.data

Target_trn = reviews_trn.target


# Extracting data and target values from Test data

Data_tst = reviews_tst.data

Target_tst = reviews_tst.target


Cvect = CountVectorizer()

Cvect.fit(Data_trn)


Data_trn = Cvect.transform(Data_trn)

print("Data_trn:\n{}".format(repr(Data_trn)))
```

Output [1]:

Data_trn:

<75000x124255 sparse matrix of type '<class 'numpy.int64'>'

with 10359806 stored elements in Compressed Sparse Row format>

You can check that the shape of Data_trn after bag of words representation is 75000 x 124255 with a vocabulary of 124,255. Once again, the Bag of words representation is stored in SciPy sparse matrix which only stores non-zero entries. If you want to get details of vocabulary, you can perform the following steps:

Input [1]:

```
names_feature = Cvect.get_feature_names()

print("Number of features: {}".format(len(names_feature)))
```

Output [1]:

```
Number of features: 124255
```

Input [2]:

```
print("First 20 features:\n{}".format(names_feature[:20]))
```

Output [2]:

```
First 20 features:

['00', '000', '0000', '0000000000000000000000000000000001',
 '0000000000001', '000000001', '000000003', '00000001',
 '000001745', '00001', '0001', '00015', '0002', '0007', '00083',
 '000ft', '000s', '000th', '001', '002']
```

Input [3]:

```
print("Features from 50010 to
50030:\n{}".format(names_feature[50010:50030]))
```

Output [3]:

Features from 50010 to 50030:

['heatman', 'heatmiser', 'heaton', 'heats', 'heatseeker', 'heatwave',
'heave', 'heaved', 'heaven', 'heavenlier', 'heavenliness', 'heavenly',
'heavens', 'heavenward', 'heaves', 'heavier', 'heavies', 'heaviest',
'heavily', 'heaviness']

Input [4]:

print("Every 5000th feature:\n{}".format(names_feature[::5000]))

Output [4]:

Every 5000th feature:

['00', 'aluin', 'banquière', 'brandie', 'chcialbym', 'corruptible',
'devagan', 'eisenburg', 'fetiches', 'ghar', 'heathen', 'indy', 'kerchner',
'locasso', 'meistersinger', 'narrators', 'overwhelmingly', 'portugese',
'recreating', 'samharris', 'silveira', 'stolen', 'themself', 'undeveloped',
'weidler']

We can observe that data is very big, and maybe some of it is useless, which is why we should apply a better feature extraction. We first need to apply classification so that we can compare its performance with one after removing some features.

Applying Logistic Regression on Movie Reviews

Input:

Importing required libraries

from sklearn.datasets import load_files

from sklearn.feature_extraction.text import CountVectorizer

```python
from sklearn.model_selection import cross_val_score

from sklearn.linear_model import LogisticRegression

import matplotlib.pyplot as plt

import numpy as np


# Reading input data

reviews_trn = load_files("aclImdb/train/")

reviews_tst = load_files("aclImdb/test/")


# Extracting data and target values from Training data

Data_trn = reviews_trn.data

Target_trn = reviews_trn.target


# Extracting data and target values from Test data

Data_tst = reviews_tst.data

Target_tst = reviews_tst.target


Cvect = CountVectorizer()

Cvect.fit(Data_trn)


Data_trn = Cvect.transform(Data_trn)
```

```python
scores = cross_val_score(LogisticRegression(), Data_trn,
Target_trn, cv = 5)

print("Accuracy: {:.2f}".format(np.mean(scores)))
```

Output:

Accuracy: 0.71

Applying Logistic Regression with Gridsearch on Movie
Reviews

Input:

```python
# Importing required libraries

from sklearn.datasets import load_files

from sklearn.model_selection import cross_val_score

from sklearn.linear_model import LogisticRegression

from sklearn.feature_extraction.text import CountVectorizer

from sklearn.model_selection import GridSearchCV

import matplotlib.pyplot as plt

import numpy as np


# Reading input data

reviews_trn = load_files("aclImdb/train/")

reviews_tst = load_files("aclImdb/test/")
```

```python
# Extracting data and target values from Training data

Data_trn = reviews_trn.data

Target_trn = reviews_trn.target


# Extracting data and target values from Test data

Data_tst = reviews_tst.data

Target_tst = reviews_tst.target


Cvect = CountVectorizer()

Cvect.fit(Data_trn)


Data_trn = Cvect.transform(Data_trn)


prm_grd = {'C': [0.001, 0.01, 0.1, 1, 10]}

grd = GridSearchCV(LogisticRegression(), prm_grd, cv = 5)

grd.fit(Data_trn, Target_trn)

print("Cross validation score: {:.2f}".format(grd.best_score_))

print("Parameter with best performance: ", grd.best_params_)
```

Output:

Cross validation score: 0.72

Parameter with best performance: {'C' : 0.1}

You can observe that cross validation score using value of C = is achieved. We should check performance on test data as well which will further describe the performance of algorithm.

Input:

```
Data_tst = Cvect.transform(Target_tst)

print("{:.2f}".format(grd.score(Data_tst, Target_tst)))
```

Output:

```
0.70
```

We have checked the accuracies of logistic regression with and without GridSearch. We need to apply a better feature extraction here, as well. We should look to remove useless or less impactful features. It can be observed that we have used CountVectorizer, which converts all words to lowercase characters, which means 'Some', 'some" and sOme will correspond to the same token.

It is a good thing to have as some words can be mistakenly written in uppercase and can be differentiated with the same word in lowercase, but despite this feature of CountVectorizer, we have observed that there are still some useless features or words which need to be removed.

Stopwords

We can remove the useless words by using stopwords. It removes words that are repeated over and over again.

Input [1]:

```python
# Importing required libraries
from sklearn.datasets import load_files
from sklearn.model_selection import cross_val_score
from sklearn.linear_model import LogisticRegression
from sklearn.feature_extraction.text import CountVectorizer
from sklearn.model_selection import GridSearchCV
import matplotlib.pyplot as plt
import numpy as np


# Reading input data
reviews_trn = load_files("aclImdb/train/")
reviews_tst = load_files("aclImdb/test/")


# Extracting data and target values from Training data
Data_trn = reviews_trn.data
Target_trn = reviews_trn.target


# Extracting data and target values from Test data
Data_tst = reviews_tst.data
Target_tst = reviews_tst.target
Cvect = CountVectorizer(min_df = 5).fit(Data_trn)
```

```python
X_train = Cvect.transform(Data_trn)

print("X_train with min_df: {}".format(repr(X_train)))
```

Output [1]:

X_train with min_df: <75000x124055 sparse matrix of type '<class 'numpy.int64'>'

with 10359846 stored elements in Compressed Sparse Row format>

We can observe that with demanding at least five occurrences, we have reduced features from 124255 to 124055, which means reduction of 200 features. Now we need to check the accuracy of logistic regression algorithm after reducing useless words.

Input [2]:

```python
grd = GridSearchCV(LogisticRegression(), prm_grd, cv = 5)

grd.fit(Data_trn, Target_trn)

print("Cross validation score: {:.2f}".format(grd.best_score_))
```

Output [2]:

Cross validation score: 0.72

We can observe that even after reducing useless words, accuracy of logistic regression algorithm is unchanged. Although the accuracy has not improved, we have reduced the number of features by getting the same performance, which means we have done good by reducing words that are meaningless.

Applying Logistic Regression with Gridsearch and Stopwords on Movie Reviews

Input [1]:

```python
# Importing required libraries
from sklearn.datasets import load_files
from sklearn.model_selection import cross_val_score
from sklearn.linear_model import LogisticRegression
from sklearn.feature_extraction.text import CountVectorizer
from sklearn.model_selection import GridSearchCV
import matplotlib.pyplot as plt
import numpy as np


# Reading input data
reviews_trn = load_files("aclImdb/train/")
reviews_tst = load_files("aclImdb/test/")


# Extracting data and target values from Training data
Data_trn = reviews_trn.data
Target_trn = reviews_trn.target


# Extracting data and target values from Test data
```

```python
Data_tst = reviews_tst.data

Target_tst = reviews_tst.target


Cvect = CountVectorizer(min_df = 5, stop_words = 
        "english").fit(Data_trn)

X_train = Cvect.transform(Data_trn)

print("X_train with stop words:\n{}".format(repr(X_train)))
```

Output [1]:

X_train with stop words:

<75000x123865 sparse matrix of type '<class 'numpy.int64'>'

with 10359836 stored elements in Compressed Sparse Row format>

We can again observe that with applying stopwords, we have reduced features from 124,055 to 123,865, which means a reduction of 190 features. Now, we need to check the accuracy of the logistic regression algorithm after the reduction.

Input [2]:

```python
grd = GridSearchCV(LogisticRegression(), param_grid, cv = 5)

grd.fit(Data_trn, Target_trn)

print("Cross validation score: {:.2f}".format(grid.best_score_))
```

Output [2]:

Cross validation score: 0. 73

Applying Logistic Regression with tf-id Vectorizer and
Stopwords on Movie Reviews

Input [1]:

```
# Importing required libraries

from sklearn.datasets import load_files

from sklearn.model_selection import cross_val_score

from sklearn.linear_model import LogisticRegression

from sklearn.model_selection import GridSearchCV

from sklearn.feature_extraction.text import TfidfVectorizer

from sklearn.pipeline import make_pipeline

import matplotlib.pyplot as plt

import numpy as np


# Reading input data

reviews_trn = load_files("aclImdb/train/")

reviews_tst = load_files("aclImdb/test/")


# Extracting data and target values from Training data

Data_trn = reviews_trn.data

Target_trn = reviews_trn.target
```

```python
# Extracting data and target values from Test data

Data_tst = reviews_tst.data

Target_tst = reviews_tst.target

ppe = make_pipeline(TfidfVectorizer(min_df = 5, norm = None),
                    LogisticRegression())

prm_grd = {'logisticregression__C': [0.001, 0.01, 0.1, 1, 10]}

grd = GridSearchCV(ppe, prm_grd, cv = 5)

grd.fit(Data_trn, Target_trn)

print("Cross validation score: {:.2f}".format(grd.best_score_))
```

Output [1]:

Cross validation score: 0.73

Applying Natural language toolkit on Email

We will be processing some emails now. We will first look at the original email and the one after some processing to get a better understanding. You can use any email and carry out the process on it.

Input [1]:

```python
# Importing required libraries

from nltk.stem import SnowballStemmer

import string
```

```
# The first part is to give an appropriate path of the file and read
the file.

d6=[]

d=open("2","r")

d1 = d.read()
```

Output [1]:

Message-ID: <26985403.1075859469480.JavaMail.evans@thyme>

Date: Wed, 26 Dec 2001 09:41:22 -0800 (PST)

From: susan.bailey@enron.com

To: stephanie.panus@enron.com

Subject: FW: People on Termination List

Cc: stewart.rosman@enron.com

Mime-Version: 1.0

Content-Type: text/plain; charset=us-ascii

Content-Transfer-Encoding: 7bit

Bcc: stewart.rosman@enron.com

X-From: Bailey, Susan
</O=ENRON/OU=NA/CN=RECIPIENTS/CN=SBAILE2>

X-To: Panus, Stephanie
</O=ENRON/OU=NA/CN=RECIPIENTS/CN=Spanus>

X-cc: Rosman, Stewart
</O=ENRON/OU=NA/CN=RECIPIENTS/CN=Srosman>

X-bcc:

X-Folder: \Susan_Bailey_Jan2002\Bailey, Susan\Deleted Items

X-Origin: Bailey-S

X-FileName: sbaile2 (Non-Privileged).pst

Stephanie,

Please add the following individuals set forth below to list of recipients to receive the Master Termination Log.

Also, please add Steve Hall to that list.

Thanks,

Susan

-----Original Message-----

From: Rosman, Stewart

Sent: Wednesday, December 26, 2001 11:37 AM

To: Bailey, Susan

Subject: People on Termination List

Sean Crandall

Diana Scholtes

Jeff Richter

Chris Mallory

Mark Fischer

Tom Alonso

Input [2]:

```python
# Once the contents are available in Python, the next step is to
remove the metadata from the email.

# the string 'X-FileName'. This string is present in every email and
can be 'split'.

d2=d1.split('X-FileName')
```

Output [2]:

```
% First part of d2

Message-ID: <26985403.1075859469480.JavaMail.evans@thyme>

Date: Wed, 26 Dec 2001 09:41:22 -0800 (PST)

From: susan.bailey@enron.com

To: stephanie.panus@enron.com

Subject: FW: People on Termination List

Cc: stewart.rosman@enron.com
```

Mime-Version: 1.0

Content-Type: text/plain; charset=us-ascii

Content-Transfer-Encoding: 7bit

Bcc: stewart.rosman@enron.com

X-From: Bailey, Susan
</O=ENRON/OU=NA/CN=RECIPIENTS/CN=SBAILE2>

X-To: Panus, Stephanie
</O=ENRON/OU=NA/CN=RECIPIENTS/CN=Spanus>

X-cc: Rosman, Stewart
</O=ENRON/OU=NA/CN=RECIPIENTS/CN=Srosman>

X-bcc:

X-Folder: \Susan_Bailey_Jan2002\Bailey, Susan\Deleted Items

X-Origin: Bailey-S

% First part of d2

: sbaile2 (Non-Privileged).pst

Stephanie,

Please add the following individuals set forth below to list of
recipients to receive the Master Termination Log.

Also, please add Steve Hall to that list.

Thanks,

Susan

-----Original Message-----

From: Rosman, Stewart

Sent: Wednesday, December 26, 2001 11:37 AM

To: Bailey, Susan

Subject: People on Termination List

Sean Crandall

Diana Scholtes

Jeff Richter

Chris Mallory

Mark Fischer

Tom Alonso

Input [3]:

Once the email body is retrieved, the next step is to remove

punctuation, and split the text into individual words.

```
for c in string.punctuation:

    d3= d2[1].replace(c,"")

    d4=d3.split(' ')
```

Output [3]:

% d3

: sbaile2 (Non-Privileged).pst

Stephanie,

Please add the following individuals set forth below to list of recipients to receive the Master Termination Log.

Also, please add Steve Hall to that list.

Thanks,

Susan

-----Original Message-----

From: Rosman, Stewart

Sent: Wednesday, December 26, 2001 11:37 AM

To: Bailey, Susan

Subject: People on Termination List

Sean Crandall

Diana Scholtes

Jeff Richter

Chris Mallory

Mark Fischer

Tom Alonso

% d4

:

sbaile2

(Non-Privileged).pst

Stephanie,

Please

add

the

following

individuals

set

forth

below

to

list

of

recipients

to

receive

the

Input [4]:

```python
# Now apply SnowballStemmer on each word. [hint: use .append()
method to make a continual list of words]

stemmer = SnowballStemmer("english")

for i in range(len(d4)):
```

```python
    d5=stemmer.stem(d4[i])

    d6.append (d5)



# The resulting list of words is then 'joined' again into a single
string.

d6 = " ".join(d6)
```

Output [4]:

```
% d5



alonso



% d6

: sbaile2 (non-privileged).pst



stephanie,
```

pleas add the follow individu set forth below to list of recipi to receiv the master termin log.

also, pleas add steve hall to that list.

thanks,

susan

-----origin message-----

from: rosman, stewart

sent: wednesday, decemb 26, 2001 11:37 am

to: bailey, susan

subject: peopl on termin list

sean crandall

diana scholtes

jeff richter

chri mallory

mark fischer

tom alonso

In the above example, we have successfully processed an email. We began with an email that contained far too much information, most of which we were neither interested in nor looking forward to.

We then processed the same email and removed meta descriptions and other unnecessary words to bring out only the information we were interested in. The end result is an information extracted from the email that is relevant and needed.

While this process is lengthy, it does beg the question, why would you do all that when you can copy and paste the email body yourself? Remember, we are undergoing Machine learning and naturally, we are expecting to deal with a bulk of data. There is every likelihood that you will not be dealing with data that is only comprising of a single email. By training the model to filter out unnecessary information for hundreds of thousands of email in the shortest span of time, you are saving yourself quite a lot of process. The machine will now be able to carry out the same for you instead, at a rate far quicker than an individual can deliver.

To conclude this chapter, we have learned how to handle data that comprises of text. Unlike previous chapters, where we were manipulating numeric values and methods to plot graphs and visualize the data, this chapter dealt with 'strings' of text as you would normally find in emails and movie reviews.

Major organizations use sentiment analysis to tailor recommendations using this information for the members of the general audience. Through using such methods and algorithms, we can train the model of the machine to learn and store words as 'vocabulary' and then ensure that the machine can use these to gain valuable data and analyze the same. Through effective analysis, we can have quite a lot of work carried out in the least timeframe possible.

In the final chapter, we will be looking at the real world applications of Machine learning. While there are quite a lot of these in existence, we will only be focusing on a select few to provide data scientists and machine learners a better understanding of the applications in the real world.

Chapter 6: Machine Learning Real World Applications

Machine learning is an all-important field throughout the world. Its application can be seen in many apps, software, and research-based projects of various magnitudes. Machine learning has been around for quite some time now; however, recently it has garnered a massive attention from the worldwide audience and computer experts.

It can be used in medical fields for diagnosing various diseases using classification or regression methods, within social networks to locate your friends, get suggestions and a feed that is tailor-made for your liking, and in forecasting weather conditions by providing the model with a number of features that can further train and classify, predict or forecast weather when required. It is capable of processing extensively large data for large organizations or small-sized data for smaller organizations as well.

Where can you use machine learning?

We can use machine learning in many applications when it comes to the real world. Before we go ahead, let us quickly stroll through the previous examples discussed to remind ourselves of some practical examples. Then, we shall look at four more large-scale uses of machine learning. For this book, we will not be covering small scale usage of machine learning. After all, we are trying to learn to be a part of a bigger picture.

In the beginning, we discussed how the spam filter used a list of blacklisted words which helped the filter to identify spam words or emails. This filter can be used as one of the examples of intelligent applications. This problem can be solved by a human as well, but in that case, a person requires thorough understanding of processes in order to come up with such a model. Manual or hand-coded rules can be useful but not in every case.

Similarly, in another example we learned that the hand-coded method fails in a specific aspect, and that is the detection of a face in an image. Although every smartphone these days can detect and identify faces in the pictures, this was far from possible in the past. The reason behind failure in detection and identification of faces in an image in the recent past is due to the difference in perception of pixels between a human and a computer.

Apart from these, The application of machine learning can be seen across various sectors of our daily lives. These include and are not limited to the following:

1.   Financial institutions – Financial institutions like banks have greatly benefited from machine learning and have used machine learning to create complex algorithms to learn and identify suspicious or fraudulent transactions. There were times when a transaction could not be identified at such a rapid pace and most of the people who carried out these illegal activities got away with it. Now, things are different. With large processing power and memory available for the systems of today, financial institutions can run transactions through a trained model and immediately identify if any transaction, regardless of how genuine it looks, is flagged as suspicious or fraudulent. These transaction checks have greatly improved the leakages in reserves and allowed the world to host better banking systems where the money and financial records remain safe and secure, away from prying eyes.

2.   Sentiment Analysis – Major streaming platforms across the globe, such as Netflix and Amazon Prime, are using sentiment analysis to analyze the behavior of the user and learn of what the user might like or dislike. This saves quite a lot of time and guess work as the entire profile is categorized by labels such as likes, dislikes, and only then recommendations are proposed for the users. This creates a high chance that

the user might end up clicking on the said recommendation. This isn't just

limited to streaming services, many other websites use the same approach, such as Facebook, twitter and many more. This is why you normally end up getting feeds that are more likely to engage you.

3.   Healthcare – We have looked at a few variations of machine learning methods using Iris and Breast Cancer datasets. However, the reason we used those is because machine learning plays a vital

role in the health sector. With top-notch machineries, equipment and analysis tools, machine learning provides ground-breaking results in the least amount of time imaginable. What was once done in days can now be done within minutes. No longer do you need

to consult various doctors regarding a scan just to find out the condition of your ailment. Now, the clever machines and models continue to evolve and learn to decode the films and scans to predict the answers with amazing accuracy. The bright side is, this field will continue to use machine learning for generations to come.

4.   E-Commerce – Sure enough, businesses that operate online, such as Amazon, eBay, Alibaba, use machine learning to understand the buying patterns, wishlisted items and items the users might browse through to come up with recommendations. For any business person, it is imperative to propose or recommend items which have a high likelihood of being sold to a specific type of customer. Through machine learning, that is being done every single minute of every day. The more you browse such e-commerce websites, the more data they compile to refine their accuracy in recommending products. Eventually, you will be spoiled for choice as these recommendations, almost all of them, will be too tempting to resist. The fact of the matter is that these existed within the website before as well, the only difference is, you may have skipped past these. Now, since the machine has learned of your shopping behavior and the kind of items you are interested in, the model will propose the ones which are most likely to be sold to you.

The world continues to evolve and with it the data that is being collected. Every day we spend hours on our cell phones and computers, scrolling through websites, products and even social media pages. This data is growing larger and larger for every single one of us. Imagine the amount of data that exists on the internet now. Processing that will require hundreds of years, if not thousands, if done by human beings.

Machine learning has drastically changed everything for us and taken over the arduous task of carrying out such large operations in unbelievably short span of time. Not only does that save us time, it saves us quite a lot of effort and possibly money as well. Now, we can create our own models and use the data we have gathered to tailor the kind of recommendations we would like the customers to see, effectively increasing our chances for great sales.

Before we end the chapter, below are some working data using a few more datasets. Have a look through and try to find out what is being done here. You can try and alter the variables, the methods and see how that would affect the overall output of the same.

Applying Machine Learning methods on Wine Data

Input [1]:

```python
# Importing required libraries
import pandas as pd
from sklearn.cluster import KMeans
from sklearn.preprocessing import StandardScaler
from sklearn.pipeline import make_pipeline


df = pd.read_csv('wine_data.csv')


samples = df.iloc[:, 2: 10].values
model = KMeans(n_clusters = 3)
labels = model.fit_predict(samples)


ct = pd.crosstab(labels,df['class_name'])
print("Crosstab with simple Kmeans:\n",ct)
```

Output [1]:

```
Crosstab with simple Kmeans:
class_name  Barbera  Barolo  Grignolino
row_0
0                 5      15           6
```

	class_label	alcohol	...	od280	proline
count	178.000000	178.000000	...	178.000000	178.000000
mean	1.938202	13.000618	...	2.611685	746.893258
std	0.775035	0.811827	...	0.709990	314.907474
min	1.000000	11.030000	...	1.270000	278.000000
25%	1.000000	12.362500	...	1.937500	500.500000
50%	2.000000	13.050000	...	2.780000	673.500000
75%	3.000000	13.677500	...	3.170000	985.000000
max	3.000000	14.830000	...	4.000000	1680.000000

Input [2]:

```python
print(df.describe())
```

```python
scaler = StandardScaler()

scaler.fit(samples)

scaled_samples = scaler.transform(samples)
```

```python
# Applying KMeans and pd.crosstab on the scaled_samples

Model = KMeans(n_clusters = 3)

labels = model.fit_predict(scaled_samples)

ct = pd.crosstab(labels,df['class_name'])

print("Crosstab with StandardScaler and Kmeans:\n",ct)
```

Output [2]:

[8 rows x 14 columns]

Crosstab with StandardScaler and Kmeans:

class_name	Barbera	Barolo	Grignolino
row_0			
0	0	55	4
1	46	0	13
2	2	4	54

Input [3]:

```python
#%% Pipeline

Scaler = StandardScaler()

Kmeans = KMeans(n_clusters = 3)

pipeline = make_pipeline(scaler,kmeans)
```

```python
pipeline.fit(samples)

labels = pipeline.predict(samples)

ct = pd.crosstab(labels,df['class_name'])

print("Crosstab with pipeline:\n",ct)
```

Output [3]:

Crosstab with pipeline:

class_name	Barbera	Barolo	Grignolino
row_0			
0	1	5	44
1	47	0	22
2	0	54	5

Applying Machine Learning methods on Banknote Authentication Data

Input [1]:

```python
# Importing required libraries

from sklearn.model_selection import train_test_split

import pandas as pd

from sklearn.tree import DecisionTreeClassifier
```

```python
from matplotlib import pyplot as plt

file = pd.read_csv('bank_note.txt')

data = file.values

x = data[: , 0:4]

y = data[: , 4]


#Data Splitting

x_train, x_test, y_train, y_test = train_test_split(x, y, test_size = 0.3,
                                                    random_state = 15)


clf = DecisionTreeClassifier(criterion = 'gini', min_samples_split = 65,
                             max_features = 3,
                             max_depth = 150)

clf.fit(x_train,y_train)

out = clf.predict(x_test)

acc = (sum(out == y_test))/len(out)

print('Accuracy of the classifier is {:.4f}'.format(acc*100))


#Data Plotting

plt.plot(x_train[y_train == 0,0],x_train[y_train == 0,1],'rs',label =
```

```python
'Original')

plt.hold

plt.plot(x_train[y_train == 1,0],x_train[y_train ==
1,1],'g.',label='Fake')

plt.legend()

plt.xlabel('variance of Wavelet Transformed image')

plt.ylabel('skewness of Wavelet Transformed image')


plt.figure(2)

plt.plot(x_train[y_train == 0,2],x_train[y_train == 0,3],'rs',label =
'Original')

plt.hold

plt.plot(x_train[y_train == 1,2],x_train[y_train == 1,3],'g.',label =
'Fake')

plt.legend()

plt.xlabel('curtosis of Wavelet Transformed image ')

plt.ylabel('entropy of image')
```

Output [1]:

Accuracy of the classifier is 93.4466

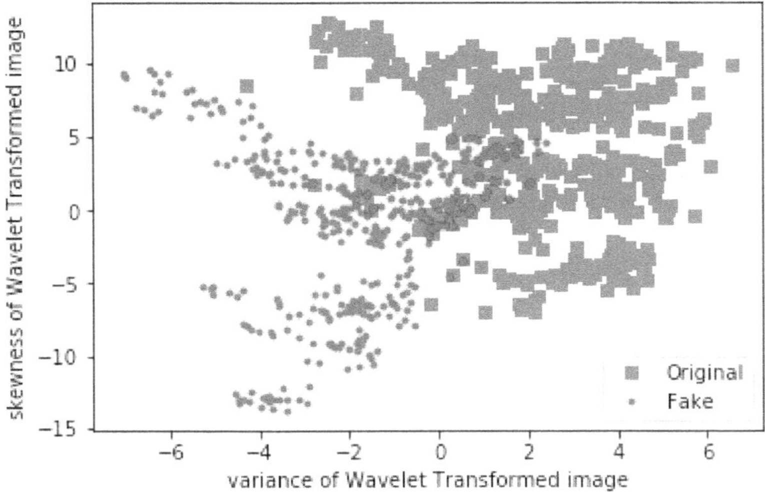

Prediction of first two features of Banknote Dataset using Decision Tree Classifier

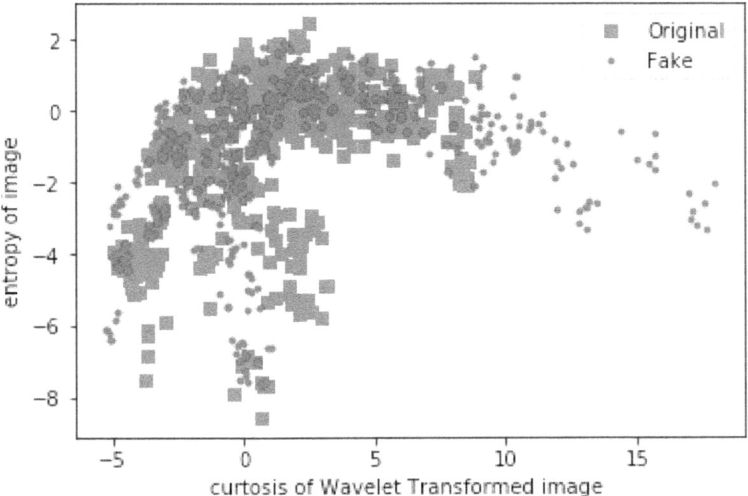

Prediction of last two features of Banknote Dataset using Decision Tree Classifier

Both of these datasets are collected from
https://archive.ics.uci.edu/ml/datasets.php. You can use this
repository to download and use any dataset you might like. It is
recommended that you continue practicing your codes and machine
learning by downloading various machine learning datasets. These
will help you grasp the concepts far better than just repeating
everything the book has to offer.

Conclusion

Admittedly, the book comprises of quite a few codes, all of which
may seem daunting and rather overwhelming at first. If you have a
good understanding of the Python programming language, you
should easily be able to relate to the code and understanding what
is being done at a certain given point. While our main objective was
to ensure we visit some of the more technically advanced
approaches and test out various models, check their accuracy and
put them to work, we cannot deny that at the heart of the entire
Machine Learning lies Python; a beautiful and intriguing language
that continues to amaze the world.

In the start of this book, we looked upon various components, went
through some details and established that this book caters to people
with a good knowledge of Python and other important libraries. The
purpose of this book was to allow you to seek out further datasets,
libraries and components which would allow you to enhance your
Machine Learning skills by using practical, real world examples.

We then discussed many machine learning methods and their
applications as well. We also learned that machine learning can be
divided into two types, supervised machine learning and
unsupervised machine learning. Supervised machine learning
contains the information of output label. Supervised machine
learning is further split into two types, classification, and regression.
Classification is used to predict discrete labels while regression is
used to predict continuous numbers or floating-point numbers.

Classification is further divided into two categories, binary
classification and multi-classification. Binary classification divides
two classes while multi-classification separates multiple classes. In

other words, we can say that binary classification provides either a yes or no as an answer. We discussed the example of classification of emails as an example of binary classification.

We also visited examples of regression such as prediction of an individual's annual income from his/her education, age and other related 'features' where predicted output will be an amount of any value. The predicted output can be any number, varying on the kind of data provided.

Unsupervised machine learning does not contain the information of the output label. It applies multiple methods including Euclidean distance. It contains k-means, agglomerative and DBSCAN methods which divide the datasets without knowing the information of output label.

Multiple methods of each category have been applied. We observed that linear kernel worked better than other kernels in classification. Some methods worked well by increasing the value of C while others performed well by reducing the value of tolerance.

We also observed that we should limit the number of features while training and predicting output otherwise we can lead to lack of accuracy.

We observed that K-means clustering performed well but in simple problems. For problems which were complex in nature, it failed.

Agglomerative and DBSCAN methods performed better than K-means clustering, especially in difficult cases. We also observed that many scales can be used to increase the efficiency of algorithms. It was also shown that many scales can be used as preprocessing especially before applying classification as some methods are sensitive to scales and perform well with application of scales such as SVM and NN.

Finally, we analyzed some text data and were successfully able to remove unnecessary data from the said email while retaining the one that we require the most.

While the book has left out hundreds of other applications of machine learning, and thousands of datasets which could have been used, it is done deliberately to allow the aspiring learners to carry out experimentations and come up with better solutions through effective approach and model training. Where possible, the links were shared so that you can gain access to such training model datasets.

Machine learning has gained quite a pace and promises to be a worthy field of interest for those willing to pursue a career in it. We have barely uncovered the tip of the iceberg, there is quite a lot remaining that we might not know yet. Machine learning will soon revolutionize ad impact quite a lot of things, which makes this the perfect time to get into some practice and start making your way to the top.

While you can continue to read various books and scroll through a gazillion videos available all over the internet, the best way to master machine learning is to implement the codes and try writing new ones. Come up with genuine ideas by visualizing a scenario and then focusing on the task. Learn and then teach the same to the model by supplying the appropriate data. The end results will always bring out something unique each time.

Great programmers and inventors have gone through extensive trial and error methods to come up with contributions which have helped the society, if not the world. However, you hold a distinct advantage over such success stories; they relied on man hours while you now have a machine to carry out the same extensive work but in a fraction of the time you may have taken otherwise. Use the knowledge and use it well!

Remember, there is no such thing as being "too late to learn." All it needs is commitment and a will to learn. Great inventors used the same age-old principles to come up with brilliant, ground-breaking inventions. Do not let the thought of being late to begin learning something new get to you. Your creativity is yours, and you are unique in your own way. With the knowledge you have gathered, let your creativity flow and practice. Who knows, you might very well be the next great mind to rise.

Let Machine Learning help you achieve great new success. This field holds significant potential and the future is only looking to grow bigger. Despite all the competition, despite the sheer number of aspiring students and masters, there is much to be done in this world to help others and create a more safe, secure and efficient environment. All it takes is one brilliant idea to change everything.

Whether you wish to bring a revolutionary new model to analyze blood samples, or detect fraudulent online transactions, you have all the time in the world to come up with something truly unique.

The beauty about the entire Machine Learning process is that you can explore far greater and more promising opportunities for yourself. The field is quite vast and you can get into various projects and institutions. Here are a few of the top ones which use or need Machine Learning:

1. Virtual Assistants - We are referring to technologies like Siri for iPhones. The world of voice recognition and virtual assistants is rapidly evolving. Now, even the television remote controls come with voice assistance. Machine learning plays an important part to make these applications successful. By gathering the data of your selection, your voice samples, and your day-to-day commands, you start getting more personalized recommendations and outputs. This is just the start; there is a long way to go as the world has just started getting used to such virtual assistants.

2. Face tracking - Whether you use facial recognition apps for surveillance purposes or for cinematography, face tracking requires complex algorithms to train the model in order to learn what face it needs to track and how to keep its focus on the subject of choice. We are still in early days which is why there is quite a lot to be done in this field as well. The applications will further diversify the use of machine learning in CCTVs, surveillance, video making, aerial/drone imaging and much more.

3. Search engine queries - We have already seen how search engines tend to immediately understand what we are trying to search. Now, you know how! They use algorithms to try and understand the behavior of the user and identify what the user is trying to search for. Using features like their geographical location, age, and browsing habits, the search engines present results tailor-made for them.

4. Customer support - This might be a bit of a surprise, but the fact of the matter is that not always do you get to speak to a live customer service representative. There are

quite a few occurrences where you will end up speaking to a 'bot' that is collecting the data and understanding what you are trying to find out. Using the abundant resources from the page, the bot will present the information to you accordingly while trying to gauge the exact nature of the query. This is far from perfect which is why if you can come up with an accurate model, you might be just moments away from becoming the next success story.

5. Traffic updates - Have you ever accessed the maps on your smartphone and come across warnings that the road you are travelling on is experiencing delays and severe traffic jams? Have you ever wondered how come your cell phone knows that? Using GPS satellites, the number of phones or GPS modules installed within cars, the speed at which they travel, the machines immediately compute if the road is facing blocks or letting the traffic flow easily. The problem is that not many GPS modules are active or installed, which does kind of create discrepancies and there is a certain lag within the actual situation and the data that it represents on the screen. While there is Machine Learning already at play, it does need upgrading. There is quite a lot of room for improvement and even new models to come and replace the old ones.

Finally, Machine Learning is still in its genesis. While the concept has lurked around for quite some time, it is only recently that things have truly started to manifest and bring forth successful stories and results. The applications go far beyond health care and financial institutions. The world awaits new ideas, there is always someone out there looking for a person of your caliber, understanding and knowledge. Train yourself by practicing and be the next success story; or better yet, train your machine to be one for you!

Bibliography

1.	Muller, A, C. & Guido, S. (2017). Introduction to Machine Learning with Python. Sebastopol, CA: O'Reilly Media Inc.

2.	Raschka, S. (2015). Python Machine Learning. Birmingham, UK: Packt Publishing Ltd.

3. Heyy Babyy, Retrieved 10/2019, from, https://www.imdb.com/title/tt0806088/reviews

4. Large Movie Review Dataset, Retrieved, 10/2019 from. http://ai.stanford.edu/~amaas/data/sentiment/

Python Data Analytics

Introduction

Data is an essential part of the Information Technology ecosystem and is utilized to perform multiple operations in Machine Learning and Data Science. In order to analyze data for different types of predictions and business operations, it is mandatory to focus on mathematical models, graphs, data insights, databases, and statistics for developing deep learning models. Python programming language is considered as the best source for developing data science and deep learning models. Being a general-purpose programming language, Python is widely being used to gain insights from data and also serves as a powerful language to store, access and manipulate data in lists.

Python programming language is easy to understand, implement and interpret because it is an exceedingly powerful and effective general-purpose language. Over time, there have been several tools and integrated development environments created for data science and data analytics which support Python. Learning Python data science is also considered as the process of gaining knowledge and insights from diverse and huge datasets by analyzing, processing and organizing data. Programming of data science is flexible but involves the application of highly complex mathematical processes for which beginners are required to learn the basics of Python programming language.

Data science is based on complex algorithms and models for which a powerful programming language is required to handle mathematical processing.

Chapter 1: Python Data Science and Machine Learning

Artificial Intelligence, Machine Learning, and Data Science are the most commonly used technologies that are capable of performing complex operations and also bring long term benefits to businesses and industries. Over the past few years, researchers and developers have been working on creating machine learning models and algorithms that have the power to make accurate predictions and get trained by utilizing input data. Machine Learning is a data-driven system development algorithm that is based on data analysis, feedback, and data models which also help in refining algorithms for improving model accuracy and performance. Mainly, the machine learning systems analyze data to detect patterns and make accurate predictions by applying the predefined rules.

Data science is associated with data representation and scientific methodologies to transform algorithms for developing new solutions. By utilizing structured and raw data, data scientists make use of algorithms, mathematical models, and statistics to derive a specific solution. Generally, data science is based on the processes of data extraction, data cleansing, visualization, analysis and actionable insights generation. Furthermore, the approach also helps in predicting and understanding user behavior or recommendations. Machine learning is a major part of data science because it inherits aspects from algorithms and statistics to process the generated data and information extracted from multiple resources.

When it comes to dealing with enormous amounts of data, machine learning and data science algorithms are implemented together for processing information and gaining actionable data insights. It is mandatory to obtain knowledge about probability, statistics and technical skills to create data science models with complete functionality. Machine learning is also a part of artificial intelligence and is capable of performing major tasks such as data extraction, processing, and loading.

In order to develop state of the art and high performing data science models, developers are required to upgrade themselves with new skills and programming techniques. This includes in depth understanding and implementation of supervised and unsupervised techniques. In particular, data science covers major topics like data integration, distributed architecture, data visualization, and deployment in production model.

Why Learn Python for Data Analysis?

Python is an essential language for data analysis because it is flexible and easy to learn. Developers who want to create machine learning and deep learning models can use Python scripts and libraries which are easy to implement. Furthermore, the language is simple to learn which makes it ideal for beginners. Without spending much time and effort on coding, developers can utilize the functionality of Python to accomplish tasks without any hassle.

Due to its increased performance and functionality, Python has a large following and is vastly used in industrial and academic processes. There is a wide range of useful analytics libraries available for Python and users can approach to various community platforms to discuss their problems with other Python developers. Libraries such as Pandas, Numpy, and Matplotlib allow data analysts to carry out different functions smoothly.

Basics of Python for Data Analysis

Python is a general-purpose programming language that includes dedicated libraries for predictive modeling and data analysis. These built-in library packages can be used to import data from Excel spreadsheets and for processing sets for time series analysis as well. Pandas is a helpful Python Data Analysis Library that supports advanced manipulation through its powerful data frames and advanced numerical analysis features. Moreover, Pandas is built through NumPy which is one of the best libraries for data science development. Other major libraries such as SciPy, Scikit-Learn, and PyBrain are popular machine learning libraries that bring modules for developing data preprocessing and neural network models.

Better understanding and implementation of NumPy will make it convenient to work on tools like Pandas for which learning basics of Python programming language is necessary. Basics of NumPy include indexing of arrays, development with N-dimensional arrays, universal functions, statistical methods, and transposing an array to create data science models and algorithms.

NumPy

NumPy stands for "Numerical Python" and is a library that is comprised of a collection of multidimensional arrays. This library can be implemented to perform both logical and mathematical operations on arrays related to linear algebra and random number generation process. Data manipulation in Python is also performed through NumPy array and the latest Python programming tools such as Pandas are all based on this library. NumPy operations include access of data and subarrays to reshape, split and join the arrays.

In NumPy library, Ndarray is an N-dimensional array type that describes items of the same type which can also be accessed through a zero based index. Syntax to create ndarray using an array function in NumPy is defined as follows:

Numpy.array(object, dtype = None, copy = True, order = None, subok = False, ndmin =0)

For example:

Import numpy as np

A = np.array([4,5,6])

Print x

Output: [4,5,6]

2-D and 3-D arrays

2 dimensional and 3 dimensional arrays in NumPy can be defined by using the following basic syntax:

For 2 dimensional arrays:

C= np.array([3,4,5),(6,7,8)])

Print(c.shape)

(2,3)

For 3 dimensional arrays:

C= np.array([

[[3,4,5], [6,7,8]],

[[7,5,4], [34,5,22]]

])

Print (d.shape)

(2,2,3)

Now, we can also create random arrays for which random function is used. Here is an example to specify the maximum value and size of an array in NumPy:

Random_array = np.random.randint(15, size =5)

Print(random_array)

Output: [1 3 56 98 45]

Boolean array

Array12_b = np.array([2,5,10], dtype='bool')

Arr2d_b

Array([True, False, True, dtype = bool)

Size and Shape

shape

print('Shape: ', arr2.shape)

dtype

print('Datatype: ', arr2.dtype)

size

```python
print('Size: ', arr2.size)

# ndim
print('Num Dimensions: ', arr2.ndim) #>
```

```
Shape: (3, 4)
#> Datatype: float64
#> Size: 12
#> Num Dimensions: 2
```

Min, Max and Mean Operations on ndarray

```python
# mean, max and min
print("Mean value is: ", arr2.mean())
print("Max value is: ", arr2.max())
print("Min value is: ", arr2.min())
```

```
#> Mean value is:
#> Max value is:
#> Min value is:
```

Adding Two Arrays

```python
print(two_dim_array + two_dim_array)
```

Output:

```
[[ 4  2 6 15]
 [20 12 55 34]]
```

Function to convert an input to an array:

Numpy.asarray(data, dtype=None, order=None)[source]

Linspace and logspace functions:

Numpy.linespace(start, stop, num, endpoint)

Numoy.logspace(start, stop, num, endpoint)

SciPy

SciPy Python library is a built-in package which provides different resources to work on NumPy arrays. The library is mostly used in scientific computing, technical computing, mathematics and Engineering. It can operate on an array of NumPy library and also contains different types of sub packages which can be used to solve complex problems in scientific computation.

Packages:

Name	Description
Scipy.io	File input and output
Scipy.linalg	Linear Algebra
Scipy.special	Special Function
Scipy.interpolate	Interpolation

Scipy.stats	Statistics operations
Scipy.optimize	Optimization and fit.
Scipy.signal	Signal processing
Scipy.ndimage	Multidimensional image processing
Scipy.spatial	Spatial data structures and algorithms
Scipy.sparse	Sparse
Scipy.fftpack	Fast Fourier Transforms

Basic Functions

These are the basic functions that can be performed with SciPy library in Python:

Defining Data Types

```
import numpy as np

arr= np.arange(3, 5, dtype = np.float)

print arr

print " This is an Array data type :".arr.dtype
```

Output:[3. 4. 5.]

NumPy Vector

```
import numpy as np

list = [6,4,2,7]

arr = np.array(list)

print arr
```

Output: [6,4,2,7]

Installing the SciPy library:

```
Pip install scipy
```

Importing ScipPy library:

```
Import scipy
```

Single and Double Integrals

SciPy also supports general purpose integration which has only one variable present between two points. For example:

```
import scipy.integrate

f= lambda x: 12*x

i = scipy.integrate.quad(f, 0, 1)
```

print (i)

Output:

(6.0, 6.661338147750939e-14)

Source:
https://docs.scipy.org/doc/scipy/reference/tutorial/integrate.html

For double integral, dblquad function is used which is comprised of two variables with y being the first argument and x being the second argument.

import scipy.integrate

f = lambda x, y : 12*x

g = lambda x : 0

h = lambda y : 1

i = scipy.integrate.dblquad(f, 0, 0.5, g, h)

print(i)

Output:

(3.0, 6.661338147750939e-14)

Input and Output

To load and save a .mat file, we can use loadmat, savemat, and whosmat functions for a MATLAB file. For example:

import scipy.io as sio

import numpy as np

vect = np.arange(10)

```python
sio.savemat('array.mat', {'vect':vect})

mat_file_content = sio.loadmat('array.mat')

Print mat_file_content
```

Source: https://docs.scipy.org/doc/scipy/reference/tutorial/io.html

Linear Algebra

Mathematics is the basic concept of Python. To perform calculations, SciPy offers fast linear algebra operations because it is created through **BLAS** and **ATLAS LAPACK** libraries. Method for solving a linear algebra system is defined as follows:

Problem: 1x + 2y =5

3x + 4y =6

Solution:

```python
# Import required modules/ libraries

import numpy as np

from scipy import linalg

# Create input array

A= np.array([[1,2],[3,4]])


# Solution Array

B= np.array([[5],[6]])


# Solve the linear algebra

X= linalg.solve(A,B)
```

```python
# Print results

print(X)


# Checking Results

print("\n Checking results, following vector should be all zeros")

print(A.dot(X)-B)
```

SciPy library also supports gradient optimization, integration, and special functions that are a part of numerical computation. Being an open source project, SciPy can also be used as a system prototyping and data processing environment like R-lab or MATLAB. Furthermore, high level classes and commands for data visualization and data manipulation increase the functionality and performance of SciPy Python library.

Pandas

Pandas Python library is designed with powerful data structures to support data analysis and data manipulation in data science. The library is mainly used for performing web analytics, statistics, finance and economics operations through Python programming. For processing and analysis of data, developers can consider Pandas library because it has the capability to load, organize, analyze, manipulate, and model the data for all kinds of datasets and inputs. Pandas is an efficient and fast DataFrame object which can work on both customized and default indexing.

Furthermore, developers can perform label-based slicing, sub setting, and indexing of large datasets through Pandas library. Other features include data alignment, integrated handling of missing data, reshaping of data sets and tools for loading data into memory objects. Generally, Pandas only supports Series and DataFrame data structures that are built through Numpy array.

Operations

Creating a data frame by using a dictionary of existing NumPy 2D arrays:

```
d_dic ={'first_col_name':c1,'second_col_names':c2 } df = pd.DataFrame(data = d_dic
```

Getting column names in a list:

```
Df.columns.tolist()
```

Reading data from a text file or CSV file:

```
df = pd.read_csv(file_path, sep=',', header = 0, index_col=False,names=None)
```

Reset an index to another list, array or an existing column:

```
new_df = df.reset_index(drop=True,inplace=False)
```

Remove a column:

```
Df.drop(columns = list of cols to drop)
```

Slice a dataframe for a given condition:

```
mask = df['age'] == age_value
```

or

```
mask = df['age].isin(list_of_age_values)
```

```
result = df[mask]
```

Sorting values by column:

```
df.sort_values(by = list_of_cols,ascending=True)
```

Applying a function to all elements in a data frame:

```
New_df = df.applymap (f)
```

Generally, Pandas is based on two major components that are Series and DataFrame. Series is referred to as a column, whereas a DataFrame is a multidimensional table comprised of a collection of Series for Pandas.

Creating DataFrames

DataFrames in Pandas can be created in multiple ways. Here is a sample code for generating DataFrames through dictionary:

```
dict = {"country": ["Brazil", "Russia", "India", "China", "South Africa"],

"capital": ["Brasilia", "Moscow", "New Dehli", "Beijing", "Pretoria"],

"area": [8.516, 17.10, 3.286, 9.597, 1.221],

"population": [200.4, 143.5, 1252, 1357, 52.98] }


import pandas as pd

brics = pd.DataFrame(dict)

print(brics)
```

Source: https://www.learnpython.org/en/Pandas_Basics

Creating DataFrame through CSV:

```
# Import pandas as pd

import pandas as pd


# Import the cars.csv data: cars

cars = pd.read_csv('cars.csv')
```

```
# Print out cars

print(cars)
```

Indexing DataFrames

To index a Pandas DataFrame, we can use the simple technique of square bracket notation as follows:

```
import pandas as pd

cars = pd.read_csv('cars.csv', index_col = 0)
```

```
# Print out country column as Pandas Series

print(cars['cars_per_cap'])
```

```
# Print out country column as Pandas DataFrame

print(cars[['cars_per_cap']])
```

```
# Print out DataFrame with country and drives_right columns

print(cars[['cars_per_cap', 'country']])
```

Importing Excel File

Importing an Excel file is possible through Python, for which we can use Pandas built-in library. We can use the read_excel function to import and manipulate data from a predefined Excel file. The syntax to import an Excel file in Python is defined as follows:

```
import pandas as pd

df = pd.read_excel('path')

print (df)
```

Capturing Data

To import an Excel file into Python Pandas, we have to first capture the file path where the Excel file is located on your computer. For example:

C:\Users\Admin\Desktop\Sample.xlsx

Applying Python code:

import pandas as pd

df = pd.read_excel (r "C:\Users\Admin\Desktop\Sample.xlsx")

print (df)

Syntax to run the code:

pip install xlrd

import pandas as pd

df = pd.read_excel (r "C:\Users\Admin\Desktop\Sample.xlsx")

df = pd.DataFrame(data, columns= ['Price']

print (df)

Matplotlib

Matplotlib Python library is used to design and create 2D graphs and plots. The process is done with the help of Python scripts and it is based on a named pyplot. This pyplot provides extra features such as styles, font properties, and formatting. The package can be imported into Python script by using the statement as mentioned below:

from matplotlib import pyplot as plt

Developers can use Python Matplotlib library features to design plots, histograms, error charts, power spectra, scatter plots, and bar charts. The library provides complete functionality for all kinds of font properties, axes properties, and line styles as well.

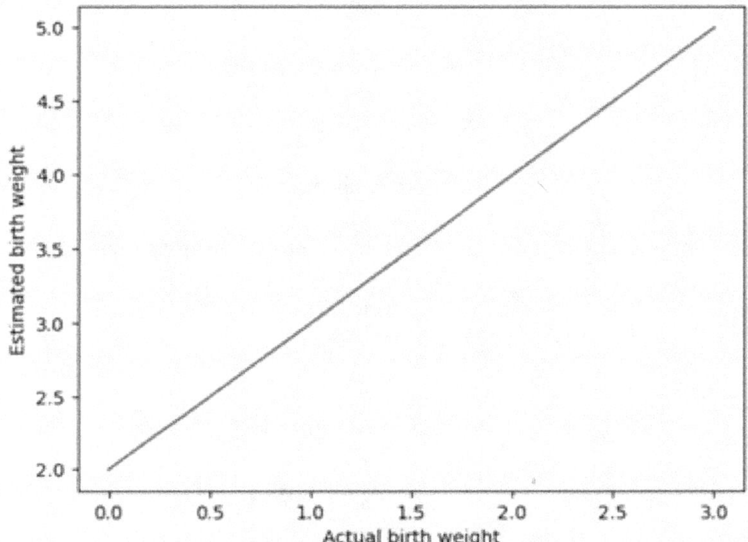

Source: https://data-flair.training/blogs/python-matplotlib-tutorial/

In the above graph, the methods xlabel() and ylabel() are used for setting labels for the x and y-axes. The values are taken from the list of parameters for y-axis whereas the values for x-axis are the four points 0.0, 1.0, 2.0 and 3.0.

Method to create pyplot interface:

Import matplotlib.pyplot as plt

Plt.plot ([2,3,4,5])

Data scientist can visualize the data to perform different types of data analysis operations. Here is an approach to plot a simple graph from matplotlib:

from matplotlib import pyplot as plt

plt.plot([1,2,3],[4,5,1])

plt.show()

Resulting graph:

Scatter Plot

For creating a scatter plot in Matplotlib, the following code based on the scatter method is used:

Fig, ax = plt.subplots()

ax. Scatter(iris['sepal_length'], iris['sepal_width])

ax.set_title('Iris Dataset')

ax.set_xlabel('sepal_length')

ax.set_ylabel('sepal_width)

Line Chart

Line chart can be created by calling the plot method in Matplotlib as follows:

Columns = iris.columns.drop(['class'])

X_data = range(0, isis.shape[0])

Fig, ax = plt.subplots()

For column in columns:

Ax.plot(x_data, isis[column])

ax.set_title('Iris Dataset')

ax.legend()

Chapter 2: Basics of Python

Python IDE's

An Integrated Development Environment is a tool which provides facilities like build automation, testing, code lining and debugging for different programming languages. Python IDEs are best suited for developing machine learning and deep analytics models. Here are some of the best IDEs for Python programming:

Sublime Text

Sublime Text is an amazing code editor that provides high customizability and is best for beginners. Along with other popular programming languages, Sublime Text also supports Python execution and comes with a predefined support for the language. The editor can be downloaded free of cost and is considered as a full-fledged Python development environment. Sublime Text packages are written in Python programming language which provide a wide range of extensions and packages to support complex programming.

Atom

Atom is an open source integrated development environment designed and developed by Github. Users can download and install the IDE along with predefined development packages such as linter-flake8 and python-debugger. Being highly customizable, users can install packages and set up the environment to meet their development requirements.

Eclipse

Eclipse is an all-rounder integrated development environment that is available for Windows, Linux, and OS X. The tool has a rich marketplace of add-ons and extensions which makes it suitable for machine learning and Python development. Furthermore, PyDev extension allows the developers to perform Python debugging and utilize code completion facility as well.

Basic Syntax

For writing your first Python program, you are required to be well aware of the basic syntax and requirements of Python programming language. A Python program can be written and executed in two basic modes which are known as Interactive mode and Script mode. In Interactive mode, developers are supposed to write a program and execute it, whereas in the Script mode, files and code can be saved and accessed through Python program (.py file).

Identifiers

Identifiers are used to identify a module, class, function, or a variable in a program. In Python programming language, an identifier can be a letter from A to Z or from a to z followed by zero or more digits, underscores, or letters. Furthermore, Python language does not allow characters such as %, $ or @ within identifiers. Being a case sensitive language, programmers need to carefully place identifiers to execute the program without any error.

Python syntax can be executed by writing the following line in the command line:

```
>> print("Hello world!")
```

Hello world

Variables and Data Types

Similar to other major programming languages such as Java, C and C++, Python has predefined data types and rules for using variables. For Python programming, you must remember that a variable can have both short and descriptive variables like x, y, age or year. A variable name should always start with a letter and cannot start with a number. Moreover, variable names are case sensitive in Python and developers need to be careful when declaring variables in the program.

Data Types

Python has built-in or default data types which include text, numeric, sequence, mapping, Set and Boolean and Binary type. To get the data type in Python programming language, "type()" function can be used in the program.

Here are some examples to set data types in Python:

Sample	Data Type
x = " Python"	Str
x = 5	Int
x = 5.0	float
x = range (5)	range
x = ("Red", "Blue")	Tuple
x = ["Red", "Blue"]	list
x = True/False	Boolean

x = b "Python"   bytes

Decision Making and Basic Operators

Decision making is an essential part of any programming language because it specifies the program to take actions according to the given conditions.

If statement

Syntax:

if expression:

statement

Sample program:

```
#!/use/bin/python

Var1 = 50

if var1:

print"1- Expression value"

print var1

var2 = 0

if var2:

print "2- Expression value"

print var 2

print "Value:"
```

If-else statement

Syntax:

if expression:

statement

else:

statement

Nested If statements

In a nested if statement, we can have an if, elif and else present within another if, elif and else statement. The syntax for implementing this statement is defined as follows:

If expression1:

Statement(s)

if expression2:

statement(s)

elif expression3:

statement(s)

else:

statement(s)

Functions and Modules

Python has built-in functions which can be used to create complex machine learning and deep learning models. Built in functions are also known as user defined functions. For defining a function in Python programming language, we can use the syntax as described below:

Def function name(parameters) :

"function docstring"

function suite

return [expression]

For example:

Def printme (str):

"Sample string passed into a function"

print str

return

Modules in Python programming allow developers to organize their code and develop code modules that can be used further in the program. A module is also referred to as a file made up of Python code which includes arbitrarily named attributes, classes, variables and functions. For example:

def print func(parameter):

print "Sample: ", parameter

return

Furthermore, we can also import an existing module into the Python source code by using the import module support. Here are some of the import statement modules for Python programming language:

- import statement
- from.. import

- statement:from

- modname import*

Object Oriented Programming

Python is based on object-oriented programming modules which enables developers to perform different tasks through classes and objects. In OOP, a class is a user defined prototype which is defined for an object and contains a set of attributes, data members, class variables and instance variables. A class variable is shared with each instance of the class and is usually defined outside the class method. Furthermore, class variables cannot be used more often as compared to instance variables.

Instance variable is defined inside a method and only belongs to the current instance of a class. In object-oriented programming, function overloading approach is referred to as the implementation of more than one behavior to a specific function. To implement classes in a program, we are required to make use of objects and methods in the class definition. Here is the syntax to create a class in Python:

Class ClassName:

"class documentation string"

Class_suite

Sample student class in Python:

class Student:

'Base class for all Students"

empCount = 0

def __init__(self, name, Grade):

self.name = name

self.grade = grade

Student.stuCount += 1

```
def displayCount(self):

print "Total Students%d" % Student.stuCount


def displayStudent(self):

print "Name : ", self.name,  ", Marks: ", self.marks
```

To access class attributes, we can use the following syntax:

```
stu.1displayStudent()

stu.2displayStudent()

print "Student %d" % Student.stuCount
```

In a Python class, there are several built-in attributes that can be accessed by using the dot operator. For example, dict, doc, name, module and bases.

Class Inheritance

In object-oriented programming, a class can be created by deriving it from an existing class. The child class inherits the attributes from its parent class and they can also be used to override data members, functions, and methods from the parent class. Furthermore, the derived classes are the same in functionality as their parent class. For example:

```
class A:          // Class A definition

                ..

class B:          // Class B definition

                ..

class C(A, B):  //Subclass A and B
```

Python syntax:

class SubClassName (ParentClass1[, ParentClass2, ..]):

"class documentation string"

Class_suite

Source:
https://www.tutorialspoint.com/python/pdf/python_classes_objects.pdf

---

Regular Expressions

Regular expression or RegEx is referred to as the sequence of characters which is implemented to create a search pattern. For developing machine learning and data analytics models, regular expressions are widely used for pattern matching and training of models. Python comes with a built-in regular expression module which is also known as re module or RegEx module. To import the module, we can use the "import re" statement in the program.

The re module is comprised of different functions which can be used to search a string for match. For example, search, split, sub and findall are the major functions that are used for pattern matching and learning in machine learning models.

Implementation:

findall () function

```
import re

str = "Machine learning"

x = re.findall("in", str)

print(x)
```

Search() function

```
import re

str = "Machine learning"
```

```
x = re.search("\s", str)
```

```
print("Position of first white-space character:", x.start())
```

Split () function

```
import re
```

```
str = "Machine learning"
```

```
x = re.split("\s", str)
```

```
print(x)
```

Match and Search functions

Match function has the capability to match re pattern to the string. The syntax for match function is defined as follows:

```
re.match(pattern, string, flags=0)
```

In the search function, the first occurrence of re pattern is searched within optional flags and the string. The syntax for search function is defined as follows:

```
re.search(pattern, string, flags=0)
```

Furthermore, regular expression literals can also include an optional modifier. The optional modifier has the capability to control different aspects of matching and they are also considered as an optional flag.

Exception Handling

An exception occurs during program execution and can disrupt the smooth flow of program instructions. When an exception occurs in a Python program, it can be handled through 'try' and 'except' statements as explained below:

```
try:
```

```
statements
```

except Exception 1:

//if exception 1 occurred, execute this block

exception 2:

//if exception 2 occurred, execute this block

else

No exception occurred

There are different exceptions and assertions which can occur in a Python program. For example: Exception, StopIteration, SystemExit, StandardError, OverflowError, ArithmeticError, ZeroDivisionError, AssertionError, ImportError, KeyboardInterrupt, LookupError, IndexError, KeyError and NameError. It must be noted that a single try statement can have various except statements and they are only used when the try block has statements that might throw any type of exception. Furthermore, the Python program might also execute a generic except clause and handle any type of exception.

File Handling

File handling is an essential part of every web or desktop application. The approach is used to create, read, update and delete files from the database of the program. In Python programming, file handling is generally performed with open() function and includes filename and mode parameters.

Opening a File

To open a file through a Python program, we can use four different modes defined as follows:

Read: Opens file for reading and initiates an error in case the file does not exist.

Write: Opens file for writing and automatically creates a file if it is not available.

Append: Opens file for appending and creates if not available.

Create: Creates the required file and initiates an error if the file already exists.

Basic syntax for file handling operations:

To open a file: f = open("samplefile.txt"0

To open a file on server:

f = open("samplefile.txt", "r")

print(f.read())

Closing a File

f = open("Filename.txt","r")

print(f.readline())

f.close

Writing into Existing Files

f = open("samplefile.txt", "a")

f.write("New content")

f.close()

f = open("samplefile.txt", "r")

print(f.read())

Create new file: f = open("Newfile.txt", "x")

Deleting Files

To remove or delete a file in Python, you are required to import OS module for which os.remove() function is recommended. The syntax for deleting or removing a file in Python programming language is defined as follows:

import os

os.remove("Samplefile.txt")

Deleting a Folder

To delete a specific folder, we can use the following syntax:

import os

os.rmdir("Folder")

Chapter 3: Data Handling

Importing and handling datasets are the key functionalities of machine learning and artificial intelligence models. In Python programming language, there are different approaches and techniques that could be implemented to create data science projects and perform data handling operations. Comma Separated Value (CSV) files are the best suitable file format for storing and transferring data. Python provides the ability to read, write, and manipulate data to and from CSV files through Pandas library and data frames which makes it easier for data scientists to design and build machine learning models.

Importing Data with CSV files

Before building machine learning models, data scientists have to find the best suitable ways to gather and utilize datasets so that the models could be trained properly. Comma Separated Value (CSV) files are the ultimate source to import and export data for machine learning models. In Python programming language, Pandas library is used to deal with operations for importing and loading CSV files. Before using the file system, it is mandatory that you know where the data is located and what is the current working directory. All the information and data in computers is stored in directories which are generally known as folders.

There are different factors which need to be focused when importing data from CSV files. A CSV file has a predefined header that helps in assigning names to each column of data and in case the header is not available, you will have to define the names and attributes manually. Furthermore, you can also explicitly specify whether or not your CSV file had a header when loading the data. Generally, CSV files have a "#" sign at the start of a line which is used to indicate comments in the file. Depending upon the method, we can use different comments and characters to give information regarding the CSV file.

Loading CSV Files

CSV files are an essential part of machine learning models for which Python API comes with a predefined CSV module and reader() function to lead CSV files. After the loading is complete, the CSV data can be converted into a NumPy array to be used for building machine learning models.

Function to load CSV data through NumPy:

```
#load CSV
import numpy
filename = "Samplefile.csv"
rawdata = open(filename, 'rt')
data = numpy.loadtxt(rawdata, delimiter=",")
print(data.shape)
```

Function to Load CSV Data Through Pandas

We can also import data or CSV files through Pandas read.csv() function which is best suitable for building machine learning models. The syntax to implement read.csv() function is defined as follows:

```
#load CSV from Pandas
import pandas
filename = 'Samplefile.csv'
data = pandas.readcsv(filename, names= names)
print(data.shape)
```

Loading CSV File Data through Python Standard Library

Python language comes with a predefined API which provides reader() function and CSV module to load CSV files into the program. Once the data has been loaded, the CSV file can be converted into a NumPy array for utilizing it in machine learning models. Basic syntax for loading CSV file data through Python standard library is described as follows:

```
#load CSV
```

```
import csv

import numpy

filename = "Samplefile.csv"

rawdata = open(filename, 'rt')

reader = csv.reader(rawdata, delimiter=',')

x = list(reader)

data = numpy.array(x).astype('float')

print(data.shape)
```

Source: https://machinelearningmastery.com/load-machine-learning-data-python/

File System

Importing CSV files and data is possible by using Pandas and Python standard library. Before starting with importing data, it is mandatory that the developer is aware of file system location of data and the current working directory. 'ls' command is used to list all content in the current working directory whereas the 'cd' command gives you the name of the sub directory in which you can change your working directory. Furthermore, 'pwd' command can be considered to print the path of your current working directory and '..' command to navigate back to the parent directory of your current working directory.

To execute Shell commands directly from IPython, we can use IPython console which includes various magic command lines capable of performing multiple operations with a single command. When importing external files, we are required to focus on some important aspects to avoid any problems in execution of the program. You must make sure that data type variable is in a consistent date format and consider special values as missing values. Furthermore, check whether the header row is present or not and make sure that no truncation of rows occurs while fetching external data.

Importing Data File from URL

Here is the simple Python syntax to import file from URL in read_csv() function:

sampledata = pd.read_csv(http://sampleurl/file.csv)

Importing R data file

To import R data file, we can use pyreadr package and load .Rds and .RData format files from the R data frame by using the following syntax:

import pyreadr

result = pyreadr.read_r('C/desktop/sample.RData')

print(result.keys()

df1 = result["df1"]

Import Data from SQL Server and Tables Stored in SQL

We can read information and data from SQL Server by building a connection for which database details including server and user ID are required. Python syntax for importing data from tables in a database is defined as follows:

import pandas as pd

import pyodbc

conn – pyodbc.connect("Driver={SQL Server};Server=servername;UID=username;PWD=password;database=RCO_DW;")

df = pd.readsqlquerry('select*from dbTable WHERE AGE > 20', conn)

df.head()

Summarizing Data

Python gives us the power of packages, libraries, and data frames to perform manipulation and aggregation on data sets. Pandas library has built in functions which allow programmers to split a specific data set into subsets on a known criterion. Furthermore, you can also apply a function or a set of functions in your code to combine different results together. The goal of Pandas library is to perform data analysis by giving appropriate functions and data structures.

Splitting Data

After the data has been loaded, we can divide it into groups for which the following Python syntax is recommended:

bytreatment = data.groupby("Treatment")

bytreatment["Relalative Fitness"].describe()

Application of Data Functions

Grouped data can be manipulated into different forms by using statistical techniques in machine learning and deep learning models. In this regard, the describe() method is used to produce statistics for grouped data such as mean(), median() and max(). Furthermore, other arbitrary functions can also be applied over groups of data by using aggregate agg() method . For example:

bygroup.treatment["Sample"].aggregate(np.sum)

Or

bygroup.treatment["Sample"].aggregate(np.sum, np.mean, sp.std, len])

Furthermore, JSON files can also be used to store and manipulate data as text in human readable format. Pandas library comes with built in JSON files for which read_json function can be used. JSON is also known as JavaScript Object Notation and is saved with .json extension.

To input data using JSON file, we can use the following Python syntax:

```
import pandas as pd

data = pd.read_json('file/input path.json')

print (data)
```

Source: https://www.shanelynn.ie/summarising-aggregation-and-grouping-data-in-python-pandas/

Similarly, JSON function can also be used to read specific columns and rows from a CSV file. Pandas library supports read_json function which is implemented to read specific columns and rows after the JSON file is loaded into the DataFrame. Moreover, we can also use the .loc() method to load JSON file which is also known as the multi-axes indexing method.

Groupby method returns a groupby object which originally describes how the rows of original data have been split. The output of aggregation and groupby operations are different for Pandas Dataframes and Pandas Series for which we have to select the operation column separately. Moreover, the groupby output will be based on an index or multi-index rows depending upon the selected grouping variables.

Python Aggregation

Aggregation is generally performed through NumPy and Pandas libraries in Python. In most of the cases, the file data is not of a similar type or format and we are required to combine or group data into sets for further processing. However, in most of the cases, an aggregation function includes different rows combined together by the implementation of statistical algorithms like count, maximum, average, mean, mode, or median. In Python, data is aggregated to ensure the privacy of datasets and make it easier to analyze.

The most important aspect of using data aggregation is to meet legal and privacy concerns for a machine learning model. It is required that the data should be called to the group by using groupby() function to map values. The values can then be indexed and rely on the transform() function to develop aggregated data through NumPy and Pandas algorithms in Python programming language. Sample program showing aggregation in Python:

```
import pandas as pd

import numpy as np


df = pd.DataFrame(np.random.randn(10, 4),

index = pd.date_range('5/4/2010', class=5),

columns = ['1', '2', '3', '4'])



print df


r = df.rolling(window=3,min_class=2)

print r
```

Source: https://www.w3resource.com/python-exercises/pandas/python-pandas-data-frame-exercise-4.php

Unstructured Data

Data that is formatted in columns and rows can be simply converted into different structures to be implemented in the development of machine learning models. XLS, CSV and TXT files are the best examples of structured data because they have a predefined limiter and fixed width. On the other hand, there is data which does not have a specific format and is also known as unstructured data. Python libraries and predefined functions can be used to process unstructured files and utilize the data for processing.

The following example illustrates the reading of unstructured data in Python:

```python
filename = 'input_data.txt'

with open(filename) as fn:

    # Read each line
    ln = fn.readline()

    # Keep count of lines
    lncnt = 1

    while ln:
        print("Line {}: {}".format(lncnt, ln.strip()))
        ln = fn.readline()
        lncnt += 1
```

Output:

Line 1: Python is a high-level programming language.

Line 2: It has a design philosophy that general-purpose interpreted,emphasizes code readability, notably using significant whitespace, interactive, object-oriented, and high-level programming language.

Line 3: It has grown from humble beginnings into one of the most popular programming languages on the planet.

Source: http://python-ds.com/python-processing-unstructured-data

Data Preparation for Analysis and Evaluation

Machine Learning and Artificial Intelligence models learn from the datasets and information they are fed with. Depending upon the labels and attributes of data, the models get trained to perform various operations and tasks in the future without human intervention. Data preparation is the first step that is performed after the data has been collected from one or more sources so that it is cleaned and transformed. Moreover, it is often merged with different sources having various levels of data and structures of data quality.

In order to create meaningful data insights, machine learning engineers and data scientists have to prepare data for analysis and outline the best sources to combine vital information and data.

How to Prepare Data

To prepare data for machine learning and predictive analysis models, we are required to focus on some simple approaches which will help us in collecting high quality data. After the objectives of model for predictive analysis have been defined, we can begin with data preparation. At first, you must identify your data sources because structured and unstructured data is available in different formats and types. Furthermore, data is mostly owned by a third party for which you need to acquire permissions to utilize the data.

Secondly, select the variables to add into your analysis for which you can start with multiple variables and eliminate the ones which offer no predictive values for the model. In most of the cases, derived variables have a greater direct impact on the model as compared to the raw variables which can in return affect performance of the machine learning model. To evaluate the quality of data, we need to understand the limitations and state of data because accuracy of the model is directly dependent upon data quality.

Although selecting and cleaning data is time consuming and requires a lot of hard effort, there are several effective data preparation techniques which can be followed to yield best results. Accuracy of machine learning models is directly dependent on the quality and accuracy of the training data.

How to Determine the Quality of Data

To explore the quality of input data, we need to understand the limitations and statistics that are required to operate the machine learning model with high accuracy. Make sure that the data is complete and perform any filtration before feeding the training data into the machine learning model. Furthermore, you are required to fill in the missing values or eliminate them if not needed. To perform analyzation and quality assurance, we can implement regression algorithms. Classification algorithms have the capability to analyze discrete data whereas the association algorithms can be considered for data having correlated attributes.

Datasets which are used to train and test the model should contain relevant business information. This will help companies to support their customers in a better way and provide them with the most suitable services as well. Smaller data files which have a good native structure can be opened through spreadsheets or editors, whereas larger or complicated datasets need to be handled with extraction or transformation software. Statistical adjustments can be applied to data which requires scale and weighting transformations. This will also help in cleaning data reviews for consistencies because generally inconsistencies may be found because of extreme, out of range or faulty logic.

In Big Data systems, preparing large datasets is time consuming and requires effort. To begin with the procedure, following data preparation rules on the sample data will reduce latency of iterative exploration and will make it easier to figure out large datasets. Data cleaning approach is used to find and eliminate errors in data.

Creating and Formatting New Variables

After the training data has been collected and finalized, the next step is to set up the variables which will directly respond to research queries and questions. Generally, datasets do not include measured variables and you are required to set up each variable individually. These operations include creating change scores, combining multiple categories of nominal variables, centering predictions and creating indices from scales.

Newly created and original variables need to be formatted properly for major reasons. Firstly, if you do not format a missing value or a dummy variable it will directly affect data analysis and predictions of your machine learning model. Secondly, it will save a lot of time and effort if a faulty variable is removed at first because setting all missing data codes and formatting date variables or numerical numbers will also remove any future discrepancies.

In Python development, we can take support from built-in libraries such as Pandas and NumPy to classify datasets and make separate groups. Data which is collected randomly features different categorical values and we need to label each variable before making it a part of training data. Based on the knowledge of business analytics goal and results of different data cleansing strategies, we can arrange the relevant data into a usable format without any hassle.

Underfitting and Overfitting

Underfitting and overfitting are two of the major issues which arise when building machine learning models and need to be overcome when handling input data. Underfitting occurs whenever a model is unable to detect relationships from data and it also indicates the essential variables to be included. On the other hand, overfitting begins whenever a machine learning model includes data having no predictive power and is only suitable for the given dataset.

Furthermore, if the machine learning algorithm or a statistical model captures vulnerable data it is known to be affected with overfitting. As a result, the algorithm shows high variance and low bias which in return affects its overall predictive powers. Overfitting and underfitting result in poor predictions on new data sets and greatly affect the performance of machine learning models. Nonetheless, we have to focus on validation and cross validation when building machine learning models to avoid overfitting and underfitting in each case.

Datasets which are used for the training of machine learning models are featured with multiple predictors. This helps businesses to avail accurate predictions and data insights in the long run from machine learning models.

Generalization

Machine learning models are known to learn from training data. The learning of target function from training data in the model is referred to as inductive learning because the aim of machine learning models is to apply specific rules and scenarios while generating outcomes. Generalization tells us how well the machine learning models have adapted the rules and information from training data and allows the model to make accurate predictions for the future. Overfitting and underfitting can surely make a machine learning model useless because they make it impossible for the models to learn from given datasets.

Generalization is also used to describe the ability of a model to react to new data and it usually happens when a model is being trained on a specific training dataset. If a model is trained well and accurately on training data, it will be unable to generalize the data and will make relevant predictions in future. Supervised machine learning models also make predictions based on the training data for which the outcome is already known. Predictions and outcomes from the model are then compared with the actual data and the model's parameters are changed to achieve desired results.

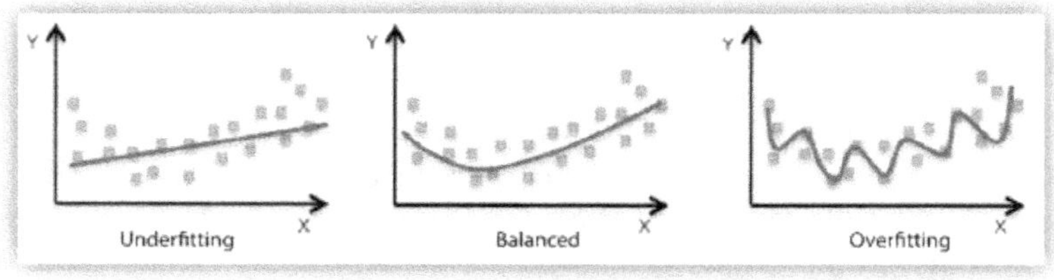

The above figure demonstrates underfitting, balanced, and overfitting graphs for a machine learning model. Based on the training data, the model notes that there is not a specific trend in data to capture relevant information, and because of this it is unable to make accurate predictions for new training data. This concept is known as underfitting and is illustrated by a straight blue line. In the middle, the line is representing a balanced model and shows the trend in data that could be easily generalized. Furthermore, on the right the line showcases a model which is too specific and inaccurately models the training data. This concept is also known as overfitting.

Chapter 4: Building Machine Learning Models

Interpreting machine learning and deep learning models is a complex task for which in depth understanding regarding data handling and ML algorithms is necessary. Nowadays, most of the businesses are relying on deep learning and AI models to drive their strategy and achieve best outcomes. Modern day examples of machine learning models are face recognition systems, self-driving vehicles and voice recognition systems such as Siri and Alexa. In-depth knowledge about statistics and linear recognition models is mandatory to design and build efficient machine learning models by using Python modules including Matplotlib, Pandas, and NumPy.

Data Science

Data science is a source of finding certain patterns in datasets and training data which are utilized by machine learning models to make accurate predictions. Initially, activities to build machine learning algorithms such as data mining were performed through basic statistical methods, but with the evolution of programming languages and modules, Python and R deliver support to different computing packages that are based on statistics-focused approaches.

There are different steps involved in the collection of data. At first, data is collected from various sources and is then classified into structured and unstructured data categories. Next, the derived data is explored and transformed to remove any discrepancies. Aggregation and labeling of data are usually performed by a data scientist for which various machine learning and artificial intelligence algorithms are implemented. Once the goal is clear, we can set an evaluation protocol and decide how the ongoing progress will be measured. This will also help in determining the performance and capability of the machine learning model.

The process of training a machine learning model through data science techniques involves the selection of ML algorithms. There are different ways to deploy machine learning models for which we can make use of data modeling techniques.

Acquisition and Data Gathering

Before the training model is loaded with the annotated data, we must focus on predictive maintenance approaches. These approaches also help in upgrading performance of ML models and also improve their efficiency with time. With the availability of new data, we are given opportunities to make better decisions and consider best suitable variables for predictive maintenance.

Failure of machine learning models can also be minimized through root cause analysis. Predictive maintenance is generally performed through root cause analysis for which machine learning engineers have to determine the likelihood and occurrence of events. To get started with predictive maintenance, we need to feed high quality data into machine learning models and get the required insights as well. If there is a lot of usage information such as maintenance logs, it is compulsory that correct identifiers and variables are used to identify connectivity between the data sets.

DataRobot is a highly efficient automated machine learning platform that allows researchers and machine learning engineers to develop models that deliver accurate predictions and long-term insights. Furthermore, it also streamlines the data science process so that users get high quality predictions within a short period of time.

Data Pipelines

A machine learning system undergoes an extensive number of data processing workflows and has to perform multiple operations like cleaning and ingesting data. The process of developing and deploying continuously can lead to complications which need to be handled immediately to avoid any kind of unwanted scenarios. Machine learning pipelines have different parts and steps which are used to train the model. These models are cyclical and iterative because each step is directly linked with the other one. One after another, each process is repeated and to build better machine learning models, we need to derive scalable and accurate development techniques.

Data that is extracted from large datasets is also known as Big Data and is responsible for actionable insights in future. New connections and precise predictions can be performed with the support of data pipelines and it is not all about storing data, but we need to focus on achieving better outcomes. Today, most of the machine learning models are trained through neural networks and have the capability to perform a specific task in multiple ways. Machine learning deployment and development pipelines are separate from each other for which the data is supposed to be retrained or upgraded.

Furthermore, the pipeline approach also helps in releasing new versions and upgradations of machine learning models for which real time data is utilized. There are several tools, libraries and frameworks available for data scientists to work with pipeline methods. After the data has been collected and processed through data pipelines, the next step is to filter, aggregate and consolidate it before transferring the dataset to a permanent data store. Databases like SQL Azure and SQL Server are best suitable for handling machine learning data. Moreover, a machine learning pipeline helps to automate machine learning workflows and improves performance of models as well.

Challenges for Machine Learning Pipelines

Developing machine learning pipelines requires the data scientists to perform extensive research and evaluation. Generally, the process is divided into three sub categories which are data quality, data accessibility, and data reliability. Each of these categories is responsible for the performance, efficiency, and management of machine learning pipelines. Machine learning models need to be fed with accurate and complete training data so that they deliver the best suitable outcomes. The greater the availability of high-quality training data, the more accurate and reliable outcomes are achieved.

When it comes to data reliability, data scientists are supposed to determine the reliability of data and analyze its accessibility and source of generation as well. In most cases, implementation of a repository for data outcomes which serves as a single source of truth is necessary. Moreover, single source repositories allow machine learning models to run from multiple locations through a data center. Data reliability also helps in avoiding varying and duplicate versions of data so that analytical teams are always provided accurate and reliable data.

One of the major challenges that is being faced by data scientists for building machine learning model pipelines is data accessibility. Before the model is implemented into the system for commercial use, it undergoes deep cleaning and cleansing. This activity is performed to remove redundant and irrelevant data during the pre-analysis stage. In the development of machine learning model pipelines, feature extraction approach allows the developers to extract existing features along with their associated transformations into the latest formats to describe variances between data. Once the data is cleansed, it can easily be aggregated and combined with other cleansed data.

Object Storage in Machine Learning Pipelines

Machine learning pipelines tend to get better with time. True value occurs when more data points are collected along with different data assets which are collected from multiple sources. The activity of correlating new data formats into the data center is a complex task and various sets of applications are required to handle massive data load. In machine learning model development, cloud storage and object storage systems play a vital role because they serve a great purpose and support custom data formats as well.

Data analysts and scientists also consider mapping of statistical methods to solve key problems for object storage in machine learning models. For quick business implementation, data scientists prefer to store everything locally and not in a public cloud because it takes more time and effort to extract information when needed. There is an abundance of machine learning content and immediate access is mandatory to maintain the performance and efficiency of machine learning models. Furthermore, each step in the process is iterative and cyclical which makes it convenient to upgrade and manage the algorithms.

Architecture of Machine Learning Pipelines

Machine learning pipelines are designed and architected through a predefined model. As it involves batch processing and handling of data to perform different operations, a machine learning pipeline has special features which allow it to make accurate predictions and insights. A pipeline is comprised of different stages and each stage is fed with processed data from its preceding stage. In the preprocessing stage, scientists use data mining techniques for data preprocessing which also involves transferring raw data into an understandable format. Data taken from external resources in often inconsistent and incomplete for which various treatment procedures are applied to remove the inaccuracies.

Constructing pipelines gives several advantages and makes it easier to implement machine learning models. The units of computation for ML pipelines are quite easy to replace and are highly flexible as well. Upgrading or changing a single part of the system can be done without dismantling the entire system. Every part of computation can be controlled through a common interface and if any part is not performing up to the mark, engineers can scale that component independently as well. Furthermore, the functionality and performance of machine learning pipelines can be increased by adding extensions into the system.

Pipelines are based on the approach of overnight batch processing which includes collection of data, sending of data, and processing it through multiple channels to feed the machine learning models. Predictions and features in pipelines are highly time sensitive because its performance is directly dependent on online model analytics and offline data recovery. Online model analytics represents the operational component of the system and is generally applied for real-time decision-making approaches. On the other hand, the offline data recovery method represents the learning component of ML pipelines and utilizes the historical data to create machine learning models through batch processing.

Online and Offline Layers

Gathering and funneling the incoming data into storage is the first step of creating any kind of machine learning workflow. Without undertaking any transformation, we can have an immutable record of original dataset for which the data can be fed from multiple sources or obtained from other services as well. Generally, data scientists use NoSQL document databases to store large volumes of constantly changing structured and unstructured data.

Online ingestion service is the gateway to streaming architecture in machine learning pipelines because it decouples and completely manages the workflow as well. The information from data sources is processed and transferred to storage components for which the system ensures better reliability, low latency, and high throughput.

Offline layers in the machine learning pipelines utilize ingestion services to confirm data flows into the raw data store. To perform this activity, a repository pattern is used to interact with a data service and also with the data store. As soon as the data is received and saved in the data store, it is automatically assigned a batch ID which allows efficient querying and traceability.

Ingestion distribution in machine learning pipelines ensures that there is a separate pipeline for each dataset and all of them are processed and managed independently. Furthermore, the data is partitioned within each pipeline to take benefit of multiple server cores and processors in the system. Furthermore, spreading the data preparation through multiple pipelines horizontally and vertically also reduces the overall time to complete the workflow.

For example:

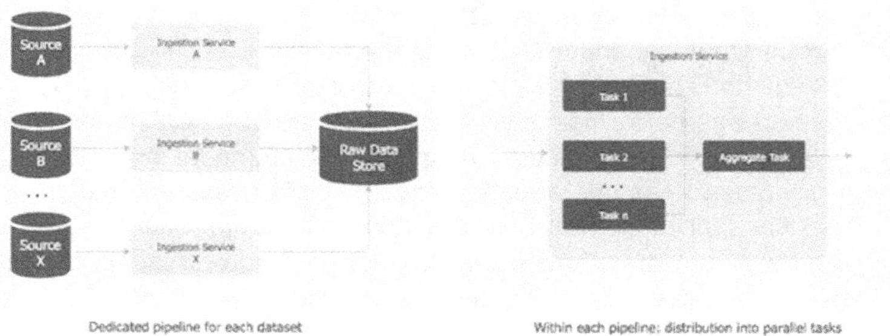

Source: https://towardsdatascience.com/architecting-a-machine-learning-pipeline-a847f094d1c7

As briefed in the diagram above, we can notice that ingestion services operate regularly on a predefined schedule or depend on a trigger. As it is supposed to fetch data from thousands of sources each day, the producer system automatically releases a message to the broker so that the embedded notification service gives prompt response to the subscription.

In both of these layers, we can see that a distributed pipeline is developed which examines the condition of data and searches for various trends, formats, differences and skewed data. Furthermore, it is mandatory that the correct design pattern is chosen before developing machine learning pipelines in order to ensure consistency and better outputs from training data.

Data Segregation

Data segregation splits the subsets of the given data in order to train machine learning models. Apart from training, data segregation also analyzes model performance and efficiency for the system. The machine learning systems are designed to utilize quality data and perform pattern prediction for data on which it is not trained. This allows ML models to deliver accurate insights and predictions on each scenario. There are several strategies to perform data segregation in machine learning pipelines. Data segregation is not separately a machine learning pipeline and is known as an API to facilitate specific tasks.

Model training of machine learning pipelines is usually performed offline because the schedule is strictly dependent upon the criticality of application. Moreover, service and maintenance time can also affect learning of a machine learning pipeline for which schedulers can be implemented.

Parallelization

Machine learning models have a dedicated pipeline which allows all of the models to run concurrently. To apply the parallelization technique, we are required to parallelize all of the training data which is partitioned. Each of the partitions has a copy of the original model and it is preferred that all of the fields of instance perform computation on their own. Furthermore, a machine learning model can also be parallelized by itself for which the model is completely partitioned. Each partition is responsible for handling and updating each portion of parameters. This approach is best suitable for Linear machine learning models such as SVM and LR.

Training of machine learning pipelines is implemented with slight error tolerance. The model training service is supposed to get training configuration parameters and hyper-parameters from configuration services. This approach allows the model to utilize the configuration service and fetch the training dataset from Data Segregation API. As a result, the dataset which is sent to all of the other models is complete and is based on the original configuration.

In machine learning model pipelines, the Model Evaluation Service is applied to request evaluation dataset from Data Segregation API. This activity is done for each model which is directly sourced from the model candidate repository and also applies relevant evaluators as well. As a result, the evaluation is saved back to the repository and becomes a part of the hyperparameter and iterative process techniques.

Importance of Metadata

Python programming language is best suited for the development of machine learning models and pipelines. Data scientists and analysts who are determined to achieve the best predictions and efficiency from ML models get support from Python libraries and functions. One of the major tasks for developing machine learning models is the extraction of metadata. Once a pipeline or model is trained sufficiently, it can be made operational for industries, businesses, and brands to yield accurate data insights.

Traditionally, file-based network attached storage (NAS) architecture was used to figure out data which had to be traversed with each operation. With thousands of directories waiting to be processed, the activity took a lot of time and effort. As a solution, object storage and ML training approaches were implemented in the architecture of artificial intelligence and deep learning models. In an object storage platform, data including text documents, files, or videos can be stored as a single object. To make things manageable, metadata is attached with the files which provides descriptive information regarding the captured data.

Model Evaluation

Evaluating a machine learning model is a crucial step of the development procedure. Although ML models yield satisfying results when trained on proper data sets, we are required to evaluate the performance, efficiency, and reliability to achieve best results in future. There are several evaluation metrics defined to examine the accuracy and response of machine learning models. We can see how the model generalizes and forecasts on unseen data as it directly affects the performance of machine learning pipelines as well. To evaluate the aspects in a better way, we need to understand how the model actually works and whether we can trust its predictions or not.

Generally, the methods for evaluating the performance of machine learning models are separated into two categories, namely cross validation and holdout. Both of these methods utilize a test data to evaluate model performance and it is never feasible to use the data which we used to build the model to examine it in future.

The following techniques are the best source of measuring performance and evaluating the efficiency of machine learning models:

Confusion Matrix

Confusion matrix is an approach which provides a complete detail of correct and incorrect classifications. For a confusion matrix, we need to remember a few key points so that the efficiency can be calculated properly. Accuracy is the part of the total number of correct predictions made by the model, whereas the positive predictive value is considered as the part of positive cases identified correctly. Negative prediction value in machine learning models is the part of negative cases which were identified correctly, whereas specificity identifies the proportion of actual negative cases that are identified correctly.

At first, we can take an N x N matrix and consider N as the number of classes for prediction as follows:

	Class1 Predicted	Class 2 Predicted
Class 1 actual	TP	FN
Class 2 actual	FP	TN

A confusion matrix can be examined through the following important terms:

1. True Positives - Occurs for cases in which Yes was predicted whereas the actual output is also the same.

2. True Negatives - Occurs for the cases in which NO was predicted whereas the actual output is also the same.

3. False Positives - Occurs for the cases in which Yes was predicted whereas the real output is NO.

4. False Negatives - Occurs for the cases in which No was predicted whereas the real output is YES.

Classification rate or accuracy for a machine learning model can be calculated from the equation below:

$$\textbf{Accuracy} = \frac{TP + TN}{TP + TN + FP + FN}$$

Taking the example of a cancer detection model, we can consider that the actual chances of having cancer are quite low for which a probability of 10 out of 100 is possible. We will never want to miss any patient in this case who has cancer but remains undetected. In this case, detecting every patient as not having cancer yields an accuracy of 90% for which the machine learning model can be held accountable.

F1 Score

The F1 score in machine learning and data analytics models is known as the harmonic mean of recall and precision. The score utilizes the contribution of precision and recall calculations to analyze the performance of a machine learning model. Moreover, if the model performs well in F1 score, it will have a higher ratio of making accurate predictions as compared to the model which has a lower F1 score.

Formula to calculate F1 score:

$$F_1 = \left(\frac{recall^{-1} + precision^{-1}}{2} \right)^{-1} = 2 \cdot \frac{precision \cdot recall}{precision + recall}$$

Logarithmic Loss

Logarithmic loss approach is used to evaluate the performance of a classification model. To evaluate logarithmic loss through mathematical calculation, we need take prediction input probability ranging from 0 to 1. With the increase of logarithmic log or log loss, the predicted probability changes from the actual label to minimize the end value.

PR Curve

Precision and Recall curve are the best way to represent properties of a classifier. PR curve is the curved formed between recall and precision for different threshold values. For example:

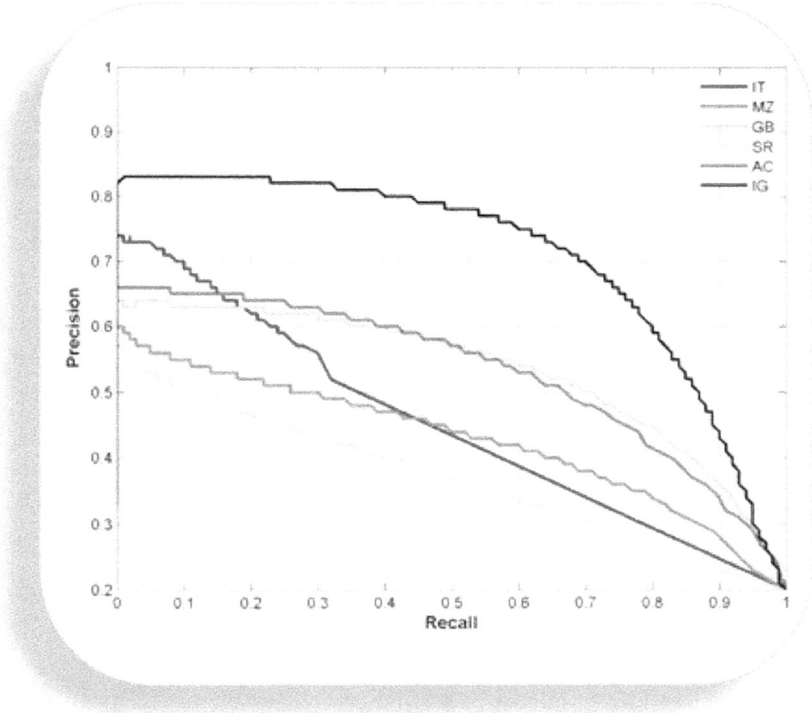

Source: https://github.com/MenuPolis/MLT/wiki/PR-Curve

From the above graph, we can notice that precision is represented by the fraction of blue circle or retrieved documents that are used as TP. Upon a low precision value, the system will have to search through different irrelevant searches to find the required value. Furthermore, we can repeat the search by eliminating an unwanted meaning of the searched word. For machine learning models, precision is considered as a measure of usefulness whereas recall is known as a measure of completeness.

Chapter 5: Machine Learning Algorithms

Before starting a data science or machine learning project in Python programming language, understanding the ideas, concepts, and functionality of ML models is compulsory. Whether you want to load data into the model or evaluate its performance, the parameters set in machine learning algorithms can help in achieving the best outcomes. As discussed earlier, data can be extracted, uploaded, and managed through Python libraries like NumPy and Pandas. In machine learning, the most commonly used format for data is known as Comma-Separated Values or CSV format, which is also applicable for storing and handling files.

Introduction to Model Handling

With the increasing demand in big data analytics and deep learning, machine learning has become a popular approach for solving real life and business problems. The approach is widely used in system development for various fields including health care, computational finance, computer vision, image processing, and computational biology. Furthermore, data science plays a vital role in automotive, energy production, and natural language processing systems.

The models are programmed to find natural patterns in data and generate insight for making accurate predictions in the future. Basically, machine learning models are divided into two major categories called supervised learning and unsupervised learning. Because machine learning models have the capability to find non linear dependencies between input data, we need to check before making any changes in our data because it can create cascading effects on downstream systems and model accuracy.

Linear Regression in Python

Artificial Intelligence and machine learning systems have the capability to handle large amounts of data which makes them best suited for powerful computers. Linear regression is one of the major parts of machine learning and deep learning algorithms because it is based upon the fundamentals of statistics and mathematics.

Regression

The term "Regression" refers to the search for relationships amongst variables in datasets. It is considered as a statistical measurement to determine the strength of a relationship between an independent variable, and the approach is widely implemented in the finance industry. Regression analysis is one popular technique used by researchers and data scientists to understand the phenomenon of interest and findings of different observations.

To implement regression in machine learning models, we are required to find a function that maps variables and features to others in an effective way. Dependent features are also known as dependent responses, outputs, or variables, whereas the independent features can be referred to as independent predictors, inputs, or variables in machine learning. Generally, regression problems result due to unbounded and continuous dependent variables for which the data needs to be handled with different techniques.

Why is Regression Important?

Regression is a useful approach to forecast a response by the support of new predictors and datasets. For machine learning models and deep learning analytics, linear regression is a widely used regression technique because it delivers great ease of comparing and interpreting results. Furthermore, implementation of linear regression in machine learning models is now possible with Python libraries and functions.

The below graph represents linear regression in machine learning models:

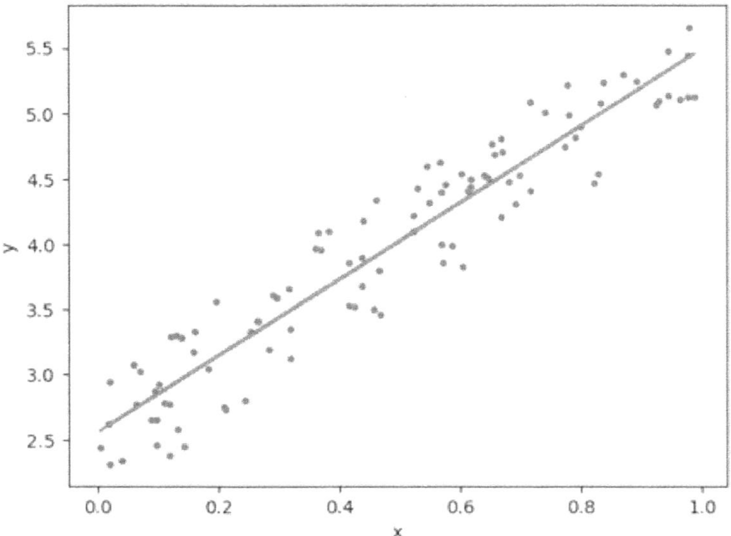

Equation to represent linear regression model:

$$Y = \theta_0 + \theta_1 x_1 + \theta_2 x_2 + ... + \theta_n x_n$$

Python implementation for creating random dataset to train machine learning models:

import numpy as np

import matplotlib.pyplot as plt

generate random data-set

np.random.seed(0)

x = np.random.rand(100, 1)

y = 2 + 3 * x + np.random.rand(100, 1)

plot

plt.scatter(x,y,s=10)

plt.xlabel('x')

plt.ylabel('y')

plt.show()

Source: https://towardsdatascience.com/linear-regression-using-python-b136c91bf0a2

In linear regression model graphs, we can notice the error line between the observed and predicted values which is also known as regression line or the line of best fit.

Types of Linear Regression Models

Linear relationship

It is the linear relationship between feature variables and response in a machine learning model. Linear relationship can be described by the following graphs:

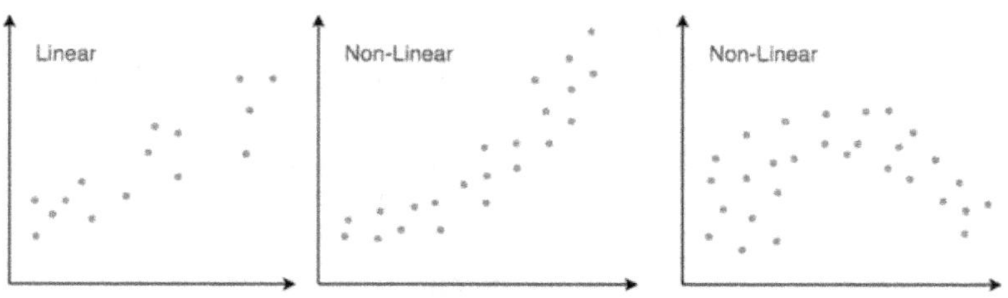

Homoscedasticity

Homoscedasticity is known as an error term that occurs as a result of a random disturbance between the dependent and independent variables.

Multiple Linear Regression

Multiple linear regression occurs in an event of linear regression between two or more independent variables in a machine learning model. The estimated regression function for two independent variables can be represented through the equation $f(x_1, x_2) = b_0 +$

$b_1x_1 + b_2x_2$. If there are more than two independent variables, we can determine the value of estimated regression function through the equation $f(x_1, ..., x_r) = b_0 + b_1x_1 + \cdots + b_rx_r$.

Polynomial Regression

Polynomial Regression is an essential part of linear regression because the polynomial dependence for inputs and outputs is considered as the polynomial estimated regression function. The equation to calculate polynomial regression is $f(x) = b_0 + b_1x + b_2x^2$.

Implementation

On a given dataset, we can use different Python libraries to implement linear regression. Here is the program to import all of the required libraries and read the dataset in Python:

```python
import numpy as np

import pandas as pd

import seaborn as sns

import matplotlib.pyplot as plt

from sklearn import preprocessing, svm

from sklearn.model_selection import train_test_split

from sklearn.linear_model import LinearRegression

df = pd.read_csv('sample.csv')

df_binary = df[['Python',]]

df_binary.columns = ['Age', 'Year']

df_binayr.head()
```

Syntax for data cleaning:

Df_binary.fillna(method = 'fill', inplace = True)

Scikit Learn

Scikit-Learn is a built-in Python library which is exclusively designed for the development of machine learning models. The library provides complete support and execution for major machine learning algorithms including random forest, k-neighbors, and linear regression. Furthermore, libraries such as NumPy and SciPy can also become a part of Scikit-Learn Python library to develop state of the art and high performance machine learning models. Scikit-learning library is designed to make machine learning development easier through Python programming language because of its various data handling and plotting techniques that help to visualize data.

Loading Data Sets

Loading datasets is the first step of developing ML models through Sci-kit learn Python programming technique. Each process and activity in data science starts with loading data, and this approach is more suitable for observed data. Before loading data into the program, make sure it is free of any independencies or mistakes so that accurate data visuals and results could be attained. Furthermore, finding datasets is challenging, for which you can also create your own sets of data to implement within the Sci-kit learn algorithm.

To load data into the program, we are required to import datasets module from sklearn and implement the load_digits() method. Python syntax to load data:

#import datasets from sk-learn

from sklearn import

digits = datasets.load_digits()

print

The dataset's module includes other methods to load and fetch reference datasets and we can also consider this in the case of artificial data generators. Moreover, the dataset can be inherited through the UCI Repository as well.

Exploring Data

After you are done with loading data, the next step is to start exploring the dataset for which Python libraries provide simple methods to be implemented. Scikit-learn library does not provide information related to data and if you are importing data from another source, there is a slight detail given about data which can be used to generate insights during model development.

If you are using the read_csv() module to import data, you can have a dataframe which contains just the data. No information related to the dataset is given in this case, but you will implement head() and tails() methods to inspect data. Data exploration is an essential step in the development of machine learning or data science projects. Even a quick evaluation for data can give true insights related to quality and reliability of the datasets.

Predicting and Learning

Datasets including numbers, images, or text files can be examined through sklearn.svm.SVC estimator class. The estimator class in Python can be set by using the following syntax:

from sklearn import svm

clf = svm.SVC(gamma= 0.005, C =50)

In Scikit-learn library, the estimator for classification can also be implemented through fit(x,y) and predict(T) methods. For classifier, we can use the clf estimator which must learn from the model. Furthermore, the method is completed by passing the training set to the fit method in the Scikit-learn library and for the training set, we can use all images or text from our dataset.

How to Split Data into Training and Test Sets Through Scikit-learn

To assess a machine learning model's performance, we can divide the data set into two parts which can also be named as a test set and a training set. Training set is used to train the system whereas the test set is implemented to evaluate the trained or learned system. In Scikit-learn, we can apply train_test_split() method along with the random_state argument to split data sets in the program. For example:

```
from sklearn.cross_validation import

X_train, X_test, y_train, y_test, images_train,

images_test = train_test_split(data, digits.target, digits.images,
                    test_size=0.25, random_state=42)
```

Creating a DataFrame

Before splitting, we are required to create a DataFrame for which importing Pandas library is mandatory. Python syntax for creating a DataFrame is defined as follows:

```
import numpy as np

from sklearn.preprocessing import MinMaxScaler

sampleData – np.random.randint(50, 100)

sampleData

scalar_model = MinMaxScalar()

feature_data = scalar_model.fit_transform(sampleData)

feature_data
```

Output for the above program:

```
In [22]: scalar_model = MinMaxScaler()
         feature_data = scalar_model.fit_transform(demoData)
         feature_data

/anaconda3/lib/python3.6/site-packages/sklearn/utils/validation.py:475: DataConversionWarning: Data with input dtype
int64 was converted to float64 by MinMaxScaler.
  warnings.warn(msg, DataConversionWarning)

Out[22]: array([[0.        , 0.27602906, 0.13174946, 0.17372881],
                [0.95081967, 0.75302663, 0.42548596, 0.05508475],
                [0.8989071 , 0.31234867, 0.32613391, 0.77118644],
                [0.38251366, 0.49394673, 0.        , 0.31144068],
                [0.7704918 , 0.22760291, 0.83585311, 0.875     ],
                [0.43169399, 0.52542373, 0.26133909, 1.        ],
                [0.20491803, 0.07021792, 0.31317495, 0.74788136],
                [0.83060109, 0.57869249, 0.16846652, 0.52118644],
                [0.98907104, 0.3220339 , 0.20086393, 0.15466102],
                [0.13934426, 0.        , 0.3650108 , 0.        ],
                [0.38251366, 0.58595642, 0.35205184, 0.56567797],
                [1.        , 1.        , 0.23326134, 0.20762712],
                [0.24590164, 0.62227603, 0.09071274, 0.53813559],
                [0.86338798, 0.7748184 , 0.15982721, 0.72669492],
                [0.1147541 , 0.63196126, 0.47732181, 0.87711864],
                [0.85519126, 0.95883777, 0.80345572, 0.59322034],
                [0.54644809, 0.93220339, 0.82289417, 0.70127119],
                [0.05464481, 0.1622276 , 0.91144708, 0.81355932],
                [0.60928962, 0.08232446, 1.        , 0.53601695],
                [0.46994536, 0.07263923, 0.15593952, 0.68008475]])
```

Splitting data into train and test:

```
from sklearn.model_selection import train_test_split

X_train, X_test, y_train, y_test = train_test_split(X,y, test_size = 0.50, random_state = 50)
```

Source: https://www.dataquest.io/blog/sci-kit-learn-tutorial/

Splitting and scaling are the most crucial steps in machine learning model development for which scikit-learn approach gives the best suitable methods to handle data sets.

Building Pipeline

Pipelines are the best source for feeding data to machine learning models. Raw data is entered into the pipeline to perform various operations for which we are required to standardize categorical data and continuous variables. The Python syntax to implement pipeline in a machine learning model is defined as follows:

```
from sklearn.preprocessing import StandardScaler, OneHotEncoder, LabelEncoder

from sklearn.compose import ColumnTransformer, make_column_transformer
```

```
from sklearn.pipeline import make_pipeline

from sklearn.linear_model import LogisticRegression
```

Scikit-learn also provides different functions to run cross validation and parameter tuning. In cross validation, the training set is run multiple times to evaluate the performance and efficiency of models, whereas the grid search approach includes various hyperparameters to check the machine learning model. Logistic classifier is one of the best sources to tune an ML model and can also be used to speed up training.

Effective Data Visualization

Data visualization is one of the major aspects of machine learning and data science. To begin with construction of ML models through Python programming language, we need to understand each of the underlying dataset and explore variables in great depth. Effective data visualization is the core tool for designing and developing machine learning models with high performance and great efficiency. Python data visualization is done through Seaborn, Pandas, and Numpy libraries.

Three important considerations for data visualization are accuracy, clarity, and efficiency. Efficiency makes use of efficient visualization approaches to highlight specific data points, whereas accuracy makes sure that only appropriate graphical representation is taken to deliver the message. Furthermore, clarity portion makes sure that the given dataset is relevant and complete. This allows data scientists to study new patterns which are derived from data in specific places from the graph.

To install Seaborn, we can use the following syntax:

```
pip install seaborn
```

Scatter Plot

Python programming can be used to design and create graphs of different categories. Scatter plots are the same as line graphs and we can utilize both vertical and horizontal axes to visualize the data points. As they are comprised of a large body of data, a straight line is formed because of the closer data points. Note that a stronger correlation between two variables yields a completely straight-line graph.

Details of Line Properties

Property	Value Type
Animated	True/False
Alpha	Float
Clip box	A matplotlib.transform.Bbox inst
Clip path	Patch
Linewidth	Float value in points

Implementation for Scatter Plot in Python:

```python
import matplotlib.pyplot as plt
```

```
import pandas as pd

import seaborn as sns

import warnings


warnings.filterwarnings('ignore')


fig = plt.figure(figsize=(5, 10))

df = pd.read_csv('SampleData')

ax = sns.regplot(x="wt", y="mpg", data=df)
```

Histogram Plot

Histograms are the graphical representations for a probability distribution and can be created through matplotlib and bar chart function in Python. For example:

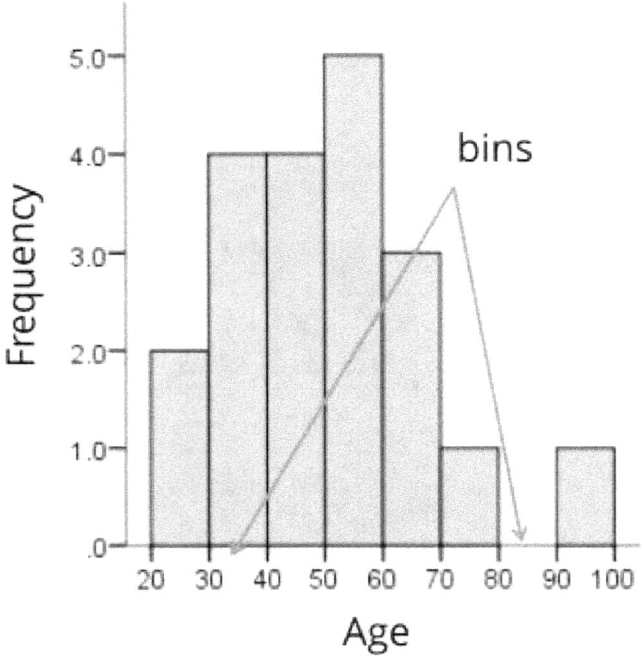

Python implementation:

```python
import pandas as pd

import seaborn as sns


df = pd.read_csv('SampleData')


fig = plt.figure(figsize=(5, 100))

sns.distplot(df.Temp, kde=False)
```

Bar Plots

In Python, we can also create bar graphs or bar plots to display and compare the frequency or number of data. Remember that the data can be of different discrete categories because bar plots have more frequency as compared to other types of graphs. Bar plots can be implemented through Python with Pandas barplot method. For example:

```python
import pandas as pd

import seaborn as sns


df = pd.read_csv('SampleData', index_col=0)


df_grpd = df.groupby("cyl").count().reset_index()

fig = plt.figure(figsize=(12, 8))

sns.barplot(x="cyl", y="mpg", data=df_grpd)
```

Source: https://pythonspot.com/matplotlib-bar-chart/

Pie Chart and Error Bars

Pie charts are created to show proportional data or percentage. Through pie charts, we can summarize huge datasets in visual form and display the relative proportion of different classes of data. On the other hand, error bars are used to show the graphical representation of variability of data and is mainly used to point out errors in data. This approach is also best suited for performing data analysis by overviewing statistical differences between the two groups of data.

Error bars demonstrate how a model and function are used in data analysis. It shows us the variability in data and also indicates any possible errors. To implement these graphs, we can take support from Seaborn Python visualization library. Seaborn provides high level interface for creating attractive statistical graphics and is widely used for visualizing data and plotting. Furthermore, Seaborn provides built in themes for better visualizations and includes built in statistical functions.

Naïve Bayes Model

Naïve Bayes classification theorem is implanted to calculate the probability of data belonging to a specific class. Classification is done by overviewing the previous knowledge about data and is used to solve both binary and multiclass classification problems. Naïve Bayes is a fast and straightforward classification algorithm which is best suitable for large volumes of data. The algorithm has the capability to perform different activities such as text classification, recommender systems, and spam filtering which makes it one of the greatest algorithms used in developing machine learning models.

How is Classification Performed?

To perform classification, data scientists need to understand the given problem and identify datasets to make specific labels. These attributes can also be considered as features of data which are directly affected by labels. Classification is divided into two phases known as evaluation phase and learning phase. In the evaluation phase, the model tests classifier performance on the basis of different parameters including recall, precision, accuracy, and error. For the learning phase, the classifier trains the model on the provided dataset so that it can deliver the best results when implemented in the machine learning system. Computation through Naïve Bayes theorem can be performed by the following equation:

$$P(h|D) = \frac{P(D|h)P(h)}{P(D)}$$

P(h) is the probability of hypothesis h and is also named as the prior probability of h, whereas P(d) is known as the probability of data or prior probability regardless of the hypothesis. P(h|D) is the probability of hypothesis h for given data D and is also named as posterior probability. P(D|h) represents the probability of data d in case of true h hypotheses and is also named as posterior probability.

Naïve Bayes Classified Development in Scikit-Learn

In the below example, we will define the best methods to define dataset, encode features and generate a machine learning model through Python programming language.

Defining the Dataset and Encoding Features to the Data

Basic syntax:

weather=['Sunny','Sunny','Overcast','Rainy','Rainy','Rainy','Overcast','Sunny','Sunny',

'Rainy','Sunny','Overcast','Overcast','Rainy']

temp=['Hot','Hot','Hot','Mild','Cool','Cool','Cool','Mild','Cool','Mild','Mild','Mild','Hot','Mild']

play=['No','No','Yes','Yes','Yes','No','Yes','No','Yes','Yes','Yes','Yes','Yes','No']

```python
from sklearn import preprocessing

#creating labelEncoder

le = preprocessing.LabelEncoder()

weather_encoded=le.fit_transform(wheather)

print weather_encoded
```

Generating model and loading data

```python
from sklearn.naive_bayes import GaussianNB


#Create a Gaussian Classifier

model = GaussianNB()

# Train the model using the training sets
```

```
model.fit(features,label)

#Predict Output

predicted= model.predict([[0,2]]) # 0:Overcast, 2:Mild

print "Predicted Value:", predicted

#load Data

from sklearn import datasets

wine = datasets.load_wine()
```

Implementation of Split() function

```
# Import train_test_split function

from sklearn.cross_validation import train_test_split
```

```
# Split dataset into training set and test set

X_train, X_test, y_train, y_test = train_test_split(wine.data,
wine.target, test_size=0.3,random_state=109)
```

Source: https://machinelearningmastery.com/naive-bayes-classifier-scratch-python/

Evaluating Accuracy of the Model

```
from sklearn import metrics

print(“Accuracy:”, metrics.accuracy_score(y_test, y_pred))
```

Source: https://www.datacamp.com/community/tutorials/naive-bayes-scikit-learn

Advantages of Naïve Bayes

Naïve Bayes is a fast approach to obtain accurate model predictions with low computation cost. Furthermore, this theorem can work efficiently on large datasets and performs ideally in case of discrete response variable as compared to continuous variable. As compared to other machine learning models such as logistic regression, Naïve Bayes yields better results in cases of independence holds as well.

K-Means Clustering

The K-Means clustering algorithm is a major part of machine learning algorithms which is based upon three important steps. These steps are named as Initialization, Assignment, and Update. K-Means clustering algorithm is used to partition n observations into k clusters for managing datasets and making accurate predictions in machine learning models.

In the Initialization step, the k means or centroids are generated at random, whereas the Assignment portion allows the creation of k clusters by associating each observation with another nearest centroid. The Update portion allows the centroid of clusters to become new mean and Update and Assignment portions are repeated iteratively until the desired outcome is achieved. As a result, the sum of squared errors is reduced between centroids and their respective points.

To implement K-Means algorithm in Python, we are required to import the following modules at first:

import pandas as pd

import numpy as np

import matplotlib.pyplot as plt

import random

from sklearn import preprocessing

Syntax to read data:

```python
data = pd.read_csv('Sample.csv')

data = data[:30]

max_clusters = 5

data['Age'].fillna(np.mean(data['Age']), inplace = True)

data['Fare'].fillna(np.mean(data['Price']), inplace = True)

data['Age'] = preprocessing.scale(data['Age'])

data['Fare'] = preprocessing.scale(data['Price'])
```

Expectation-Minimization Algorithm

Expectation-Minimization is an essential part of the K-Means algorithm and it plays a vital role in machine learning model development. This algorithm has the capability to guess cluster centers and repeat the process until the model is fully converged. E-step is used to assign points for nearest cluster center, whereas the M-step is considered to set the clusters to mean. E-step is also known as expectation step because it involves updating of expectations which is used to study point location for each cluster.

Furthermore, the M-step is named as maximization step and it involves maximization of fitness function and is best suited to define the location of cluster centers. In Python programming, there are predefined syntax and libraries to implement K-means algorithm for achieving different outcomes from the machine learning model. K-Means cluster algorithm is limited to linear cluster boundaries which are always linear. In particular, K-means can be implemented in Scikit-Learn through SpectralClustering estimation method for which the following syntax can be used:

```python
from sklearn.cluster import SpectralClustering

model = SpectralClustering(n_clusters=2,
            affinity='nearest_neighbors',

            assign_labels='kmeans')
```

labels = model.fit_predict(X)

plt.scatter(X[:, 0], X[:, 1], c=labels,

s=50, cmap='viridis');

Graphical Output:

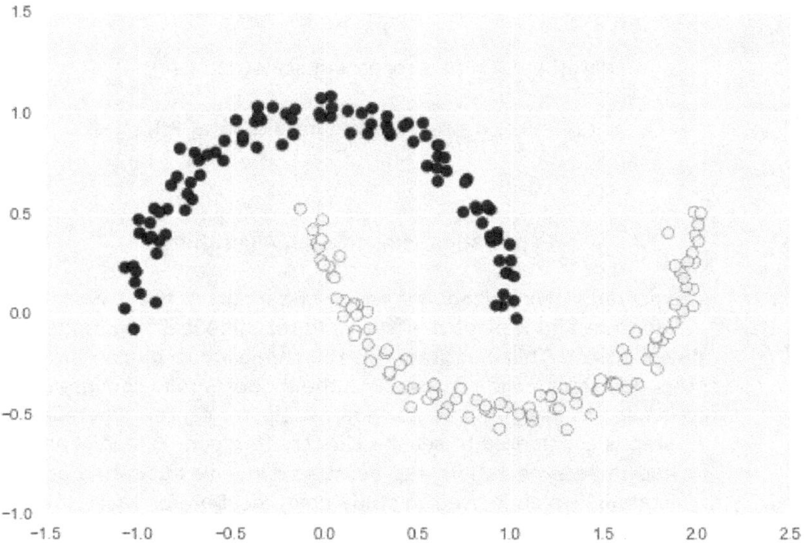

Mean Shift Algorithm

Mean shift algorithm has the capability to assign and outline data points to clusters by turning points towards the mode. This is a hierarchical clustering algorithm based on unsupervised learning techniques and is also named as Mode-seeding algorithm. To apply Mean shift algorithm in Python programming language, we need to perform kernel density estimation and represent the data in mathematical format. This makes it easier for the model to process data and use it for delivering accurate insights and predictions.

Kernel is also known as a function to perform convolution in datasets and is suitable for developing high performing machine learning models. Here is a simple program in Python to demonstrate how Mean shift algorithm works:

```python
clusters = [[2, 2, 2], [7, 7, 7], [5, 13, 13]]

X, _ = make_blobs(n_samples = 150, centers = clusters,

cluster_std = 0.60)

# After training the model, we store the

coordinates for cluster centers

ms = MeanShift()

ms.fit(X)

cluster_centers = ms.cluster_centers_


# Plot the data points and centroids in 3D graph

fig = plt.figure()

ax = fig.add_subplot(111, projection ='3d')

ax.scatter(X[:, 0], X[:, 1], X[:, 2], marker ='o')

ax.scatter(cluster_centers[:, 0], cluster_centers[:, 1],

cluster_centers[:, 2], marker ='x', color ='red',

s = 300, linewidth = 5, zorder = 10)

plt.show()
```

Output:

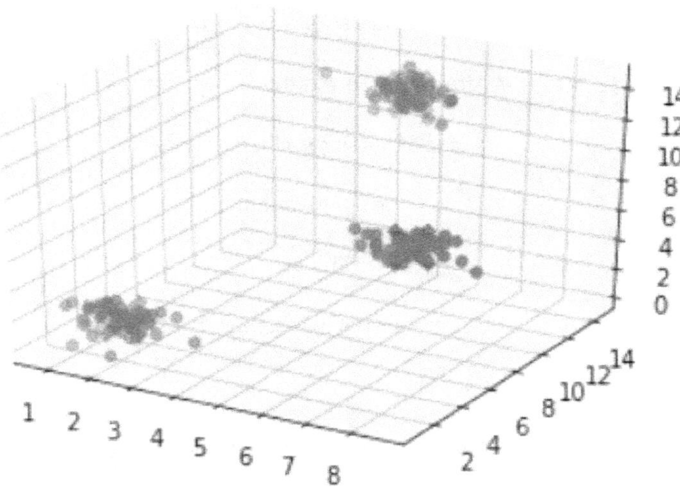

Source: https://www.geeksforgeeks.org/ml-mean-shift-clustering/

There are several advantages of using Mean shift algorithm in machine learning models. The algorithm is good for finding a variable number of modes and is an application independent tool. Furthermore, the model does not assume any prior shape on data clusters like elliptical or spherical.

Chapter 6: Deep Learning and Artificial Intelligence

Machine learning is a branch of computer science which is based on the study of algorithms having the capability to learn and predict on their own. Each algorithm is based on a predefined set of rules and procedures that are used to perform specific operations in machine learning models. These algorithms are also known as Artificial Neural Networks (ANN) in deep learning which is also a subfield of machine learning. Python provides simple and easy to implement approaches for developers and data scientists to program machine learning models and enhance their performance as well.

To develop, maintain, and evaluate deep learning models, we can take help from Python libraries such as Pandas, TensorFlow, and Keras. As they are based on efficient numerical modules, you can get started with deep neural networks and utilize built-in modules to develop high performing machine learning models.

Introduction to Artificial Neural Networks

It is important to learn the basics and functionality of artificial neural networks before starting with deep learning in Python. Neural networks are based on the perception of neurons in the human brain and how they work to perform specific operations. The human brain is the greatest example to be inspired from because it is composed of millions of neurons working together to control different operations in the human body. The brain is capable of performing complex computations within seconds, which is surely the biggest inspiration for artificial neural networks.

Understanding Data

Before developing neural networks or deep learning models, getting information about data and its qualities can deliver long term advantages. At first, check the description folder to overview variables of datasets and learn about details and other vital information as well. Generally, a neural network is comprised of an input layer which is your actual data and is present in numerical form. There are various hidden layers in neural networks which are present between input and output layers. With a single layer, the model is capable of handling linear relationships, whereas in the case of hidden layers, the model can handle non-linear relationships as well.

TensorFlow and Keran are best suited for building multiple layers in a neural network. Here is the syntax to implement these libraries in Python:

pip install tensorflow

import tensorflow.keras as keras

import tensorflow as tf

Once we are done with importing TensorFlow, we can start to prepare our data and make it ready for training in machine learning models. The syntax is defined as follows:

mnist = tf.keras.datasets.mnist

(x_train, y_train),(x_test, y_test) = mnist.load_data()

Keras

To implement Keras, you are required to install and configure Python 2 or 3 along with SciPy and NumPy libraries. TensorFlow and Keras can be installed and configured without complex coding because there are predefined Python modules which you can easily add in your program.

Starting with the first step, we need to load our dataset for which the following two classes form Keras library can be implemented to define the model:

from numpy import loadtxt

from keras.models import sequential

from keras.layers import Dense

Source: https://machinelearningmastery.com/keras-functional-api-deep-learning/

Defining Keras Model

To define Keras model, we need to develop a sequential model and add layers until the required network architecture is complete. There are specific heuristics to determine the best network structure for which data scientists implement the process of trial and error experimentation. A fully connected layer can be defined by Dense class and we can also specify the number of nodes or neurons present in the layer by the help of activation argument. Python syntax to define Keras model is defined as follows:

```
model = Sequential()

model.add(Dense(10, input_dim=5, activation= 'relu'))

model.compile(loss- 'binary_crossentropy' , optimizer = 'adam',
metrics= ['accuracy'])
```

Evaluation and Prediction

For evaluating Keras model, we can use the evaluate() function on the model and pass the same input and output for training as well. Moreover, this activity will also generate a prediction for every input and output including the average loss or accuracy metrics. Implementation in Python for evaluating the model and predicting values in Keras is defined as follows:

```
accuracy = model.evaluate(X, y)

print('Accuracy: %.2f %(accuracy*100))

predictions = model.predict(X)

predictions = model.predict_classes(X)
```

Machine Learning

Machine learning is a branch of Artificial Intelligence which is based on statistical methods and cognitive behavior. The concept also allows computers to learn on their own without being programmed repeatedly whenever the system is exposed to new data. The process of prediction and training is based on specialized algorithms which are developed to perform specific tasks in machine learning models. For developing machine learning systems in Python programming language, major libraries including SciPy, NumPy, Matplotlib, Pandas, Keran and Scikit-learn need to be installed and configured at first.

For efficient learning and accurate predictions, machine learning models should be fed with data having certain attributes and variables during training. Majorly, machine learning tasks are categorized as predictive modeling, clustering, and concept learning whereas the ultimate goal of developing ML models is to take decisions without human intervention.

Categories of Machine Learning

Machine learning is divided into three main sections: Supervised learning, Unsupervised learning, and Reinforcement learning. Supervised learning is the most used paradigm for building machine learning models because it is absolutely easy to understand and implement. With the passage of time, ML models become capable of learning the relationship between examples and their labels until they become fully trained to make accurate predictions.

Supervised and Unsupervised Learning

Supervised learning algorithms have the power to model relationships and dependencies to achieve specific target prediction output. Common algorithms for implementing supervised learning are Nearest neighbor, Decision Trees, Naïve Bayes, and Neural networks. Unsupervised learning is based on machine learning models that are trained with unlabeled data. The models are not given any supporting training datasets and they have to learn through patterns and attributes in data. Common algorithms for developing unsupervised machine learning models are K-Means clustering and Association Rules. Unsupervised learning algorithms are mainly used in the development of descriptive modeling and pattern detection systems because there are no labels or output categories defined.

Another major category of machine learning is named as Semi-supervising learning. For supervised and unsupervised machine learning models, there are labels for data given in some cases whereas in other scenarios, there are no labels for observation in datasets. Categories and techniques of machine learning are selected after complete observation and evaluation of external factors such as cost, security, reliability, and maintenance. These factors play a vital role in machine learning model development as well.

Reinforcement Learning

The reinforcement learning method has a capability to utilize observations from interaction with external factors and environments to make specific decisions in a machine learning model. Agents in reinforcement learning models consistently learn from the environment and repeatedly try for exploring a new range of possible states. Being an important part of machine learning and artificial intelligence, reinforcement learning allows systems and software agents to automatically determine ideal behavior within a certain context to boost performance.

There are several algorithms to implement the reinforcement learning model in Python. Usually, reinforcement learning models are created for a specific problem and all of the solutions are given by the model itself. Common algorithms for reinforcement learning are Q-Learning, Deep Adversarial Networks, and Temporal Difference.

Deep Neural Networks

What are Neural Networks?

Deep neural networks are comprised of various algorithms which are modeled according to the functionality and connectivity of the human brain to recognize specific patterns. The human brain has the capability to predict, analyze, and make decisions overviewing any given scenarios and perform tasks successfully. Neural networks classify and cluster data and utilize the given variables and attributes to make relevant predictions and perform certain tasks as well. A deep neural network is actually a neural network with a certain level of complexity because it is based on more than two layers.

By using mathematical modeling, neural networks process data in different ways because they are designed to simulate the activity of the human brain. Furthermore, the model performs specific types of ordering and sorting by utilizing artificial intelligence and machine learning approaches. Patterns recognized by neural networks are numerical and include vectors through which any real-world data such as sound, time series, or text could be translated. Moreover, they also group unlabeled data as per its similarities when provided a labeled dataset.

Neural networks are comprised of various components. These include an input layer, an output layer, and some hidden layers as well. To complete the network architecture, we can select an activation function for each hidden layer along with a set of biases and weights between the layers. We can easily create a neural network in Python through the following syntax:

```python
class NeuralNetwork:

    def __init__(self, x, y):

        self.input    = x

        self.weights1 = np.random.rand(self.input.shape[2],8)

        self.weights2 = np.random.rand(4,1)

        self.y        = y

        self.output   = np.zeros(y.shape)
```

Generally, the values for biases and weights determine the strength and effectiveness of predictions. Training of neural networks involves fine tuning of biases and weights from input data for which we are required to perform different iterations. Each iteration of training involves the calculation of feed forward and updating of biases and weights through back propagation approach.

Recurrent Neural Networks

Recurrent Neural Networks are also known as RNNs and are

basically used in the implementation of Natural Language Processing or language modeling because they allow data to flow in any direction. As they can repeat the same task for each element of the sequence, the output is usually dependent on the previous computations and RNNs are known to have built-in memory that records the previously calculated information.

Training Neural Networks

Training neural networks is an essential part of machine learning model development. As we are required to find the most suitable values of weights and bias of a neural network to achieve the desired output, the training must be performed by using effective techniques such as the iterative gradient descent method. Once random initialization is complete, we can make predictions on subset of data through forward propagation process and update each weight by an amount proportional to dC/dq or the derivative of cost functions with respect to the weight. The calculation can also be referred to as the learning rate and implemented through a computational graph as well. Gradients can be calculated through back-propagation algorithm for which we can implement chain rule of differentiation as well.

Back propagation algorithm is implemented by analyzing data through a computational graph which has each neuron expanded to several nodes. The computational graph does not have any kind of bias or weights on the edges, so weights become their own nodes.

Gradient Descent

Gradient descent optimization technique is used to find out which weight produces the fewest errors and is used to translate signals from input data into a correct classification. A neural network learns and adjusts to several weights so that it can map signal meaning in the best suitable manner. Furthermore, each weight factor in deep network is based on several transforms because the signal of weight has to pass through different sums and activation over the layers. The idea behind deep learning is to adjust a model's weight and increase its performance and capability to make accurate predictions.

Deep learning can process millions of images and classify them as per their similarities. As it performs automatic feature extraction, we can perform complex tasks without human intervention even by training machine learning models on unlabeled data. During processing, neural networks try to learn and recognize correlations between the features and optimal results. This activity is done by drawing specific connections between feature signals and labeled data.

Optimization

The training process of deep learning neural networks is dependent upon input data, labels, and attributes. As they learn to map inputs and outputs over a training dataset of examples, the process is usually iterative and involves finding a set of weights that are best suited for the network. An iterative training process for neural networks is best for solving optimization problem and searches for model weights that yield minimum loss or error when evaluation examples in training datasets. Remember that optimization is a search procedure and can become challenging when implemented in deep neural network models.

To perform optimization and training for deep learning neural networks, the best method is back propagation of the error algorithm. Generally, we can handle the difficulty in terms of features of error surface or landscape which the algorithm has undergone changes so that it can navigate on its own and select the right path as well.

Artificial Neural Networks

The Artificial Neural Networks are based on the working and functionality of biological neural networks and are capable of modeling non linear relationships between inputs and outputs. Being statistical models, Artificial neural networks are widely implemented in machine learning systems because they are based on the approach of learning and observing datasets. Optimization techniques such as cost function allow ANN's to determine best values of each tunable model parameter and improve the learning rate as well. Furthermore, these optimization techniques allow developers and data scientists to develop state of the art machine learning models which are capable of making accurate predictions and insights.

Machine learning models are complex because of the increased abstraction and higher problem-solving capabilities. Due to the increased number of hidden layers, the number of paths between each neuron and given layer increases which in return makes the ANN system more complex. Tuning and model architecture are major components of Artificial Neural Networks. Each of these characteristics allow ANN to make a significant impact on the reliability and performance of the deep learning model.

Remember the fact that Artificial Neural Networks are extremely powerful and they can often become complex. Furthermore, they are also named as black box algorithms as their actual working and functionality is impossible to understand. In contrast with deep learning algorithms, these models are also dependent on optimal model selection and model tuning approach for maximizing performance and output. Furthermore, statistical techniques and deep learning leverage concepts are a major part of Artificial Neural Networks.

How Do They Work?

Artificial Neural Networks have the capability to make decisions and calculations on their own. As the model works as a supervised learning approach, it is fed with enough examples and similar scenarios which allow ANN's to make accurate predictions on their own. This process is usually done through back propagation approach because Artificial Neural Networks are represented as weighted directed graphs. In these graphs, node is designed by artificial neurons for which the connection between neuron inputs and neuron outputs is represented through directed edges and weights.

Each given input is multiplied with its corresponding weights and the output is directly dependent upon the details and labels of the weight for solving a specific problem. Furthermore, the weights are represented through the strength of interconnection in between neurons of the artificial neural network. In case the weighted sum is zero, we can add a bias to make output non-zero or update the system to meet the model's requirements. Weights of inputs can range from zero to positive infinity and to keep the response according to the limits of desired values, we can create a specific threshold value as well.

Furthermore, activation functions can also be implemented in artificial neural networks which comprise of a set of functions implemented to achieve a desired value. Some of the common activation functions are named as Sigmoidal, Tan hyperbolic sigmoidal, and binary.

Architecture of ANN's

Artificial Neural Networks or ANN's contain a huge number of artificial neurons, and this is the main reason they are named as artificial neural networks. The architecture is comprised of an Input layer, an Output layer, and a Hidden layer. The input layer has artificial neurons which are subject to receive input from external resources and are responsible for learning and recognition as well. For the output layer, the information that is fed into the system is analyzed and recognized before it is sent for further processing. Moreover, the output layer also accepts or rejects the training data by overviewing the labels and attributes to make sure that the information is best suited for the artificial neural network. The illustration below will better help you in understanding the architecture of artificial neural networks:

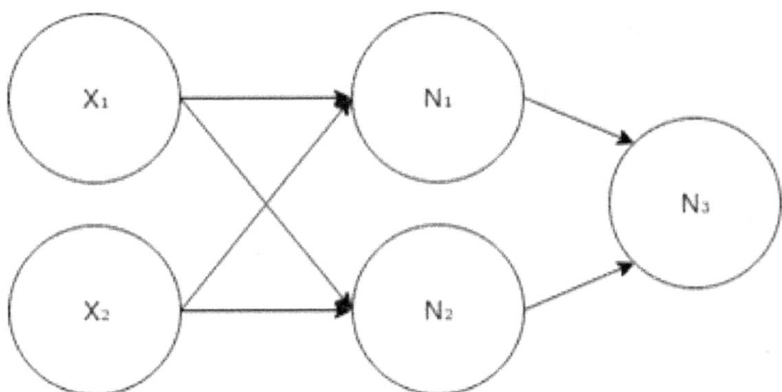

Hidden layers are present between input layers and output layers. Their job is to transform the input into meaningful data so that the output layer can utilize it in the best manner. Each of the artificial neural networks is interconnected and the hidden layers cover each portion of data present in the system. This makes it easier to complete the learning process and allows the system to make relevant updates without any hassle.

Advantages

Artificial neural networks have several key advantages that make them ideal for solving complex problems in machine learning and artificial intelligence. Having the capability to model non-linear relationships, ANNs can solve real life problems by defining relationships between inputs and outputs from non linear data as well. Furthermore, artificial neural networks can learn from initial inputs and generalize relationships to predict unseen data and make the model capable of performing complex operations without any hassle. Unlike other prediction models, artificial neural networks never impose any restrictions over input variables which allows researchers to train the model through different techniques.

Applications of ANNs

Character recognition and image processing are the greatest applications of artificial neural networks. As this network has the power to process large sets of input data, it can also define non-linear relationships and help in the development of character and image recognition applications. Artificial neural network models are widely implemented in fraud detection and security systems because they have the capability to perform facial recognition in real time.

Moreover, artificial neural networks also serve as a useful tool for food quality and safety analysis. This covers the development of microbial growth models through which prediction of food safety and interpretation of spectroscopic data is performed.

Chapter 7: Data Science in Real World

Data science is a combination of statistics, mathematics, and programming. In order to develop data science and machine learning models, we are required to have in depth knowledge and information regarding the subject so that accurate training data can be fed into the system. On the other hand, business thinking and domain knowledge are also essential for developing high performing machine learning models and data science projects.

Python is a completely suitable programming language for developing machine learning and data science models because it is absolutely easy to learn and implement. Furthermore, we can perform specific tasks and operations by utilizing built-in Python libraries such as Pandas, NumPy and Scikit-Learn.

How Can We Implement Data Science in Real Life Scenarios?

Most industries and businesses are now using systems that are based on the latest machine learning and data science models. This helps in automating processes and allows businesses to make accurate predictions for the future to increase sales and boost profits. Traditional information systems are not capable of bringing long term benefits to companies and businesses because of outdated technology. To make things better, data scientists and machine learning experts have utilized the concepts of computer science, mathematics, and statistics to develop systems which are capable of making accurate predictions and learn from the training datasets as well.

There are several key advantages of data science in business and real life for humans. An experienced data scientist can also serve as a trusted advisor and strategic partner to the company by providing accurate data insights and predictions for the future. This activity is done through measuring performance across the entire organization and recording performance metrics. Furthermore, data scientists perform different tests to determine the status of an organization's current analytics system to bring further improvements.

Data Science Applications

Most of the advanced applications and systems developed nowadays are based on machine learning and data science models. The impact and performance of machine learning systems is a lot better as compared to traditional computing systems which is the main reason why machine learning and artificial intelligence are widely being researched. By using data science, companies and businesses have become intelligent enough to sell products and promote their services in a shorter time frame.

Here are a few major applications of Data Science:

Image recognition

You might have noticed that once you have uploaded any image with your friends on Facebook, you start to get suggestions for adding tags. This feature of automatic suggestion is based on an image recognition algorithm which has the capability to detect specific patterns and yield outcomes with matching data. Furthermore, image recognition systems are widely being used by security agencies and financial institutes to detect people involved in fraudulent activities in real time.

Speech Recognition

Speech recognition systems allow users to perform different tasks by communicating with their devices such as smartphones or computers. Google Voice, Cortana, and Siri are the finest implementations of speech recognition systems that were originally designed with machine learning and data science models.

Virtual Assistants

Chatbots from different websites and applications are the finest implementation of deep learning and artificial intelligence. Virtual assistance is now available in mobile applications through which patients can avail healthcare guidance and basic support without any hassle. Furthermore, you can book appointments and make schedules with chatbots through virtual assistants and receive vital information as well.

Risk and Fraud Detection

Financial institutions such as banks are the biggest users of automated fraud detection and risk management systems. Banks can now analyze user data and information to check credit history for thousands of people instead of checking for everyone individually. Furthermore, companies can avoid bad debts and losses by overviewing and managing transactions in real time.

Data Analytics in Detail

Data analytics is an approach which is used to analyze data sets and draw conclusions regarding the available data. To tackle the increasing demand and requirements of businesses and companies, research for specialized software and systems is being performed by data scientists and machine learning engineers to improve scientific models and theories. Online analytical processing and business intelligence are the major forms of advanced analytics. Data analytics systems can make businesses improve operational efficiency and increase revenue by meeting customer demands and increasing sales.

Process and Working

Analyzing and evaluating data are the basic concepts of data analytics. Most of the work in the development of data analytics systems includes collection, integration, and preparation of data which has to be used for model training. The models are then tested and upgraded to produce accurate results. For development of data analytics models, the first step is data collection for which scientists take support from particular analytics applications and work with data engineers to implement the information in the best possible manner.

Data combined from different sources needs to be refined with data integration tools so that it can be transformed into a common format. Once the labels and format are properly analyzed, we can load the data into an analytics system such as Datawarehouse or

Hadoop cluster for fast processing. Moreover, data scientists have to find and solve data quality problems so that the accuracy of analytics applications is never compromised. Furthermore, data cleansing and data profiling techniques can be used to make sure that the data set is consistent and free of mistakes. This will help in achieving accurate insights and predictions in future.

Analytical models are built by taking support from predictive modeling tools and programming languages such as Python or Scala. Once the model is developed, it undergoes proper testing for which different types of test training datasets are used. The process is repeated until the model completely learns and adapts characteristics from training data so that it can make accurate predictions when implemented into the system. Furthermore, the model is also run in production mode for which full datasets are used and if any problem arises, it is solved immediately to ensure reliability and performance of the analytics model.

Types and Categories of Data Analytics

Generally, data analytics is divided into four major categories which are predictive, prescriptive, diagnostic, and descriptive analysis. Each of the categories has unique characteristics and is capable of performing various operations for business analytic models. Starting with predictive analysis, the category is best for gaining insights and predictions for the future. This approach uses historical data to identify the given records and trends which are likely to occur. Furthermore, predictive analysis tools also provide valuable insights for scenarios which might happen in the future if they are likely to occur. To implement predictive analysis, we can use machine learning techniques including decision trees, regression, and neural networks.

Prescriptive analysis approach gives us ideas for activities that could be performed to avail best outcomes. The technique uses insights from predictive analysis to make reliable data driven decisions. Furthermore, businesses can get help from predictive analysis to determine the likelihood of events and outcomes because this approach has the capability to detect patterns in large datasets. Diagnostic analytics can be helpful for obtaining reasons related to the happening of certain aspects in an analytics model. The technique takes points from descriptive analysis and works deeper to find the root cause of each event.

Moreover, diagnostic analysis also includes performance indicators which help to discover the main reason which might have affected the performance or reliability of the analytics system. Diagnostic analysis is used to identify and outline anomalies in data and information related to each anomaly is also collected. At the end, data scientists implement statistical techniques to find trends and relationships to outline the root causes of these anomalies. The fourth category of data analytics is named as descriptive analysis which summarizes large datasets into separate portions for describing outcomes in a better way.

Descriptive analysis can be considered as a way of analyzing the main reason why a specific scenario happened for which data scientists implement key performance indicators (KPI) to develop analytics models. Furthermore, other metrics like return on investment (ROI) are also based on descriptive analysis because they are implemented in systems for large scale businesses and industries to gain performance and sales insights.

Importance of Data Analytics

Analyzing big data is an essential part of machine learning model development. There is a wide range of applications of data analytics that have greatly improved the performance of business systems and have allowed companies to compete in today's world. Talking about the earliest adopters of data analytics tools, the financial sector has widely implemented machine learning and data analytics systems to secure transactions and avoid fraudulent activities. Furthermore, data analytics can also be used to detect fraud in real time and take certain actions to stop all kinds of fraudulent activities.

Data analytic also provides vital information for healthcare, environment protection, and crime prevention. These applications bring long term advantages and support for people as they can protect themselves from fraudulent activities and get medical assistance without any hassle. Data analysis, statistics, and mathematics have always been a part of scientific research through which advanced analytic techniques and tools are designed. The Internet of Things (IoT) is another great invention made through data analytics methods and its devices are comprised of sensors that collect meaningful data which is then utilized by data analytics models to make predictions and accurate insights. There are endless applications of data analytics and the increasing volume of data being collected each day reveals new pathways for machine learning and deep analytics models to learn effectively.

Data Mining

This is the method of analyzing data from various perspectives and converting it into useful information. The converted and summarized information is used to make vital decisions and training data. In machine learning models, data mining is considered as a technique of detecting, analyzing, and exploring patterns in large amounts of data and the processed information is then sorted and classified into separate categories. Moreover, classification and data prediction techniques help us in getting accurate insights and prediction results through data mining methods without any hassle.

Logistic regression, classification trees, neural networks, anomaly detection, and clustering techniques such as K-nearest Neighbors are a few examples of data mining. The characteristics of data analysis are dependent upon different aspects such as variety, velocity, and volume. In order to get better results and outcomes from data mining, we are required to address each scenario in-depth and implement the best algorithms to develop data mining models. Furthermore, framing a problem makes data scientist clear about the requirements of systems and helps data scientists to gain accurate insights from the data mining model.

Steps in Data Mining

The first step in data mining is data cleaning, in which we are supposed to check the quality of data and remove any kind of irregularities. Multiple data sources are combined to complete the data integration process so that data could be extracted from the database. Data selection and data transformation approaches are used to perform summary analysis and aggregatory operations over data while doing data mining. In data mining, we have to extract useful information and data from the data source and analyze several patterns as well.

In the final step of knowledge representation, data scientists have to represent knowledge to users in the form of metrics, graphs, trees, and tables. Data mining is widely implemented in the development of fraud detection, risk management, market analysis, and corporate analysis systems to explore and manage data.

Importance of Machine Learning

Machine learning is responsible for transforming operations for each sector including finance, health care, security, information technology, and education. Based on the idea of learning from data, machine learning is a branch of artificial intelligence that automates analytical model building and allows systems to make decisions without human intervention. Because of the ever-increasing advancements and revolutions in computing technologies, businesses can find the best solutions to boost their sales and increase profits.

The aim of machine learning is to understand the structure of data and utilize theoretical models for developing systems which are capable of making accurate predictions and data insights. Data driven decisions always bring positive outcomes for businesses because machine learning models are trained on factual data which delivers the best possible solutions for any problem. In traditional computing systems, data analysis was performed through trial and error-based approach which cannot yield accurate results when implemented over large data sets and heterogeneous data.

Data Science Lifecycle and Model Building

Building data science models by focusing on each important aspect of the data science lifecycle will help you in achieving the best results and outcomes. Discovery, data preparation, model planning, model building, operations, and results analysis are key portions of the data science lifecycle. Starting with the first steps of discovery and data preparation, data scientists need to understand the requirements, specifications, and priorities of the system. Budget and time constraints should also be kept in mind before starting the project, as it will save you from further issues as well.

In the data preparation phase, sufficient training data and information must be discovered so that the data science model is capable of making accurate predictions and evaluations in future.

Extract, transform, and load are the major approaches that should be considered while creating datasets for the system. Once the data preparation step is done, the next part is model planning where data scientists have to determine the techniques and methods to draw relationships between variables.

The next phase is known as model building in which data scientists and engineers have to develop datasets for testing and training purposes. Implementing techniques like clustering, association, and classification will make it easier to complete the model building phase. For the operations phase, data scientists are supposed to deliver briefings, technical documents, code, and final reports for the project.

Challenges in Neural Networks and Deep Learning Algorithms

Neural networks and deep learning algorithms are widely used in the development of machine learning and artificial intelligence models. Although the performance and effectiveness of deep learning models is directly dependent upon the quality and reliability of training data, there are several other factors that can be held accountable for the performance of machine learning models. Overfitting and underfitting are two of the major challenges that are faced by ML systems and to prevent further loss, data scientists have to research and implement effective techniques to improve the performance and functionality of machine learning models.

To avoid overfitting, we can apply regularization methods such as data augmentation, drop out, early stopping, and transfer learning during training of deep learning models. This will help in protecting the model from overfitting and also improves rare dependencies. For neural networks, we use the dropout approach which is a popular regularization technique to finish overfitting. Other methods like early stopping, data augmentation, and transfer learning can also be implemented to avoid the challenges that are being faced during the development of deep learning and neural network systems.

Deep Learning Limitations

Although deep learning systems are great performers, there are some external factors which can have a direct impact on their functionality and effectiveness. Usually, artificial intelligence models are given training through a supervised learning approach which includes training data that is completely labeled and classified by humans. Deep learning systems are based on the same approach and require huge training datasets to become properly trained. Complex and large models are difficult to train for which data scientists need to classify and label training data as well.

Improving Data Science Models

Machine learning models developed with the Python programming language can be updated and improved by making simple changes in the code. Although there are different checks to overview the performance and effectiveness of a data science model, we need to focus on some key factors explained below to avail best outcomes:

Determine Problems

For improving results, we need to analyze the problems with our data science model at first. Learning curves are a great source to verify a test set against the provided training data. By analyzing computational graphs, one can easily identify the weaknesses of a data analytics or machine learning model. Furthermore, you can also perform cross validation to overview performance of your model. A large difference between the results and cross validation estimates is a common problem which usually occurs with training data.

Choosing Hyper Parameters

When solving a data science problem, you need to analyze the problem and determine the best metric for getting a long-term solution. Remember that most of the algorithms perform best even with default parameter settings. However, you can optimize the efficiency of machine learning and artificial intelligence models by implementing hyperparameters as well. To perform this activity, you have to design a grid search containing possible values supported by your parameters and start to evaluate the results through a score metric.

Testing and Evaluation

Testing and evaluation will help you in determining the quality of predictions and data insights delivered by a deep analytics model. In some cases, bias can affect the performance of the model for which you can implement various techniques such as automatic feature creation and support vectors to achieve a better solution. Although these techniques will make the model perform slightly better, your understanding and expertise regarding the machine learning model are the best source to examine, test, and improve the overall performance and efficiency.

Search for More Data

No matter what amount of training data you have used, there is always room for improvement because machine learning and deep learning models always improve when a new data set is fed into the system. Increasing the size of the training set is also a vital approach to be considered. In case you have been training your model with simple data, you can feed complex or unlabeled data so that the model is capable of learning and making better decisions on its own.

Chapter 8: Deep Learning and Business

Business processes nowadays are completely transformed due to the involvement of artificial intelligence, deep learning, and machine learning systems. They are key aspects of enacting digital transformation and development of computational systems. There are several forms of prescriptive analysis that can help businesses in achieving desired outcomes within a short period of time. These procedures include automated stock transactions, intelligent traffic flow pattern optimization, autonomous data center functions, and autonomous cars. The basic fundamentals behind each of these technologies are deep learning and major concepts of artificial intelligence.

Actually, artificial intelligence is an approach to mimic human intelligence process through the application of mathematical and statistical algorithms. Machine learning is actually a subset of artificial intelligence and is a major field of computer science that focuses on interpreting structures and patterns in data.

How Does Deep Learning Work?

Deep learning is an approach based on the construct of human neural networks and is also a subfield of machine learning and artificial intelligence. The approach has the capability to learn from both structured and unstructured data to initiate automated learning from training data. In order to improve accuracy of deep learning models, data scientists need to remove weak correlations and assumptions in data. The presence of reliable and high-quality data is the key aspect to building accurate machine learning models.

For extracting more information from existing data, we can follow the feature engineering approach in deep learning. This method is used to extract new facilities and features from data and allows the deep learning model to understand variance in data as well. As a result, data scientists are able to develop models with improved accuracy and better prediction capabilities. Feature engineering is based on a hypothesis generation approach which is divided into feature transformation and feature creation methods.

In feature transformation, the algorithms work with normally distributed data. Methods such as inverse, square root, or log of the values are implemented to remove skewness from data and this approach is also known as data normalization. Numeric data can also be created by adding discrete values into the deep learning model. On the other hand, feature creation method derives new variables from existing variables and helps to uncover hidden relationships between datasets. Moreover, data scientists also take support from the feature selection process to find out the best subset of attributes to explain the relationship of independent variables with the available target variable.

Feature selection is based on major machine learning model development metrics like domain knowledge and visualization. Through domain knowledge, we can select features which might yield a higher impact on target variable whereas the visualization approach helps to visualize the relationship between multiple variables. In return, this approach makes variable selection processes easier and more effective. To enhance performance and reliability of the model, we can also consider working on statistical parameters like p-values and other modules to select the right features.

Algorithm Tuning and Method Ensemble

The performance of machine learning algorithms is dependent upon parameters and variables in the dataset. The parameters can influence the efficiency and outcome of the learning process for which data scientists follow the approach of algorithm tuning. This approach is used to figure out the best value for each parameter which in return improves the accuracy of the model. To tune the parameters, you should have in-depth knowledge about the machine learning model and datasets in advance. Furthermore, the process can be repeated multiple times until the desired outcome is achieved.

Ensemble methods are commonly used in the development and maintenance of machine learning and deep learning models. This technique combines outcomes of weak models and performs operations to produce a model with better results. Bagging and boosting are two major techniques used to implement ensemble methods on machine learning models.

Model Interpretability

Businesses and industries require information systems that have the capability to deliver accurate data insights and predictions that bring long term benefits to the organization. To deliver the best machine learning models in industry, we need to interpret and analyze the effectiveness and performance of deep learning and artificial intelligence models before starting with the implementation process. Model interpretability in machine learning is an approach which is used to assess how easy it is for humans to evaluate and understand the working process of a machine learning model.

Models such as logistic regression are ideal for use in the development of business AI models because you can add extra features and implement deep learning methods to meet system requirements. Model interpretability is immensely important because algorithm outcomes are responsible for making high stakes decisions and it is mandatory to know which features to add and which need to be removed. Additionally, in case the model is not interpretable, the company might not be legally permitted to make changes to processes by using insights.

Model interpretability can be performed with the help of DataRobot. DataRobot features several components that yield fully human-interpretable models because of the model blueprint and feature explanation techniques. Model blueprint provides insights related to the preprocessing steps on which each model is based to achieve a desired outcome. Furthermore, it also helps data scientists to justify the models and explain regulatory details if needed.

On the other hand, prediction explanations reveal the top variables that can make an impact on the model's outcome. This allows users to explain how the model has derived a specific outcome and the steps involved in deriving accurate predictions and data insights.

Deep Learning in Business Systems

Pioneers in deep learning system development have been using artificial intelligence and deep learning to advance machine learning model capabilities. These advancements have deployed at scale in order to achieve greater efficiency and speed for which a wide range of new training data is used in model training. Business systems now require deep learning models that are capable of making real time decisions and deliver outcomes that bring long term benefits to the business. The process of scoring predictive models and processing of decision requests in real time have added great value to machine learning models.

Technologies today have advanced to a point where machine learning models can be implemented and deployed at a scale to achieve better performance, reliability, and effectiveness. These advances are unleashing new pathways of data science capabilities such as the acceptance of real time decision requests from various channels and processing of decision requests in real time according to the given business rules. To handle thousands of requests per second, machine learning engineers have to design and control processes through multiple model recalibration methods.

Usage of Deep Learning in Businesses and Industries

Marketing, Sales, and Finance industries are the biggest users of deep learning models and machine learning algorithms. Modern day marketing models and approaches are designed to attract customers and improve sales by showcasing services of a company in unique ways. To make this happen, marketing departments work to find large datasets which are then implemented in deep learning models to understand customer purchase decisions and recommendations. Deep learning has the power to replace traditional heuristics-based lead scoring because it can determine relationships between data and generate useful insights as well. On the other hand, sales teams can also get support from deep learning models to analyze customer predictions.

Generally, companies and businesses get unstructured data from a variety of sources and sales teams are unable to understand purchasing trends of customers. With the help of deep learning models, businesses are now able to predict insights, deal cycles, and deal sizes which can yield the highest return on investment and sales ratio. Evaluating customer and sales interactions that are likely to yield best outcomes can deliver long term benefits to business for which deep learning models are ideal and best performing.

In the finance sector, we can see deep learning and artificial intelligence systems that are used to perform certain tasks to avoid fraud and analyze credit history of customers. Banks can now overview credit history for thousands of customers within seconds and make major decisions such as loan approval with the help of automated machine learning systems. Furthermore, machine learning systems have also eliminated the need to perform manual data entry for which predictive modeling algorithms and machine learning methods are used.

Applications

Here are some examples of the best deep learning applications that have brought significant benefits and ease to humans.

Language Recognition

Language recognition systems are based on deep learning models which allows them to differentiate dialects of any language. The dialects are determined by artificial intelligence models and can be differentiated in real time without human involvement. Language recognition and translation systems are some of the best implementations of deep learning algorithms as they can perform translation from images and text in real time as well.

Autonomous Vehicles

The biggest revolution in our transport system is the addition of self-driving or autonomous vehicles. Artificial intelligence and machine learning models in self-driving vehicles have the capability to detect patterns, humans, and other traffic for making accurate decisions.

Computer Vision and Text Generation

The deep learning approach has provided best models for image classification, image segmentation, and object detection systems. Computer vision and text generation methods are widely used in education systems because they have the capability to automate tasks and perform required text generation without any hassle.

Limitations of Machine Learning Models

Machine learning models developed with Python and R programming languages are capable of automating processing and deliver accurate insights when trained through high quality training datasets. It is simple to understand the value of ML and the great advantages it has brought in today's world. Although technology has greatly revolutionized how different tasks and processes are done, there are still a lot of limitations and consequences of automating tasks which need to be overlooked by human beings.

Information explosion has now resulted in the collection of massive amounts of data, and this amount of data is engaged with rapid development of computer parallelization and processor power. The concept of trusting machine learning models has its own advantages and disadvantages. When trained with high quality training data, artificial intelligence and machine learning systems can generate 100 percent accurate predictions and complete the given tasks without failure. Although machines can never achieve the level of human intelligence, they have significantly improved with time to bring positive outcomes.

Machine learning models can never tell us about the normative values which need to be accepted and answers to questions like how we should act in certain scenarios. The approach is extremely powerful for sensors and can be used to design and calibrate systems for delivering accurate outcomes.

Finding Useful Data

The most vital part of developing and training a deep learning model is to find accurate and high-quality data. If you feed a model with poor or unstructured data, it will surely provide inaccurate results in future. Finding quality data is difficult for which data scientists need to verify the resources and include information that is completely reliable and authentic. Furthermore, most of the machine learning models require huge amounts of data to be trained perfectly. The larger the architecture, the greater the size of data needed to produce viable results.

Reusing data in machine learning models is surely a bad approach. In case you are not able to find data in bulk, try to train your model with labeled and structured data so that it can learn within a short period of time. Whenever fake data is fed into a machine learning model, it will start to train by itself and when tested on an unseen data set, it might not deliver accurate prediction results. Like quality of training data, features also play a vital role in the predictions made by machine learning models.

Chapter 9: Advanced Python Data Science

Data is the core part of the machine learning model development process. Traditional data and Big Data are major types of data that are used to train machine learning models. It has become mandatory to build new platforms to meet the ever-increasing demand of organizations. There are several challenges and difficulties faced by traditional data because it requires collaborative efforts of people to be managed and utilizes a lot of resources and time as well.

What is Big Data?

Big data is known as the collection of large amounts of information which is processed and manipulated for analytics. This approach is divided into three major portions which are volume, velocity, and variety. In the volume section, organizations have to collect information and data from different sources including social media, industrial equipment, Internet, and business transactions. Storage mediums like Hadoop and Data lakes are widely used to store and process information in big data.

To deal with millions of transactions each minute, big data systems have built in velocity handling modules. Moreover, data streams and tons of information from the Internet can now be processed through big data algorithms without any hassle. Data is present in different formats; it can be either structured or unstructured for which the variety properties in big data are used to handle database operations.

Importance of Big Data

Big data systems can change the way we handle information. When it comes to handling large volumes of data, we need to select the most suitable tools and models to manage the available information. With the implementation of big data, companies can take data from any source and manipulate it to get accurate insights. Tools such as in-memory analytics and Hadoop can identify new sources of data and reduce the time needed to process the information. Furthermore, these tools are cost saving and can help companies in processing large volumes of data without any hassle.

There is no business that claims success without having the need to develop strong customer relations. Customers are the most vital asset for any business and if the company is not able to deliver quality services, losing potential customers becomes inevitable. The use of big data systems allows businesses to analyze customer behavior and purchase decisions by overviewing the trends and patterns in data.

Organizational Benefits

Advanced Python data science applications are designed to bring long term benefit to large scale industries and businesses. Big data systems help businesses to understand market trends, evaluate product effectiveness, and gain information regarding customer behavior. Furthermore, the approach also promotes cost saving measures and delivers high returns and meaningful insights within a short period of time. Machine learning and artificial intelligence systems have to handle big data regularly for which the model is programmed to learn and gain insights from high quality data. In return, this approach brings long term benefit to companies and businesses.

Modern day computing systems provide the power, flexibility, and speed needed to access huge amounts of big data. Furthermore, companies need new methods with reliable access and storage facilities in order to store and manage huge volumes of data. High performance tools such as in-memory analytics and grid computing have greatly increased reliability and efficiency of big data systems.

Python Machine Learning Limitations

Python is the finest general purpose and high-level programming language which is widely being used by developers to create state of the art machine learning and artificial intelligence models. Compilation of a Python program is not similar to a conventional C or C++ program because its execution occurs with the support of an interpreter. For other languages, the compiler is responsible for executing and running the program. This makes Python execution slower as compared to the execution of other programming languages. Furthermore, memory consumption of Python is higher because of the complexity of data types and implementation of libraries.

There are specific limitations of Python programming language which make it difficult for beginners to develop machine learning models through Python. Numerous kinds of runtime errors occur during the development of Python programs which need to be addressed sequentially to avoid any future problems. Moreover, Python features and extensions can be customized to make programming easier, as this is not the case with other programming languages such as C, C++ and R.

Reasons to select Python in Data Science

Python programming language allows programmers to express logical concepts and libraries without writing long lines of code. There are no extra steps to compile and execute steps as we can directly run the program through source code. Furthermore, Python has the capability to convert the source code into bytecodes so that it can be easily translated into the native language of the computer. Developers can load and link libraries directly without adding any type of additional lines of code or functions.

Memory management and exception handling approaches make Python suitable for developing data analytics and machine learning models. Python standard libraries including Pandas, NumPy, and Matplotlib are the ultimate sources to design, develop and test machine learning models. Libraries provide pre-written piece of code which can be enhanced by the developers to meet the requirements of the machine learning model. As machine learning requires continuous data processing, Python libraries can be used to access, handle, and transform data without any hassle.

For handling basic machine learning algorithms such as linear regression, clustering and classification, we can use Scikit-Learn library whereas Pandas library is best for handling high level data structures. Pandas allows data scientists to gather data from external sources and also performs filtration of information to create high quality training datasets. Moreover, Pandas also provides extra facilities such as data extraction from external resources such as Excel.

Is Machine Learning Perfect?

Despite its amazing advantages and facilities in the real world, machine learning models cannot be considered one hundred percent perfect and ideal. Although data scientists and machine learning engineers are researching to make AI models work accurately and perform near to human intelligence, there is still a lot of room for improvement. Machine learning models require loads of training datasets, and these should be of high quality as well. Data is not always available which makes the training process difficult and machine learning models start to make predictions that might not be suitable for human beings.

Machine learning requires a lot of resources and time to develop algorithms and complete the training process. As we can achieve a considerable amount of relevance and accuracy, there are several other functions and external resources required to avail maximum outcome from the machine learning models. Furthermore, interpretation of results might not be accurate in all cases, as humans are not completely aware of the functionality of machine learning models and how they are yielding predictions.

Machine Learning vs Data Science

Artificial intelligence and data science are major technologies in today's world. Although artificial intelligence is involved in data science operations, it definitely does not completely represent artificial intelligence. Data science involves various underlying data operations and supports both structured and unstructured data. In artificial intelligence, there is a limited implementation of machine learning algorithms and we are required to use vectors and embeddings.

Generally, data science is widely used in advertising, Internet search engines, and marketing industries whereas artificial intelligence models are more focused on manufacturing, healthcare, transportation, and robotics projects. Artificial intelligence and data science models can also be combined together for boosting the performance of machine learning systems. Data has become an essential factor for each industry and business for which companies are focused on developing secure storage systems as well.

Data science covers various fields such as programming, mathematics, and statistics. For data scientists to develop the best performing data science models though Python programming, getting information and accurate training datasets is immensely important. Moreover, other steps involved in data science including maintenance, visualization, manipulation, and extraction of data to forecast predictions, and occurrence of future events is also a major part of data science model development approach.

Most of the traditional artificial intelligence and machine learning algorithms were provided with goals in advance. With the evolution and development of the deep learning approach, data scientists have been able to understand the patterns and get valuable insights from data in a better way.

Differences and Constraints

There are considerable differences between artificial intelligence and machine learning. Computer systems still do not have consciousness and full autonomy like human beings which makes it difficult for data scientists to achieve one hundred percent accurate results from machine learning systems. Instead, the models only perform tasks for which they are trained, whether they are for the benefit of humans or not. Data science is the study and analysis of data, and a data scientist is responsible for outcomes the model will be delivering in the industry.

Moreover, the main requirement of data science models is to process data and complete other activities like transformation and cleaning. Artificial intelligence is a tool for data scientists and it is the best available approach to analyze data. On the other hand, data scientists are also held accountable for reviewing patterns in data by applying predictive modeling techniques. Depending on the requirements, the limitations and constraints of data science models can be managed to achieve accurate data insights and analytics in the future.

Different statistical techniques are used in data science models whereas in artificial intelligence, we take support from computer algorithms. Data science is all about finding hidden patterns in data, whereas artificial intelligence concepts are based on the autonomy and performance of machine learning models.

Useful Deep Learning Methods and Techniques

Learning about the advantages of transfer learning and latent features of pre-trained architecture can help you gain better insights and predictions from deep learning models. Remember that pre-trained weights are a good option to be considered as compared to the randomly initialized weights because they can be easily modified. Furthermore, we can also limit weight sizes and absolute value of weights to generalize the machine learning model. In this way, you can achieve maximum output and performance from your training data as well.

Moreover, you can also change the output layer and replace model defaults with a specific output size and activation function which is best suited for your domain. Make sure that you do not remove the first layers of a neural network because they are responsible for interpreting features and performing interactions throughout the domain as well.

Quality Assurance

Optimizing deep learning and machine learning models is quite simple if you are well aware of the design, algorithms, and functionality of the model. Hyperparameter settings and optimization algorithms make it easier to check the performance of a machine learning model and are ideal for conducting quality assurance checks as well. Each model is based on a specific set of hyperparameters which include number of hidden layers, number of neurons, activation functions, and optimization algorithm. Moreover, other factors such as learning rate, regularization hyperparameters, and regularization techniques are best for conducting in-depth quality checks for a machine learning model.

Most of the time, quality assurance mechanisms are not recognized by some artificial intelligence and machine learning systems. To avoid such problems, we are required to research and select the best approaches to test each machine learning model separately. Using training data to overview the performance and prediction capabilities of a machine learning model is absolutely not recommended because it might not yield accurate results in each case. Understanding statistical techniques for data such as mean, median, and mode will be helpful in reviewing data relationships at a high level.

As the machine learning model gets trained, it is likely to make accurate predictions and data insights for any scenario. Model testing is mandatory because machine learning systems are implemented in information systems of businesses and companies of each category. As they are subject to handle critical data, we have to make sure the information is never compromised or mishandled by the machine learning model. Although machine learning systems are not 100 percent accurate, we can surely improve the performance, safety, and reliability by regularly conducting quality checks.

Advanced AI

An artificial intelligence system can become super intelligent and perform activities for positive development in today's world. Powerful programming languages such as Python and R can be used to develop high end machine learning and artificial intelligence models which are capable of completing complex tasks without any hassle. Although advanced artificial intelligence can unleash the potential of machine learning systems, there are several consequences that need to be focused. As we all know, intelligent systems are given training through specific datasets and they might not make suitable predictions in each scenario, which in return can become harmful for humans.

Things to Remember

An efficient machine learning model has the capability to adapt unseen and new data. This approach can be done by generalizing the machine learning model development process for which you have to follow some specific rules and techniques. The model will better generalize if the data contains a wide spectrum of observations and is reliable by all means. To predict an accurate outcome, a machine learning model utilizes training data at first whereas the testing data is used afterwards.

Remember that machine learning, artificial intelligence, and deep learning will never take over a human level of intelligence and decision-making capabilities. In fact, the models are vulnerable to human mistakes and whenever an error is found in a machine learning system, the model is completely held accountable for the mistake. Most of the hard work for developing machine learning model lies upon data transformation.

Most of the effort and time is spent on feature engineering and data cleansing methods. These methods allow data scientists to uncover the hidden features in the training data sets so that a relationship can be developed between the layers, variables, and attributes within the machine learning model. Deep learning has achieved great acceptance in the real world because the models developed from deep learning can be implemented in a broad range of applications and fields.

Today, the use of machine learning and deep analytics has reached a new level of success and acceptance. Due to the consistent improvement and development in hardware systems, the performance, reliability, and security of machine learning models is also increasing which brings long term benefits to companies and businesses.

We should try to focus on the outcomes and predictions of machine learning models which are directly associated with human beings. Taking the example of a healthcare system, there is absolutely no room for errors or mistakes because the patient who is following instructions from the machine learning model is absolutely unaware about the negative effects in case the model delivers misleading information. Such is the case with the machine learning and artificial intelligence models that are implemented in autonomous vehicles or financial systems.

Although machine learning, deep learning, and artificial intelligence models are reliable, they might never meet the level of human intelligence because computer systems are absolutely unaware about external factors associated with humans such as ethics or relationships. If a model is programmed to perform a specific task, it will keep on learning and developing predictions to achieve best outcomes even if it is bringing loss for humans. Machine learning algorithms provide intelligent services and products which have delivered great advantages to humans.

Data analytics and deep learning are key factors that can directly affect the prediction capabilities of a model. To implement these strategies into a business model, we need to understand the core requirements of the business and implement the techniques and machine learning algorithms that can help in achieving the highest return on investment. Deep learning algorithms can bring long term advantages to businesses and humans in real life as well. Through accurate predictions and data insights, machine learning models serve as a best source for automating processes and tasks that were previously done through traditional computer systems. To achieve desired results, data scientists always focus on the maintenance and training of machine learning systems.

Conclusion

Python Data Analytics: How to learn python data science and use python machine learning. Introduction to deep learning to master python for beginners is a comprehensive guide for learning Python for machine learning and artificial intelligence. The concepts and methodologies explained in this book can be adopted to understand how data science actually works and why Python is the best programming language to develop high performing machine learning and data analytics models.

Designed for beginners, we have explained each aspect and portion of Python programming language with code samples which will greatly help our readers in developing machine learning models.

Machine learning has revolutionized business processes and the way we are performing routine activities. By learning the basics and findings of data science, researchers can understand the functionality of machine learning systems and implement their Python programming skills to develop high end data science models. Python Data Analytics: How to learn python data science and use python machine learning. Introduction to deep learning to master python for beginners is absolutely easy to understand as it is intended to help beginners in learning core concepts of Python machine learning, data analytics, and data science with the support of examples and real-life scenarios.

References

(2019). What is Data Analytics?. Retrieved from
https://www.mastersindatascience.org/resources/what-is-data-
analytics/

Assessing Data and Creating a dataset, (2017). Retrieved from
https://wp.wwu.edu/machinelearning/2017/01/29/accessing-data-
and-creating-a-dataset/

Chris, N. (2019) A Beginner's Guide to Neural Networks and Deep
Learning. Retrieved from https://skymind.ai/wiki/neural-network

James, W. (2028). Big Data VS Traditional Data. Retrieved from
http://customerthink.com/big-data-vs-traditional-data-what-to-
know-when-it-comes-to-defines-big-data/

Jason, B. (2018). Your First Deep Learning Project in Python with
Keras Step-By-Step. Retrieved from
https://machinelearningmastery.com/tutorial-first-neural-network-
python-keras/

Machine Learning Algorithms. Retrieved from
https://www.datarobot.com/wiki/algorithm/

Moussa, T. (2018). Lessons Learned from Building Scalable Machine
Learning Pipelines. Retrieved from
https://techblog.appnexus.com/lessons-learned-from-building-
scalable-machine-learning-pipelines-822acb3412ad

Victor, R. (2019). How To Develop a Machine Learning Model From
Scratch. Retrieved from https://towardsdatascience.com/machine-
learning-general-process-8f1b510bd8af